133

TABORI + RAPHAEL

-4. FEB. 1974

-1. MAR. 1974

20.

06. 02.

15. 03. 75

18. 03. 75

01. 04. 75

26. 04. 75

03. 06. 75

19. 09. 75

31. 10. 75

13. 01. 76

16. 05. 77

07. 03. 77

01. 07. 77

26. 07. 77

28. 11. 77

10. 03. 73

26. 05. 78

05. 07. 79

S U C
16. 9. 80

19. 04. 78

79

16. APR 07.

BEYOND THE SENSES

FRONTIERS OF THE UNKNOWN

A Library of Psychic Knowledge
Edited by Dr Paul Tabori

BEYOND THE SENSES: A REPORT ON
PSYCHICAL RESEARCH IN THE SIXTIES
by Paul Tabori and Phyllis Raphael

SURVIVAL AFTER DEATH
by Sir William Crookes

FRONTIERS OF THE UNKNOWN

BEYOND THE SENSES

A report on psychical research and occult phenomena in the sixties

PAUL TABORI
PHYLLIS RAPHAEL

Souvenir Press

First British edition published 1971
by Souvenir Press Ltd., 95, Mortimer Street, London, W.1.
and simultaneously by J. M. Dent & Son (Canada) Ltd., Toronto, Canada

ISBN 0 285 62011 8

Printed in Great Britain by
Clarke, Doble & Brendon Ltd.
Plymouth

CONTENTS

FOR

DR. ERIC J. DINGWALL

With friendship and affection
and no hard feelings

P. T.

INTRODUCTION

When, about twenty years ago, I became the literary executor of Harry Price, the most colourful and most tenacious of Britain's psychical researchers, I soon found that I had also become heir to all the eccentrics, zealots and plain madmen who constitute the lunatic fringe of occultism. No one in the field can escape them though if you are lucky, or rude enough, you might lose them after a while.

One of them was a gentleman in the Home Counties of England who wrote me long and half-literate letters, full of Biblical quotations and veiled references to marvels he might disclose if the spirit moved him to do so. Finally he insisted on coming to see me. He was a tall, fleshy man in a pepper-and-salt suit, with a ruddy face, a shock of white hair and a gold watch-chain across his ample middle. He looked as normal as Mr. Gilbert, the butcher with whom we have done business in Kensington for twenty years; even though he had a slight and elusive foreign accent, there was nothing in his appearance to connect him with those apocalyptic letters. He had his own small firm in a town in South-East England; the last thing I want is to humiliate or expose him, so I'd better stop at this scanty identification—though I must add that he was of Flemish birth and had come to England as a very young boy during the First World War.

He talked about Harry Price and several of the controversial and still unresolved cases with which Price had been connected; but slowly he warmed up and became more personal.

"I think it is my duty to tell you," he leant forward suddenly and jabbed a confidential finger into my stomach, "that I am the rightful King of Belgium."

There are two possible reactions to such a statement. The non-committal "how interesting!" or the forthright: "you must be kidding!" I avoided both when I said: "You can prove it, I suppose?"

He nodded. "I have all the papers. Of course, I resigned my claims—I didn't want to embarrass Poldi . . ."

"Poldi?"

"My nephew. Leopold. He has made a mess of it, I'm afraid, but I'm not sure I could have done any better. And for that short time, it wouldn't have been worthwhile, would it?"

I hastily agreed though I hadn't the faintest idea what he was talking about. It did seem magnanimous to renounce crown and sceptre of such a prosperous and pleasant country as Belgium. But then he moved closer and went on in a hoarse whisper.

"Being the rightful king was all right, I suppose," he smiled. "But it would have been only incognito."

This was even more puzzling. I saw him watching me, waiting for my reaction. I didn't quite know what to say so he decided to prod me.

"You know, naturally, who I *really* am?" he demanded.

"Well, I'm afraid I . . ."

He held out his two huge hands, palms upward. Both of them bore the sign of the cross, carved deep into the pudgy flesh—it must have been done quite some time ago for the scars had healed, their white lines running straight and true across the other chiromantic marks.

I was still silent. He bent very close for the revelation:

"I am Jesus Christ, you see."

He went on to tell me how he had gone to Fatima, the Portuguese shrine, and had met "his Father" who had given him the choice to decide when the end of the world should come—and how he, the Son of God in incognito, had taken pity on mankind and given us all a little respite. Soon afterwards he left, promising further good news. I wondered how a man like this, an obvious religious maniac, could live among people, in the midst of a large family, carrying his burning lunacy like a torch and yet doing business, filling out forms, drinking a pint at the local. I never heard from him again but his existence continued to trouble me; what if his obsessions exploded one day and he ran amuck, a saviour in search of people he could crucify?

In recent years, observing the ebb and flow of occult belief and practice, the trends in psychical research, the changes in methodology, aims and preoccupations, I often thought of my visitor in the salt-and-pepper suit. For he seems to symbolise so much that is going on in the world of the quest for proof and certainty in the realm beyond the senses. There is an undeniable boom in psychic matters. This is a little strange, for mediums and fortune-tellers, astrologers and faith healers usually flourish

during and after a world war, a global period of disasters. The
peaks can clearly be traced through 1916–1924 and 1945–52.
This is natural enough for in these periods millions of people
lose their nearest and dearest and a large percentage of those who
have suffered the grievous loss will not accept it, are psychologically incapable of recognising death as final, the separation
as total. But though the armistice of the last twenty-five years
has been an uneasy one and little, or not so little, wars have
raged like brushfires in many parts of the world, their comprehensive effect could not be compared to that of world wars one
and two. Yet, except in certain areas, the passionate interest in
the occult has grown apace through the sixties and the signs are
that there is going to be a continued preoccupation with survival after death, extrasensory perception, reincarnation, witchcraft in the new decade as well.

The causes are diverse but two principal ones seem to me the
most significant—and these are closely connected.

One is the interest of *youth* in these phenomena—and this is
a fairly recent development. In the twenties and thirties young
people had other concerns; it is reasonably exact to say that
among the members of psychical societies and research groups,
in the ranks of the spiritualist churches there were hardly any
under-thirties. (As an American pastor of such a church pointed
out, the "senior citizens" were, after all, closer to death and
therefore more interested in what was happening after they had
passed away; they also had more dear departed to get in touch
with.). Today the situation is changed almost globally. Writing
about *The Making of the Yippie Culture**, Garry Wills lists the
facets of the experimental character of this culture and explains:

> A fourth sign of the empirical society is a reversion to super-
> stition, magic, astrology, fortune-telling, tarot-cards, I Ching,
> omens, spells ("Om"), Vedanta, witchcraft, mysticism. Not only
> do these supply a street theatre of liturgy, symbol and vest-
> ments: they are also, like all magic, basically experimental.
> Magic is a way of getting certain things done. Say the right
> spell, and an automatic response is assured. Be born under the
> right star, and things will demonstrably happen. When author-
> ity has been drained from conventional religion, when the

* *Esquire,* November 1969

social symbols no longer signify anything, no longer promote communication, men are forced to invent private myths; they are thrown back on their own resources, constructing a social creed based on pure faith, on undemonstrable mysteries. Belief in astrology is mere acceptance of a working hypothesis, which allows endless experiment, verification, personal adaptation, analogical extension. Magic is also "against interpretation". Who knows what machinery makes the doors swing wide at "Open sesame"? And who cares? The real question is not how astrology works, but whether it works; and that is a question each person must answer in his own case, by experiment, by the daily lab work of checking one's life against one's horoscope.

Mr. Wills presents here something like a stall at a jumble-sale but being young himself he assumably speaks for youth. Certainly the audiences that flocked to *Rosemary's Baby* or devoured the pseudo-Gothic romances about synthetic werewolves and imitation *revenants* were mostly the young. They also buy the ouija boards; and in drugs they seek the mystic experience, the "total awareness" just as, in spite of the warnings of such an experienced old truth-seeker as Arthur Koestler,* they try to find the answers in yoga and Zen. This has brought an entirely new element and a vast new public into the occult field—as participants, as enquirers, as dupes and deceivers.

The other cause for this broadened and deepened interest in matters psychic is not linked to any age group though perhaps again more evident in youth than in the more mature. It is the loss of belief in reason in a world that has increasingly moved towards the *acte gratuite*. Pop art, the theatre of cruelty (and its various bastard offsprings), electronic music, unscripted and endless panel discussions on radio and TV, the *nouvelle vague* in films are just as much part of it as the murder of the eight nurses in Chicago or the massacre of Sharon Tate and her companions in Hollywood—or the Moscow phoney gasman's rampage. The irrational has become a haven from the bankruptcy of logic and order. This is no denunciation but a diagnosis that can be checked against your daily newspaper. If the natural and reasonable are forsaken, the supernatural and the extra-rational

* *The Lotus and the Robot,* 1959

must flourish. Our world is no longer seeking normal, logical explanations for the mysteries and rites of the occult; it is trying to substitute *mystique* for fact, the amateur's spontaneity for the professional's discipline—and of course, is constantly seeking ways to commercialize all its aspects. In a way there are fewer mediums, telepaths, clairvoyants; but there are more believers and seekers. Scientists themselves are becoming drawn into this magic circle for they discover more and more surrealistic elements in their measurable and, until recently, classifiable and explorable world; what could be more surrealistic a conception than anti-matter and mirror-worlds, the whole heritage of Nils Bohr's complimentary? Symmetry and system are being rapidly questioned; the alchemists have been proved at least partly right and the old wives' tales about henbane and hellebore, spiders' webs and green mould have been transferred into digitalis therapy and antibiotics. As in the so-called exact sciences re-discovery accounts for half of the progress, the marginal exploration of the borderlands which every scientific disciple possesses brings the teacher frequently into close companionship with totally intangible and unreal factors. Reaching the moon has raised at least as many new questions as it has provided answers to the old ones. A fourteenth century enlightened Hungarian king proclaimed that "of the witches that do not exist there shall be no talk". Today there is a good deal of talk about witches—who are called into existence by the very talk.

And this brings us back to my stalwart visitor in the pepper-and-salt suit. "Men are forced to invent private myths," Garry Wills said in his diagnosis of "yippie culture"— but these private myths very often remain incognito, disguised behind a would-be sophistication and pretended scepticism. Without straining the parallel, there are millions today who consider themselves rightful heirs to their chosen kingdoms—financial, political, sexual—and, as they are never able to take possession of their domains pretend that they had renounced them. Yet there has to be a substitute for what they never had and therefore doubly desire. To them the questions are more important than the answers. Equally, they bear the invisible stigmata—instead of a penknife, these have been etched into their minds and souls by the unbearable demands of modern life. They cannot all claim to be saviours—but they can pretend to share the ultimate mysteries, to belong to the élite that has been admitted to the innermost sanctuary where the secrets of heaven and hell are disclosed. Their hells and heavens, of course, are shaped like human beings —just like Swedenborg's.

All this is, I feel, sufficient motivation for the great occult boom. But those who have worked in these vast fields, patiently and often on very small and specialised tasks, know that the search on which they are engaged is an endless one and that there can be no discharge from their service. They might be total sceptics or, like Harry Price and others of his philosophy, men and women with completely open minds—in either case they will not deny the possibility of extrasensory or, if you like, supernatural phenomena—just as cosmologists have come to accept the possibility or even the probability of other humanoid civilizations on other planets in other galaxies.

This book is an interim report from the frontier zone, a series of summaries from the psychical battle-fields. Inevitably it has to pose more questions than it provides answers—for as you will see in the chapter *The End of Rosalie?* more often than not it takes decades for an occult investigation to be closed, if it is ever closed at all. We are starting with faith-healers whose work merits serious investigation because of claims recently made by apparently responsible individuals. While it seems that the attraction of the great miracle-making pilgrimage places is waning, the new shamans, the modern magicians are flourishing as never before. Another chapter deals with psychic surgery and its exotic practitioners who seem to attract just as many fervent partisans as enemies of their unorthodox and often violent practices. A good deal of this material has reached us from private and rather publicity-shy sources in South America and Asia.

We have tried to give a representative sampler of the vast field of telepathy and clairvoyance, perhaps the "most reputable" branch of psychical research. The results of Professor Rhine and Dr. Soal have been challenged and yet we know that even the totally materialistic Soviet scientists are working in this territory. Here, as at a triangular border, psychology, psychic research and mysticism meet and there is a good deal of cross-fertilization. There is also considerable overlapping into criminology and psychosomatic medicine.

The belief in reincarnation is as old as mankind though it has gone underground for long periods. In our age that has brought such widespread use of hallucinogenic drugs, more and more people claim that they have dragged up evidence from the collective unconscious of past existences and long-distant *karmas*. (Professor Stevenson's recent work in this field is particularly interesting.) There is a definite link here with the latest and persistent enquiries into the possibility if not the probability of survival after death.

In the chapter dealing with the famous Rosalie case we publish, for the first time, the alleged solution of a mystery of physical mediumship that has occupied the experts for over thirty years, has provoked three books and innumerable articles—a story that proves how the most experienced and the most conservative researcher can be fooled if those set to deceive him are clever and tenacious enough. It also proves that some charges of fabrication made against the principal of the tale have been completely groundless; that far from being the instigator, he was the victim.

The sexual element in contemporary psychic phenomena has become more and more obvious in recent years as more and more people (both young and old) have turned to the frontiers of the unknown for new experiences, reviving the strange practices of pre-Christian times and the Middle Ages. The hippie and yippie movements, the relationship of drugs and psychical phenomena, necrophilia and occultism all enter into this vast subject. Finally we present some indications as to the future of psychical research, the likely new paths to be opened, the way the recent and expected achievements of space travel will affect sceptics and believers alike. The new electronic discoveries and their more and more widespread use (such as miniaturization) is bound to have a definite influence upon mediumship. The growth or decline of spiritualism and of the various occult philosophies also deserve to be explored.

This book is intended as the first of a series that will serve a double purpose. On one hand we will present new and original works dealing with various aspects of extrasensory and psychical research and with some of the most interesting individuals such research has discovered and involved. One of these volumes, already commissioned, will deal with the anthropological, psychological, linguistic and historical aspects of witchcraft; the third will present a gazetteer of British ghosts. The other group of books we intend to publish are either the great classics of psychical literature which are inaccessible today, having been long out of print, or selections of material that has only been available to small, specialist groups but needs and deserves far wider readership. We hope that in the fullness of time we will produce a valuable and enduring library of psychical research which will strike a proper balance between healthy scepticism and the acceptance of the possibility of extrasensory (or, if you like, supernatural) phenomena. We have certainly no axes to grind and will do our best to preserve both a sense of proportion and a sense of humour.

This book was written in close collaboration with Miss Phyllis Raphael who has conducted many of the interviews and has done invaluable research work, particularly in the European countries and in Britain.

London, January 1971

Paul Tabori

The Faith Healers

Brent Town Hall, Middlesex, capacity twelve hundred, is packed. People are sitting on the stairs, stand serried against the back walls, sprawl in the aisles.

On the platform the place of pride is occupied by a portly gentleman with a shock of white hair and an undeniable resemblance to the late W. C. Fields—without, however, the copper-red complexion of the great comedian. He is dressed in a dark suit with a waistcoat but his arms are bare to above his elbows. His manner is one of benign self-confidence and evangelical zeal. Behind him huge white letters proclaim:

HEALERS' DAY, 1969

The star of this annual occasion is the "world's most famous spiritual healer", Mr. Harry Edwards, owner and leading spirit of The Sanctuary, Shere, Guildford, Surrey, author of *Born to Heal*, editor of the monthly *The Spiritual Healer*, prolific writer on his own work and the achievements of others in the same field, the most prominent member of the British National Federation of Spiritual Healers which arranges such mass jamborees.

The spotlight focuses on a girl of seventeen who can barely drag herself along on two sticks and is assisted to the platform. She announces her name over the microphone: Patricia Hannon of 1, Inglefield Road, Holland-on-Sea, Essex. Edwards tells her to turn her back to him. His stubby fingers move down her back, gently and persistently. He talks to her but the audience cannot hear his words. The girl's face is tense, expectant, as she faces the front rows. The hands continue their probing, the healer's lips move.

Then he invites a member of the public to examine the girl's spine. She has been born, he explains, with a deformity—but now "healing has succeeded in making her spine straighter". A white-haired lady in a tailormade touches Patricia's back gingerly.

9

No, she is not going to have any more operations, the girl says, but she will visit local healers to continue her treatment. She already feels better. Much better.

The next patient is a middle-aged lady in a sensible grey suit. For more than eleven years, she tells the audience, she has been suffering from a slipped disc after an accident. The doctors could do nothing more for her. Again, the healing hands perform their little ritual dance on her back. Again a silent prayer accompanies the ministrations. Then the lady is told to lift a heavy, leather-upholstered stool to prove that "healing has overcome" her condition. She proceeds to do so, a little hesitantly. A smile of delight spreads over her well-fed face as she succeeds. Applause ripples through the hall but decorously subdued.

Not every case is a success—that would be too much to accept or perhaps not in keeping with such well-established and traditional showmanship. Albert Howard is still on crutches when he leaves the platform and his broken back—Albert, a window-cleaner, fell some 20 feet three years before—shows no improvement. Not yet, that is. For the microphone announces that Mr. Howard, of 8 Rathcole Gardens, North London, will "continue to receive treatment from his local healer".

The parade continues—altogether about a dozen or so crippled and sick people mount the platform, are ministered to by Edwards and his army of white-coated colleagues. In the evening there is a mass healing service "so that no one who comes seeking help is left untreated".

Long before Professor Marshall McLuhan, the prophet of the electronic age summed up his disturbing creed in the five words: "the medium is the message", professor Julius Wagner von Jauregg, the Austrian neurologist and psychiatrist, winner of the 1927 Nobel Prize for Medicine, coined the axiom: *"The doctor is the medicine"*.

What he meant was the acceptance of a basic psychological fact: healing is at least two-thirds a mental process. Apart from the very basic remedies all medicine must rely to a considerable extent on the placebo effect. *It works because the doctor says it will work*. It works because it triggers off a mental reaction that in turn projects and releases physical forces—glandular or otherwise—which are still largely unexplored. That is why a proper bedside manner is often more important than the most brilliant theoretical knowledge. In spite of group therapy, computer diagnosis and the general depersonalization of medicine, the individual involvement of the healer is still essential. Indifference can be as deadly as a virus. The doctor is still the best medicine.

Faith healing is as ancient as mankind. The Egyptians believed in the healing power of the hand, practicing a kind of sympathetic magic by placing it on the stomach or the head, though the patient had to be in a suitable mood and submit to the hypnotic, suggestive influence of the healer. In the Acts of the Apostles we read of St. Paul: "And when Paul laid his hands upon them, the Holy Ghost came upon them; and they spake with tongues, and prophesied . . ." Later we are told: "And God wrought special miracles by the hands of Paul so that from his body were brought unto the sick handkerchiefs or aprons, and the disease departed from them, and the evil spirits went out of them . . ." Paul advised Timothy directly: "Neglect not the gift that is in thee, which was given thee by prophecy, with the laying on of the hands of the presbytery . . ."

And St. Paul only followed in the footsteps of his Master for Jesus also healed by touch. Jairus, as we read in the Gospel of St. Mark, begged him plainly: "My daughter lieth at the point of death: I pray thee, come and lay thy hands on her, that she may be healed . . ." And in the same Gospel there is mention of a "certain woman" who "when she heard of Jesus, came in the press behind him and touched his garment. For, she said, If I may touch but his clothes, I shall be whole. And indeed, she felt in her body that she was healed of that plague . . ." The crowd was astonished, and on the sabbath day they asked: "From whence hath this man these things? And what wisdom is this which is given unto him that even such mighty works are wrought by his hand?" When the blind man of Bethsaida is brought to him, he is again besought "to touch him". Almost every passage of the Gospels, whether of St. Mark's or St. Luke's, speaking of Jesus the Healer, remarks that He touched the ailing part of the body directly with His hands; He covered the eyes of the blind, He put His fingers into the ears of the deaf-and-dumb and moistened his tongue with His own.

It is the healing power of the Saviour that is invoked by the faith healers of today. For, unlike Wagner von Jauregg, they do not restrict themselves to any psychological explanation—most of them, actually, reject it. They believe that they have been given a divine gift—a portion of the healing fluid which St. Luke called "the power of God", *dynamis kuriou*. This is why the physical contact is so important for it is through the hand that the diseased organ or limb is supposed to receive this fluid; the hand is the carrier of this dynamic power, and with it, of the Messianic consciousness, self-assurance and firmness. As He touched the sick, Jesus usually spoke a few words of prayer— and in this, as in all the other outward forms, the later kings of France and England followed his example—and so did the greedy charlatans who developed hypnotic, suggestive healing.

The Biblical cures differed from those of later ages in that they seemed to be effective against all ills to which the body is heir. In the first centuries of Christianity the majestic figure of Christ was transformed into that of Asclepius Soter. (The Greek *soter* literally means "saviour, life saver".) Apollo, one of the gods of the art of medicine also bore this as one of his epithets— *Phoibos Soter*. Many facts seem to indicate that the healing by touch adopted by the cult of primitive Christianity was an immediate borrowing from Hellenism.

All this the modern faith healer has forgotten or never bothered to learn. To most, though not all of them, faith healing is both a vocation and a business, a divine or at least supernatural gift and a workaday profession.

After the great gathering at Brent Town Hall, we visited the Sanctuary, Burrows Lea, to watch Harry Edwards in his own setting and to talk to him about his life's work. Burrows Lea, Shere, is about an hour's drive from London, set in a most attractive country-side. The Sanctuary itself is oak-panelled and very handsome. Here the patients for whom three healing sessions a week are held wait in a double row of chairs. The sessions are open to everybody—but appointments must be made in advance.

On that afternoon there were about twenty-five people in the large room, patients and their relatives and friends. They faced a Jacobean oak altar table with a cross and a vase of flowers. Behind it a stained glass window bore the inscription : HEALING IS A GIFT FROM THE SPIRIT. The draperies were velvet; the atmosphere, respectfully silent and expectant.

Promptly at a quarter past two the door opened and Mr. Edwards entered. Both he and his three assistants—one woman and two men—wore white coats. Smoothly they made their way to the right side of the altar.

The first patient was a boy of seven, accompanied by his mother and father. He appeared to be in good health but his parents reported that X-rays showed there were faulty valves in the ducts connecting the kidneys to the bladder so that urine was passing from the bladder back into the kidneys—and this could lead to a dangerous infection. A second set of X-rays was to be taken the following week, the last were made about three years before.

The healer felt the boy, particularly around the abdomen, announced that he had made "good contact" with him and added that he would like to see the X-rays when they were ready. This ended the examination or treatment.

Next came a lady in a fuzzy hat and harlequin glasses who looked pleased and expectant in equal measure. Mr. Edwards asked her whether this was her first visit and she replied that it was her third. She complained of pressure and pain in her back. He put his arms around her, exerted pressure on her spine and rotated her torso back and forward. He asked: "Where is it hurting?", then added: "your spine is not very set." She explained that she had taken off her medical corset and he advised her that as she had already done so, she should keep it off. "I think we've done it," he added, asking whether her back still ached. "Not too much," she replied cautiously.

She was followed by a man of about fifty who had a circulatory problem. He wore glasses and said that he had been suffering from this condition for almost a year. When he got up from a seated or recumbent position, he sometimes lost consciousness. Harry Edwards told him that he shouldn't worry much about his heart but suggested deep breathing exercises. "The more oxygen you take into your lungs, the better. Feel as if you are taking in strength and healing. Maintain a continuous state of contentment."

Another patient was a man who was partially paralysed from the waist down. He walked on crutches with great difficulty. Edwards manipulated his spine and lower back, held him while he stood up and sat down, then said: "If we relieve the pressure, the messages will pass through." He demonstrated exercises for the feet and legs, suggested massage to the man's wife. "Don't try too hard," he said. "It will take time but we can look forward to improvement. Avoid depression. Don't expect too much all of a sudden. Write to me. Breathe in slowly and take in strength."

A woman patient had suffered from the effects of a stroke for nine years and was almost completely paralyzed. As Edwards manipulated her body, she began to smile, a broad and happy smile. He suggested that she should try to do more at home. "If you make a mess of it, it doesn't matter," he reassured her. Then he added: "Hold me tight . . . let me go . . . tight again . . . let go . . ." She looked almost ecstatic as she exercised the muscles which her daughter, who was with her, indicated she was able to use.

Another woman, a bleached blonde, skinny and nervous, with a rather grubby see-through blouse, complained: "Life just worries me. It's an effort to start every day . . ." Mr. Edwards spoke of her migraine and neuralgia and soothed her.

After he finished with each patient, he sent them off to the side where his assistants waited to practice the exercises he had prescribed for them. The healing session ended, as it began, with a brief prayer.

Afterwards we had a long talk with the doyen of British faith healers.

"How many people do you treat at the Sanctuary in an average year?"

"About five thousand."

"Do you keep records about the results of the treatment?"

"We couldn't possibly do that—in addition to the five thousand there are about ten thousand letters every week."

"And you answer them all?"

"We do."

"You seem to have quite a staff here."

"Certainly—but even so it's impossible to keep individual case records."

"How effective is treatment by mail?"

"Just as effective as physical contact."

"You are sure of that? or is it just an educated guess?"

"Most of all, we just know it. The greater part of our work is that way."

"What sort of cases do you find are the most frequent? You seemed to have a good many arthritic people today. Is that a rule?"

"Yes. In contact healing we find a good many physical conditions are centered around the spine. Leg trouble and so on . . ."

"Don't the Buddhists and the followers of Theodore Reik deal a lot with the spine in their psycho-therapy?"

"They deal with it on a different basis. I won't go into it because it's rather complicated. But they say that the spine has nervous centres which they call *charkars*. And of course there are a lot of nerves centred in the spine. What you saw this afternoon was the actual freeing of spines that have become cemented up. Adhesions, calciary deposits etc. cause the bones to become cemented together which leads to all kinds of trouble, especially following paralysis and sclerosis. Our healing is able to break up and disperse these adhesions and make it possible for the spine to palpitate freely as you saw it happen. It's as easy as that . . ."

"Yes, it was incredible. We also felt that it had a lot to do with you, personally, Mr. Edwards. As we sat there, we wished something were wrong with us because we wanted to establish contact with you. Your personality makes one feel quite secure. Do you feel this yourself?"

"It is not so much personality—you see, what we do is to *blend* with people. We tune into them. I think that's what you noticed. We have to do this blending—as if we were used as a conveyor and a transformer of healing energy. You see, healing is a science."

"You feel it *is* a science?"

"Oh yes."

"Have you studied medicine yourself?"

"No. I have no medical degree. But I know enough to—"

"In what way is faith healing a science?"

"We have just been talking about 'cementing' in arthritis. Now, before you can move the spine or a joint that's locked up, you must bring about a chemical change—you must alter the chemical nature of the substance that keeps the joints or the spine locked. To do that there must be energy applied to bring about this change. It doesn't happen by chance or magic."

"Then how does it happen?"

"In the physical world it means that there are other energies—counteracting energies—which are applied to break up or alter the formation—the chemical formation."

"How do you help in this process?"

"By acting as transformers, as receivers—we receive the help which is transformed through us and transmitted to the patient. Purposefully."

"You consider yourself then, a sort of catalyst?"

"Yes. You see, all healing is a planned effort. Every case demands an intelligence to carry it out and when, as you have seen, we overcome conditions that doctors cannot heal, what does it mean? It means that there is a Superior Intelligence at work."

"You feel that you are in contact with such a Superior Intelligence?"

"Yes. And it uses us as instruments to overcome these physical troubles."

"It's a sort of spiritual inspiration for which you are the catalyst?"

"It is a spiritual effect."

"But in a sense, you are spiritually inspired?"

"Oh yes. We're in tune with the Spirit, put it that way."

"How much do you think depends on the patients themselves? We noticed that you have them do certain exercises at home."

"Yes. People are people and there are times when they must help themselves. They must co-operate with the healer. If a person has had a locked hip joint and has limped for ten years and I get that joint free, it is ten to one that when they leave here, they will limp again. It's the habit. So what I try to do is to get them to co-operate with me as a healer by looking for the improvement that healing brings. To come back to spines—the exercises are destined to keep the spine free by bending it. Otherwise arthritis will creep in and cement it up again."

"Do you think many of them carry out these exercises?"

"I know they do. There are letters—and you heard those who were here giving testimony about having been healed years ago."

"What is the percentage of the cures?"

"We must get the figures correct. You see, one has to take into account the individual character of the patient. They usually come to us when the doctors are unable to do anything more for them or when they are in a real bad state as you have seen some of them here. If the doctor could have healed them, they wouldn't come to me. Of those who do come about eighty per cent report improvement, easement, no pain, symptoms disappearing. Of these eighty per cent thirty per cent report complete recovery— about a quarter of the total. Then there is about twenty per cent who do not seem to respond."

"Why do you suppose that is?"

"It can be for a number of reasons. Maybe they cling to the cause of their troubles. If it is a mental case and they maintain a mental frustration, their healing is negative. If we heal a person with failing eyesight and he goes back to very exacting work— or if an arthritic person goes and sleeps in a damp room or a damp bed . . ."

"Have you had any experiences of miraculous cures? For instance this little boy with the degenerative kidneys—there doesn't seem to be much that can be done—"

"There are lots of things that *are* done. A good deal of what you would call miracles. We have had babies and children here in whom—what's the term?—what's the place in the body there? the digestion doesn't work—the name escapes me for a moment—"

"The intestines?"

"Part of them—the small organ—"

"The colon?"

"No, that's too far down. Up here—"

"The pancreas?"

"That's it. With some children it hasn't worked properly since birth which means they haven't had any strength, couldn't grow, they would be four or five years old and no taller than this . . . and the healing comes, a change takes place, the pancreas works and they get better."

"And this happened after doctors and clinics have failed to help?"

"Oh yes. What you saw this afternoon is in the same category."

"The little boy with the kidneys—you believe that should they continue to degenerate, you will be able to affect a cure?"

"I'm going to wait until we hear more about it. The fact is that the boy hasn't suffered from any symptoms—hasn't had urine trouble, there's no pain in the kidneys. He's putting on weight, he's growing. Well, that's all happened since the healing started. So I'm simply going to wait now and see what the X-rays show next week. Perhaps he will be all right. At the moment there's nothing that can do him very much harm."

"What are your feelings about the medical profession in general? If someone comes to you directly and you feel it is something the doctors could do, would you refer him to them?"

"We often do that."

"Do you find the medical profession is hostile to you?"

"Officially it is non-co-operative. Individually and in increasing numbers, doctors do co-operate with us."

"Do you feel in any way that perhaps you function as a kind of psycho-analyst?"

"Oh, I think so. The point is, we get results, where the doctors may not—and so doctors cannot close their eyes to it and send their patients to us. Some doctors come for treatment themselves."

"And you think it is because of this catalysing effect of yours?"

"No, not at all."

"You don't think it's the fact that you're so reassuring and that you do give people a sense of security?"

"All the reassurance in the world and all the self-suggestion cannot free a stiffened spine—or a joint that's locked."

"Have you ever dealt with hysterical people? people who are under some compelling obsession—alcoholics, heavy smokers, drug addicts?"

"That's where most of our work lies. You see, it is generally admitted that almost all disease has a psychosomatic origin, due to frustration, mental upsets or what have you. And that includes cancer. Therefore when a healing takes place, we must first get rid of the cause in order to remove the symptoms. And that's why we get so many so-called incurables. Most of our work is in that field; corrective influences are directed at these people— and we do this mainly with *absent healing*, not face to face. These corrective influences are received by their consciousness and their minds, inducing a change of habits, a change of mental preoccupations or overcoming a cause that is even more fundamental. It may be disappointment in love, a block of hatred, lack of ambition or excess of it. Women who want babies and cannot have them; women who have babies and do not want them—all this sort of thing is our work. By altering or adjusting the mental attitudes of these people, we can heal. We've helped addicts. There used to be a hospital near here and they would send us all their serious cases of drug addiction. We had quite good results."

"Do you follow up in any way the *duration* of the cure? The problem of drug addiction is of course, the relapse, the recidivism."

"All I know that the doctors in charge were quite pleased with our work. I didn't bother to ask . . . It's like the case when a husband who has turned sadistic or cruel and the wife writes to me in confidence, the husband doesn't know anything about it—yet we see the change take place . . ."

"In this case do you work through the wife? You tell her to change her behaviour in some way?"

"Oh no. It is all done by absent healing."

"You don't even see the husband? You don't speak to him? He doesn't know he's being treated?"

"No. That's how all our work is done."

"You don't see the man and he doesn't even know that you are working on him—and yet there is a change?"

"Changes take place just the same. Therefore it is not just a question of faith healing. With faith healing alone you wouldn't get babies and children to respond, would you? The boy you saw this afternoon—he's still alive and doing well, you can't say he has great faith. It was four years ago when I saw him first. He was three. A child of three hasn't the ability of expressing or activating faith. And he can't maintain it for four years. Yet that boy has been kept alive because of our work . . ."

Another faith healer whom we visited is certainly unique because, so he claims, he has been dead for more than thirty years. This, of course, created certain handicaps and so he works through a living person whose name is George Chapman. It is through him that Dr. William Lang (1852-1937) is supposed to practice the art of healing.

George Chapman/William Lang share a spacious house with a garden in Aylesbury, about an hour's train-ride from London. Here, too, there is a sanctuary housed in a small modern building near the main house.

The taxi driver who took us from the railway station knew all about the place and told us that hundreds of people visit it every year; though he, the driver, didn't have any first-hand knowledge of cures he seemed to be convinced of the complete authenticity of the results. He also praised George Chapman highly as a kind and gracious gentleman.

We got there about half an hour early for our appointment and were greeted by George Chapman's son, Michael, a boy about 17 or 18 who acts as receptionist. He was pleasant and easy to talk to and since the waiting room was small and informal, it was equally easy to talk to the other patients. A pile of books called *Healing Hands* by J. Bernard Hutton was available for sale on Michael's desk and the elderly lady sitting next to us had just bought her copy. She was there to consult "Dr. Lang" about her eyes and when she went in to see him, she was a little nervous. Afterwards she told us that he had soon put her at her ease and performed a spirit operation which was painless and, he told her, would have good results. He made her lie down on his operating couch and he spoke to his associates (none of whom she could see) and clicked his fingers as he called for the necessary—also invisible—instruments. When she came out of the consultation room she seemed quite thrilled with the whole experience. We took her name and address so that we could follow up on the success or failure of her cure. She had driven down from London with a friend and when she left she forgot her purse; she had been almost half-way back to London when she noticed it and returned about forty minutes later to collect it. Some weeks later we talked to her on the telephone and she told us that she had an early state of cataracts and that up to that moment there had been no improvement. This was about a month and a half after her "spirit-treatment". She remained in contact with George Chapman through the mail every week and she had not been advised to return for further treatment. She explained that cataracts were generally operated on when they had completely or almost completely covered the eye and since she was elderly she was not anxious to wait for this to happen or to undergo surgery.

The other person to whom we spoke at length was an Indian lady-doctor who was attached to a hospital in Omagh, Northern Ireland. Her husband, also a doctor, was at the same place. They had one child and she wanted to have another but she could not get pregnant—it seemed that her womb was weakened and tilted in a way that made conception difficult. "Dr. Lang" told her that she herself had the gift of healing and that he would like her to work at a larger hospital under more experienced surgeons where her physical and spiritual gifts could be more strongly developed. The lady-doctor did not appear to be overly ambitious in this direction; she would have preferred to have another child and stay at home for a while.

She expressed complete belief in "Dr Lang" and when, on the train going back we shared a compartment and she found that the tape recorder we had brought would not play back properly, she told us that she had known all about it and had "arranged" for it not to work. Fortunately she was wrong and later the recorder functioned perfectly. She explained that "Dr. Lang" had performed a "spirit operation" on her and had said he believed the problem had been solved and that she would soon be able to have a child.

Another woman had to be carried in from her car, unable to walk, as she was suffering from spinal cancer. We had a chance to discuss her case with Chapman/Lang during our interview with the spirit healer.

When at last we were admitted to the consulting room, we found it in complete darkness, except for a red light. The healer sat on a rather old-fashioned sofa and the walls were lined with pictures of Dr. Lang and his associates. While he talked to us, he kept his eyes closed. Whether they were completely shut, it was difficult to say—in a dimly-lit room it is easy to see through a narrow slit. And any child who tried to cheat at hide-and-seek has practiced this art. Chapman/Lang's attitude was paternal and he seemed happy to talk.

In his book, Hutton claims that "Dr. Lang" couldn't possibly see him; he also maintains that when the doctor takes possession of George Chapman's body, the latter turns into a very old man. All we saw was a man who wrinkled or twisted up his face and who had obviously practiced stooping. We were also told that George Chapman enters the sanctuary about half an hour before the first patient arrives and goes into a trance. He stays in a trance until after everyone has left.

There is no doubt about it that Dr. William Lang, F.R.C.S. did exist and worked for nine years at the London Hospital in Whitechapel and also at the Central London Ophthalmic Hospital and the Middlesex. In 1881 he founded the Ophthalmological Society, published many scientific papers and developed some surgical instruments which are still in use. Hutton has done considerable research on this and he also relates many cures in his book though he is most explicit about his own. His eyesight had been always bad but when in 1963 he became ill with a non-paralytic form of polio, it worsened steadily. He could only read if he held the page within less than an inch of his face and he couldn't distinguish a person standing ten yards away. He also suffered from double vision. His wife insisted that he should call on "Dr. Lang" who then performed "a spirit operation on my spirit body". Hutton describes the same snapping of the fingers for instruments and the discussions with "medical colleagues in the spirit world". His sensations were those of incisions and sewing up but he felt no pain; when he rose from the table, he was completely blind and in a great panic. He went out to his car and he sat there for a few minutes, unable to see anything. Then gradually shapes and colours began to appear and soon he was able to see far better than he had in years. He was, before long, capable of resuming his work as a journalist and undertook to write the book in which he recorded a number of "miraculous cures" among which he certainly counted his own; to him "Dr. Lang" was completely genuine.

During our visit Chapman/Dr. Lang certainly acted the part of a kind, paternal doctor far removed from the slick Harley Street practitioners we have met. He wore eyeglasses and we could not tell whether he wore those only when he was in trance as Dr. Lang or whether George Chapman also needed spectacles. If only Lang needed the glasses, we thought, and they remained "here", in the physical world to be put on when Chapman went into a trance, we must regard them as a prop in a performance by an able actor. And once he certainly slipped when he referred to Michael Chapman as "my son"—having made an issue earlier of the young man being Chapman's son.

And yet—we were inclined to feel that the three: Chapman, "Dr. Lang" and Michael were all convinced that they acted in an honest and straightforward manner. Michael told us that he was being trained as a healer and although he had not yet gone into trance and had "Basil Lang" operate through him, he appeared to accept that this would be his life's work. He wasn't mealy-mouthed or holier-than-thou about it but genuinely modest and nice.

"Dr. Lang's" comments on the pill, organ transplants or cybernetics were not particularly impressive; but then, one had to keep in mind that he was supposed to be an old-fashioned, nineteenth-century-trained physician.

His picture of the spirit world was deliciously simple. In Hutton's book he described his death as a falling asleep and waking up briefly just as his spirit body separated from his physical body. There were the spirit bodies of his two wives and of his son Basil to help him in the spirit world. He then lay asleep in a spirit hospital where spirit doctors attended to him until he was well again.

Hutton included in his book interviews with a Dr. Kildare Lawrence Singer who had known Lang well while he studied under him at Middlesex Hospital. Years later when he was ill with cancer he went to see the "spirit doctor", never suspecting that it "would be the same Dr. Lang" who had been his teacher. Lang greeted him with : "Hello, my dear boy. I am happy to see you again . . ."

Finally we were admitted to the inner sanctum and could begin our talk with the "spirit healer". We told him that we had come early on purpose to be able to watch his other patients and talk to them.

"And they allowed you to?"

"Yes."

"I see. Only, you know, people come here for private appointments and they don't expect to be questioned. I know you won't mind me talking to you in this way but I have a kind of practice—I am quite well known—and patients must be treated very privately when they come to consult with a doctor. I very often have newspaper reporters here and I've been very firm with them and just chase them on their way. I know you don't mind me talking like this but if you came to see me as a patient, I wouldn't like you to be cross-examined, you see, because many of the patients who come here are practising doctors and surgeons."

"Yes. We spoke to that lovely Indian girl—"

"You see. I think I have more members of the medical profession than the ordinary patient—"

"Your son told us you were supposed to have a Dr. * * * here today . . ."

"You aren't writing about these people by name for any paper, are you?"

"No. This is a report for a book and we just wanted to ask you a few questions."

"And what about my patients whose names . . . such as a Dr. * * *—what do you want to know his name for?"

"We didn't want to know his name. Your son mentioned—"

"George's son . . ."

"That he was coming . . ."

"My medium's son? Why? Do you know him?"

"No. But the Indian girl asked if anyone else was coming and George's son looked into the appointments book and said, yes, he was supposed to be here. That's all."

"Well, you mustn't write anything about my patients unless they give you permission because they are . . . because I like to treat things . . . everything is treated very private . . . and I like my patients to trust me and this way . . . My patients are the famous and the unfamous and they can come along feeling safe, so to speak . . ."

"We respect your wishes."

"Well, what do you want to ask?"

"Factual things. What was your date of birth and your date of death?"

"It's in the book . . . it's all there. I was born in 1852 and I passed over in 1937. But it's all in *Healing Hands*."

"You specialized in ophthalmology? Could we ask you why you were chosen for this work? What happened on the other side that made you come through?"

"Quite simply during my life on earth I had a great love of my work. Surgery was my life. Do you understand? And so when I passed over into the spirit world medicine was still the thing I knew . . . the desire not just to practice but to help my fellow creatures in some way or other—and George was a very young man during those years and was chosen as my medium and I had to learn my new methods of treating a patient in the spirit world so I could return . . ."

"Are there other doctors you know in the spirit world who would like to do the same thing but aren't able to . . . ?"

"There are many other doctors but not enough capable mediums. There are many people who could be good mediums but they only go so far that the spirit doesn't get a chance to talk through them . . . they only go so far and many people come to see me who tell me they are mediums, they tell me that they develop a trance but a trance isn't necessary; so they work in the raw state. When I ask them who the trance control is they usually tell me that he is an Indian or a coloured gentleman and you can't get any evidence from that medium. You see? To me a medium should be able to provide evidence of survival. Now, no matter how much I speak to you about it myself, it may not give you the type of evidence you want. If I have a medical colleague or, better still, someone who knew me upon earth, then they recognize me as the William Lang they knew. But when you start talking about coloured people who died centuries and centuries ago, no one can produce any evidence to say that they would in actual point of fact . . . and so, to my mind, they are not genuine . . . If I knew of any other medium through whom a spirit doctor worked, it would be much easier for my medium to get more help—because some of the many patients who come here, he would be able to send to that other person. But the majority of healers all work in the normal state by laying on of hands . . . you see?

"What would you do, Dr. Lang, in the event of your medium's death?"

"Well, in the event of Chapman's death or the end of his mediumship, the medium who is my son . . . my medium's son . . . you understand? . . . He would be the medium for my son Basil and then my own work would finish. You see at present when I am operating on a patient I say . . ." here "Dr. Lang" snapped his fingers twice, "I say 'Basil' . . . and Basil assists me. Now when Michael is old enough—he is being trained as a medium now—my son Basil will be the spirit doctor for Michael and so it will go on that way—and Michael will marry, you see, and it will just . . ."

"Won't it be frustrating for you not to be able to work any more?"

"Oh, I shall still work, won't I? As things happen now, sometimes I step back while Basil operates and the same thing will apply then—but you see, I will be George's spirit and Michael

B

will be the medium for Basil but we . . . Basil co-operates with
me and I'll co-operate with him so my work shall go on just the
same. I'd be still working in the Chapman family. You see, it
takes many years to train a medium and it takes many years for
the spirit to be trained so that he can use his medium success-
fully. And therefore Michael's training started at birth. And now,
working in the normal state, he's a very good healer."

"So you have extraordinary communications with this family?"

"Yes, and of course, the advantage of it is that I was so well-
known on earth that the surgeons and doctors who knew me
and other people, professional people, although they are dying off
over there, my son's contemporaries who were eighteen or nine-
teen, still come to see me and so do their sons—and so I'm
kept in the picture as to what is happening in modern medicine
today . . ."

"Is that how you're keeping up with what's going on?"

"Oh yes. Last week I had two surgeons from the London
Hospital to see me with a nice list of questions and I said, well,
fair's fair. You may question me but I in turn must be allowed
to ask questions. I don't just sit here. I asked them about particular treatments and medicines they are using; so I'm gaining
knowledge all the time although I can't use it over here because
my method of treating a person is different from what one would
do here on earth—but I'm still interested to know what's going
on."

"Is it possible for you to have access to any of the medical
journals or the medical libraries?"

"Well, I know what goes on. Many people who are writing . . .
for instance, there's one young man who's writing a medical
brochure on cancer research . . . it was written here . . . He's
an American . . . but he came here and told me what he was
writing about and we discussed points and then it was all read
to me to give my opinion again and then it was sent to the
colleagues in America."

"But you couldn't possibly go through your medium to a
medical library and read up on it—should you want to know
about it?"

"It isn't necessary. When a patient comes here I look at his
spirit body and all the information I want is there, anyway."

"How do you handle incurables?"

"The word 'incurable' is one dreamed up by my profession. There is no such a thing. When a patient comes to me I tell him from the start I will do my very best to help him. I may succeed. I may fail and that's it. I don't cure every patient who comes along. But the word 'incurable' is just a word conjured up by the medical profession. You see, in medicine there's a routine, a way of doing things. You go to your doctor, he examines you and he finds some disease of this or that kind and he gives it treatment. If you don't respond to that treatment, he goes a stage further and gives you various treatments until in the end he is still unsuccessful and so the next step is to send you to the hospital. You go along to the hospital and there, too, they have their procedures of doing things—they keep to the practice which is laid down by the surgeons and the text-books and when they come to the end and you're not cured, you're marked incurable. But it's only a word."

"In other words if someone comes here with what your colleagues would call an incurable illness, such as cancer, you will try—?"

"Oh yes. But I will be honest with them. I had a lady here—no doubt you saw her in the wheelchair—and she sat down and I said, well, I'll examine you. If I see someone is a very intelligent person, I'll tell the truth straight away. I don't hide anything. If I see someone who's very nervous, I'll tell him the truth without letting him really know what I've said. You understand? Well, as soon as I examined this lady, I diagnosed cancer of the lumbar area of the spine which was spreading and she said that's what the doctors had told her. There are secondary growths, I said. And she asked: 'can you cure it?' I said I can't promise, I'll treat you—I may fail, I may succeed, I don't know. But if I succeed, you'll know. If I fail you'll be dead within eight months. Why eight months? Because this type of condition develops rapidly, spreading by the spinal core."

"How do you feel about eternal life? Do you think the medical profession is heading towards it? There is all this business of freezing people at the point of death . . . cryotherapy . . .?"

"My medical colleagues . . . well, the other day they asked me about heart transplants and I referred them to the paper written many years ago about the circulation of the blood and the action of the heart. We spoke of organs and transplants and of Man.

He can't live for ever. He has a life span. It can be expanded. In my day if you lived to sixty or seventy, it was a full life. Now people live to eighty-five or ninety. This is only because of good food, better nourishment, better clothing, housing, better medical facilities. Some of the people who are living to ninety would be better off over here. It was always my belief that if a person was suffering a great deal, he should be in the spirit world rather than go on suffering. Life is very dear to people. They want to go on living but they only live half-a-life and they should rather be over here than live under constant medical care."

"Is George Chapman aware of what happens when you inhabit his body?"

"He is completely out of his body. My medium won't meet any patients before he goes into a trance so he doesn't get any mind pictures. You know what it's like to meet somebody— maybe they're on crutches. My medium won't do this. He comes in here fifteen or thirty minutes before the patients arrive and goes into trance. He has no knowledge at all of any contact with the patients and of what is said here. He has to rely upon the patients to write to him and keep up reports by letter. He is out of his body. I can see your spirit body but I can only sense dead things, such as notebooks, chairs etc. I can only see what is spirit."

"What does a spirit look like?"

"In what way do you mean? A spirit body or a spirit soul?"

"Perhaps you can tell us the difference."

"Well, you see, you have your spirit body, your physical body and your soul which is the spirit soul. Quite simply, the spirit body is the same shape without the imperfections—rather too many imperfections—as the physical body. The physical takes the shape of the spirit body. Inside your spirit body is your spirit soul which is the soul and cannot have any imperfections. What happens, quite simply, is that diseases are set up on the spirit body which affect the physical body or the physical can affect the spiritual to some extent. When one dies the spirit body conveys the soul to the spirit world. The spirit body then dies and the soul is reborn and takes on shape again, the shape which it had when it was on earth. It is quite simple."

"Do you feel that your form of healing is more effective than that of the orthodox medical profession?"

"Not in all cases. I think very highly of the medical profession as many men of the medical profession think of me. I don't argue with them, I discuss things with them. Certain surgical work is done better by them than by me. For instance, if a person breaks a bone, it is much better to go to a doctor and have it set and plastered up. It depends. Some conditions shouldn't be touched by doctors, they should be treated by spirits. But you say, one can't say either one is better because these people . . . take that little Indian girl—isn't she beautiful?"

"She's lovely."

"That girl has a soul—a developed soul . . . Like many doctors who come to see me, she is a healer herself and therefore when she treats a patient she gives of herself, so a patient receives both spirit and medical treatment. Therefore one can't say one is better than the other . . . I would never say anything against any member of my medical profession or against medicine because I think very highly of medicine but every kind of healing has its own place."

"Are there any particular areas that you think you're best equipped to deal with as a spirit healer?"

Instead of replying, he took us over to examine the pictures of his colleagues, a photograph of his graduating class and others.

"All these surgeons . . ." he reminisced. "I commenced healing in the London hospital in the seventies . . . so there have been many, many surgeons in my life. I ended up at the Middlesex in 1914. Because there was a war on, I was asked to carry on and so my work was finished in the twenties. I didn't pass over until 1937. Now, all these surgeons are over here because of their ages, do you understand? In the spirit world . . . so all of them are with me, working as a team . . . Suppose I would diagnose some particular ailment in you . . . I would say . . ." and he snapped his fingers, "and So-and-so who was a specialist in that particular thing. I would discuss it with him and we would come to a conclusion . . . and so, whatever complaint comes here, I know what to do because I've got all those spirit-specialists working with me . . ."

"And how do they feel about birth control pills—introduced a good twenty years after they passed over?"

"It depends on the patient. You know, many patients who take these pills find it affects the lymphatic glands and they start to put on weight. So you get very beautiful slender ladies who've taken these pills—and by the age of forty they're very stout . . ."

"It must be difficult for your colleagues to keep up with medical progress, isn't it?"

"Not at all. Let's take one day last week. Today there's been just a couple of doctors. Last week there were five. Many of them come here to discuss things when they're writing a new book . . . they may come and talk to me and ask what was the position in my day. And I would ask them about antibodies or about cortisone. You see, I'm always interested in what goes on. Same as if someone were a racing driver, I'd ask him questions. I had a dancer here today and two opera singers. I asked them where they would sing next; much as I did with a pianist from America who came to see me. I don't play the piano but I asked for the programme because I know how it works and what they play. You can't be a cabbage, can you? I think no matter to whom you talk, you ought to ask questions."

"When you are not healing through George Chapman—what do you do in the spirit world? Do you talk to friends? do you play chess?"

"Yes. It's just like it is on earth."

"You mean, we have all those things to look forward to? Love and dancing and friendship?"

"Yes. When I passed over I met X. He said, I bet you're glad you're in the spirit world. Well, I'd have been just as happy living on earth. The main thing I would have missed were the pleasures of my work. No matter whether you are in this world or over here, you make your own heaven or hell. I found life on earth perfect and I found it just the same over here . . . People make too much of the spirit world. I'd have hated to come over here and not be myself. My medium would hate not to be George Chapman. You want to be who you are, not somebody floating around . . ."

"Among your colleagues in the spirit world who would you classify as the greatest contributors to medicine?"

"In the spirit world? I can't answer that . . . I'd make too many enemies."

"They'd gang up on you?"

"Yes."

"How about the world of the living?"

"I wouldn't like to say that either because in your living world there are so many men of medicine, among them as eminent as you can go, who come here to consult with me and I think so much of them. You know, there's the Lang Medal for the surgeon who has done the most within a year or so in eye surgery ... lectures and such. I'd never give it to the people who receive it each year because I think there are far better persons. You see, everybody in medicine from the nurse up does some little thing to help . . . they all make a contribution. A nurse may discuss something with a surgeon . . . he tells her things because he has to have someone young and lively to talk to and she gives him a line on something and he follows it so really the discovery may have come from the little nurse. I developed an instrument one year but it was only through talking to a young nurse and she said, Mr. Lang, I think such and such a thing would be better and she drew it for me and that instrument is still being used today . . ."

A few days later we have a meeting with George Chapman away from his home, separated from the setting in which he acts as medium for "Dr. Lang". At first glance he bears little resemblance to the spirit doctor. An extremely handsome man of forty-eight with a full head of greying hair and long sideburns, his face is unlined with the exception of a few "character lines" which make him look interesting. Well built, about 5 feet 7, he was dressed in an expensive brown corduroy suit with a matching corduroy overcoat, a shirt and a knit tie.

He told us a little about his life before he became a medium. He knew nothing about his parents; but at the age of five he acquired a guardian. At that time he was suffering from malnutrition and his ankles were very weak; but in the next five years he "built himself up" and by the time he was ten he became much interested in boxing. He grew up in a rough neighbourhood where he had to learn to defend himself—and he did. His schooling was scanty and he did not learn to read and write properly until he joined the Army in 1939. He lied about his age and got into the Irish Guards where they made him a physical training instructor.

He gave us some details about the setting of his work and the financial details. With the exception of the examination couch, all the furniture in his consulting room used to belong to Dr. Lang; he had obtained it through the members of a medical group many of whom were colleagues of Basil Lang. He explained that he had a private income and did not make his living from healing. The practice allotted him about £40.—(say $100.—) per week which he used to pay his office staff. He employed a total of fifteen people, eight of whom were typists and there was a full-time accountant. The typists dealt with the large correspondence which he answered himself—not "Dr. Lang". It seems that he invested the money he made as a prize fighter in stocks and shares.

As we talked to him, we found that we saw far more in his face of Dr. Lang than initially. He used quite frequently the phrase "do you understand?" and "you see" which were stock phrases of "Dr. Lang" and even the tonal inflection seemed to be quite similar. But of course one could not discount the fact that "Dr. Lang" was supposed to use his, George Chapman's, physical body and some resemblance was unavoidable. Yet one had the distinct feeling that Dr. Lang and George Chapman were the same person and that Chapman either had certain schizoid features—or was a very able actor.

He spoke at some length about his son, Michael who was supposed to take over for him and the late Basil Lang when he, Chapman, passed on. Michael had never gone into trance and his father had encouraged him to choose a different career—but the boy himself wanted to do this.

We asked him about his own trance.

"To go into trance you have to be able to relax. When I say this, I mean, relax every muscle, no matter what disharmonies or conflicts you may have. You must be the proper type of person who can push things away, not a worrier. Do you understand what I mean? You must be the complete you; the type of person who, as a medium, is the master of his own mind. By this I mean that one is not going to be influenced by anything that may move in the room while one is sitting there. So all I do is to sit and relax myself. I just stretch myself out, cross my arms and make myself relaxed. Then I just close my eyes and I start going to sleep. As I find myself going off to sleep, I see great mist coming towards me and then this mist, like a fog, takes the shape of a person. As this person comes closer, he takes on the features of Dr. Lang. As I see him, I can see myself floating away—myself, George Chapman, moving away and then as I start moving away, becoming a mist—and as the two meet, I know no more."

"How did you feel the first time this happened?"

"Well, let me give you a parallel. In the Forces I was stationed with a Polish squadron during the Battle of Britain. Some of the Poles had too much to drink and as usual, there was a fight between the British airmen and the Poles at one of the local village pubs. I had just come off duty and I was tired. I lay on my bed and one of the Poles got a pillow and pushed it over my face . . . if you can understand . . . feeling half asleep, dozing and then feeling as if you were being smothered . . . That was the experience and I feel the same now, being smothered, as it comes towards me. That's what you feel when you're going into trance. And when you're coming out of trance again, you start seeing the smiling face of a doctor—you see the mist going away and you see yourself coming as though this body is something unimportant you carry about and two people can use it, like an overcoat. You see one moving away and yourself moving in and you feel as if you were starting to breathe again . . . absorbing oxygen once more . . ."

"Do you feel tired afterwards?"

"Oh yes. It takes me an hour to recover. When I'm finished, Michael switches on the shower for me and I go in or I may go and take a bath in the house and then Michael brings me a couple of pints of very sweet tea and I lie in the bath drinking this—and they know they must not come near me because I am so bad-tempered. Or rather—I just don't want to know anything. Have you ever lain in bed and every nerve of your body felt as if it wanted to . . . this is the feeling I have. I'm lying in the bath and the water doesn't feel as if it did anything. You can to be yourself again . . . because what has taken place . . . all the different people coming in with their different complaints . . . you feel as if all their conditions have been clinging to you and you must buff yourself, so you're clean. Then I use a lot of cologne—which I like because it seems to get the aura of sickness off my body. Then I dry myself and take the dog for a walk, half-an-hour or so. But after that everything seems to come back and I am all right."

B*

"How do you feel about giving up your ego and having some-one take over your body?"

"No, you're not giving up your ego because the ego is you, isn't it? I'll always be myself. I'm me in every possible way. Whatever gives you your feelings, the drive to achieve something with your life is the part of you which is important, which is you. The thing which is inside you, which gives you feelings, which attracts you to some people and which makes others re-pulsive to you. The thing which makes you want to do some-thing with your life, not just be whoever you are—that makes you want to achieve something and even if you fail, you know, this is the ego I believe, the spirit that makes you. You can never take that away from a person. But the physical body, we dress it up in nice clothes, we powder it, we rub cologne on it, to make you feel good. Women go to hairdressers because they want their hair done some way to make them feel better—but all they're doing to my mind is dressing up the physical body. As for taking over my body, every time I must give special permission that it should be done. I mean, before I go into trance, I go into my healing room and I spend half an hour to prepare myself so I can move out of my body. For a trance medium the doctor can't do anything unless I can move out of my body and I, as a person, must have the ability to get my spirit body out. But my ego, my spirit self goes out within that body, the spirit body. It's still me. This, my physical body, is a vessel I'm letting them use."

"Do you feel that the ego is totally disconnected from the body?"

"Yes . . . err . . . no! It's connected with the body. It's just connected insomuch as to form part of you. The only part that survives. But the nice thing about is you open the mail and you get ten letters complaining and then, you get someone else who's cured and that's made your day. And so you feel, well, although this work is so strenuous, what I'm doing is worth while."

That was about all George Chapman would tell us but we thought the partnership of the ex-boxer and the late famous surgeon so intriguing that we pursued our enquiries—and we found two people who were both willing to talk and had im-portant things to say about this healer . . . or healers.

The first was Gordon Creighton, a retired civil servant who has had experiences both with George Chapman and with a psychic surgeon whose career we are discussing in our next chapter. Creighton who has also been connected with the investigations into UFO's (Unidentified Flying Objects, or, if you like, flying saucers), had been treated himself by George Chapman.

"I think this business of Lang is quite impressive," Mr. Creighton told us, "because I think George Chapman was originally a butcher's boy or something. Did you meet him as George Chapman?"

"No, as Dr. Lang."

"I can assure you that Chapman is nothing like him. Did you read the book *Healing Hands*? It's an important one. One of the cases mentioned in it is that of a young German woman named Ilse Kuder who suffered terrible injuries in a road accident. Well, I know her very well and the strange thing is that I'd never known that she had this horrible accident. I got to know her after that. The story of her cure is all true. So I think George Chapman is very important. Then there is Harry Edwards who is unquestionably a channel for great healing power—and Gordon Turner whom I know well and several others. The funny thing is they all somehow work in different ways, are on different levels and wave lengths. What one can do, another, can't. Some do this so-called absent treatment and some don't. I think it's all working up to something very extraordinary. The technique of this man Lang is totally different as far as I know from any of the Brazilian psychic surgeons where there is an actual removal of tissues . . ."

"Lang doesn't cut—he isn't really a psychic surgeon but a healer."

"Well, maybe his spirit double does . . . I had Lang actually work on my sinus area because I've got chronic sinusitis."

"Did it help?"

"To a certain extent, yes."

The other patient of George Chapman/Dr. Lang whom we tracked down was the lady who had been brought to him in a wheel-chair and of whom the "spirit-doctor" told us that she had spinal cancer which was spreading rapidly. Her story was so extraordinary that we asked her to put it in writing and this is what she sent us from her home, Pant Glas, Tre'r-Ddol, Machynlleth, Montgomeryshire:

Yes, it is perfectly true: Dr. Lang cured me of cancer, which gave me about six to eight months to live on his reckoning, within a fortnight of his treatment on 26th November (1969).

When you saw me being carried into his consulting room I was not exactly filled with hope. The medical profession knew me as incurable. My condition had been diagnosed in Aberystwyth and, later, in Birmingham at the General Hospital by the radiologist and cancer expert—whose name I hope I shall remember by the time I finish this letter!* I was then attended in Broadway, Worcs. by Dr. William Juckes, who now marvels at my cure. There is a curious silence from all Aberystwyth doctors, but I gather the case is much discussed! Not one doctor locally has been to see me since I visited Dr. Lang, but I have not needed them. Perhaps we might fairly attribute my slightly inaccessible hillside home as a reason?

After that visit, for the first ten days I lay in bed, completely immovable as before. My left leg was paralysed but gradually I left off pain killers to ease the back pain. I then came home and within five days could stand without pain. The following day I walked easily from room to room and typed several letters—a feat which had been impossible for the past three and a half months.

This was cancer of the spine. I have just walked half a mile through my woods and back up the steep path, feeling perfectly well and strong. I am still taking moderate care, because Dr. Lang warned me not to run before I could walk. Apart from a little rheumatism across the shoulders I am as well as ever, and strengthening daily after four months in bed. The strange thing was that I did not have to learn to walk again after such a long period in bed; I just walked.

I have another appointment with Dr. Lang early in June, so that he can then give me the All Clear, which is apparent now. I thought that medically it would be more satisfactory; then, if they like, they can take other X-rays!

The operations which Dr. Lang carried out on my etheric body were on my heart and kidneys. He wanted to release

* Dr. Guy Holme.

a sudden flow from the heart to help to seal the activity, which he stated to be great, on those cancer cells. This he seemed to achieve excellently.

My own thoughts on the matter, for what they are worth, are that while mankind bumbles about, destroying or, worse, torturing animals for medical solutions, they are destroying the very purpose they would serve. But even when Heaven gets in a rage with us, it is the tenderest sort of rage: we are sent people like Dr. Lang to solve and expound. I think it will not be long before such help from the other side is accepted generally by the medical profession before it destroys its valuable self.

So now I can go ahead with my plans to build homes here for elderly pet lovers who would otherwise have to be separated from often the only friends left to them. There is a frightening demand but no doubt it will all get sorted out in time.

Whatever Mrs. Elma M. Williams, who runs her Valley of Animals with such passionate devotion, may experience in the future, her letter is a glowing testimony to George Chapman/Dr. Lang. Others may have had less sensational cures, but even this single instance is a remarkable one—as, indeed, are many others which some faith healers have achieved.

Such a faith healer, less famous than Harry Edwards, but equally active and self-assured is Kenneth Hebblethwaite—who works at his "craft" only part time. He hit the headlines in Britain when he cured Mr. Richard Pratt, Chief Constable of Bedfordshire, of a serious back complaint. (Note the concentration on spinal and back trouble—practically a special field of faith healing.) Hebblethwaite lives at Biddenham Turn, Bedford and after press reports began to appear about his successes, hundreds of letters started to arrive, all asking for help—not only from Britain but also from America and Germany.

Money is of no interest to Hebblethwaite who is the head of seven companies concerned with building and finance; he is also a member of Bedfordshire County Council. He only devotes his spare time to healing; a deeply religious man, he carries a Bible in the glove-compartment of his Jaguar. He uses a very simple technique: he makes each patient lie on a couch, places his left hand under the head, the right hand on the forehead of the sufferer. His voice is soft as he urges them to relax. He says a prayer and that's the end of the "treatment".

We spoke to one of his grateful patients—Mrs. Daisy Longland, aged 65, of Coventry Road, Bedford who had suffered from fibrositis of the spine for almost fifteen years.

"I have spent hundreds of pounds on medical treatment," Mrs. Longland explained. "I have been to Guernsey and Germany to see specialists. I have had physiotherapy and worn steel corsets but all to no effect. The pain was sometimes unbearable."

But after a few minutes with Mr. Hebblethwaite, she sat up on the couch and cried: "It's gone, the pain's gone." She flung her arms around the healer's neck. "After all these years, it's a miracle . . ."

As she described it later: "His right hand seemed to be burning. I also felt a tingling, like pins and needles in my fingers—then a feeling of peace and tranquility came over me." She was able to bend down and touch her toes without difficulty.

Two other patients described a similar "pins-and-needles" effect and the heat which Mr. Hebblethwaite's hands appeared to generate. And when he showed us his hands after his day's healing, they were marked by three large blotches.

Mrs. Edwina Massey of Dennis Road, Kempston, Bedford, had suffered from rheumatoid arthritis since her son was born in 1965. After treatment, she sat straight up and said: "I couldn't do that before. I had to swing my legs over the edge and get up very slowly." She put her hands behind her head and touched the back of her neck. "I couldn't do that either . . . I have always had to get a neighbour to set my hair . . ." She walked downstairs normally and remarked. "I haven't been able to do that in three years. I always had to go down sideways, a step at a time."

The third patient, a 75-year-old man had been in pain since an attack of shingles in 1964. He, too, was relieved of pain "completely". Mr. Dennis Betts, a 42-year-old car salesman who was invalided out of the R.A.F. in 1966, suffering from a serious neck disorder, had an even more extraordinary tale to tell. The trouble had begun to develop in 1961 and the R.A.F. decided that it was due to an accident Betts had while drawing a lorry—aggravated later in a parachute landing. He was given a disability pension. Bett's couldn't turn his head to the side at all, had to wear a rack for support and was in constant, considerable pain. "Then I went to Mr. Hebblethwaite," he said. "The first time I only had partial relief but when I went back to see him again, I was completely cured. All the pain went and I was able to turn my head freely. Now I have joined the Territorial Army and go on assault courses with them. A few months ago I went for an R.A.F. medical check on my disability. I was passed as completely fit and they took my pension away . . ."

Still another dramatic cure recorded was that of 30-year-old Mr. Terence Bullivant, a window cleaner from Birdfoot Lane, Luton, Bedfordshire. He fractured his wrist and dislocated his elbow when he fell fifteen feet from a window ledge. The accident left his right arm three inches shorter than his left. After treatment by Hebblethwaite it was claimed that his arms returned to the same length, the pain left him and he was able to practice judo regularly.

The last case presented to us was that of Mr. Horace Mabbott, a poultry farmer aged 62 of Clapham, Bedfordshire. Late in 1967 he developed severe back trouble and could barely walk. He lay on boards for weeks without moving. "Then Mr. Hebblethwaite laid his hands on me. I got up and walked about the room and I have never felt a twinge since."

Hebblethwaite himself estimates that three out of four treatments are successful. Originally he used to see only two or three people a week but by February 1969 they had increased to three or four a day. This made heavy inroads on his time; as he had absolutely no intention of imposing any charge, he had to find a financial solution. But he was determined to go on because he believed in his own powers—"the power of God working within me"—and felt it his duty to help people.

David Lee is one of Britain's most successful popular composers. His song *Goodness, Gracious Me!*, the theme song of the Peter-Sellers-Sofia Loren hit *The Millionairess* swept the charts some years ago; his musical *Our Mister Crichton* (based on the Barrie play) had a respectable run in London and he has composed reams of theme music for television shows, not to mention mining the rich golden vein of jingles.

David is a very matter-of-fact man—in spite of his profession. The story he told us was the more striking—even though sceptics might raise a number of nagging questions. But the events he recorded were beyond doubt genuine even if their interpretation or causation might be debated.

All through his life David Lee had suffered dreadfully from attacks of hayfever and asthma. These became finally so bad that a Harley Street specialist and several doctors at the clinic he had been attending recommended a series of injections developed by a certain Dr. Pees. Lee accepted this advice and the injections were administered daily by his personal physician.

Gradually he began to notice that his eyes were being affected and that he was losing his sight. He did not connect the daily injections and his impaired vision but he did consult an eye specialist named Lorimer Fison, a man of excellent reputation who had been oculist of the Duke of Windsor. Mr. Fison diagnosed cataracts which he said had been developing over the years and had suddenly taken a turn for the worse. He added, in confidence that the injections may have contributed to this—though he was not prepared to testify publicly against the drug. David Lee explained that less than a year before this diagnosis he had a complete check-up of his eyes—at which time no evidence of any cataracts was found or communicated to him. The check-up was needed as he wears glasses and has periodical examinations as to their efficiency. Lorimer Fison advised an operation to be done as quickly as possible—though he was not prepared to guarantee complete success. Even after the operation, he said, David Lee would have to wear rather thick glasses.

The composer became very depressed. He had stopped taking the daily injections but his eyesight was not getting any better. One day at the B.B.C. he ran into Michael Bentine, the well-known comedian and told him about his problem. Bentine recommended a woman he knew, a faith healer called Florrie Dott. Lee, though sceptical, decided to follow Bentine's suggestion. About two months had now passed since he had ceased having the injections and his condition was not getting any better.

He called on Miss Dott who made him sit down and said that she did not want him to tell her what was wrong with him; she explained that she received messages as to a person's illness and that if she was told anything, it interfered with these. She

washed her hands and said a brief prayer. Then she stood behind
his chair and told him he was suffering from hayfever and had
considerable trouble with his eyes. She asked him which of these
conditions he had come to see her about. He replied that it was
his eyes. She then placed her hands over his eyes and kept them
there for about five minutes. When she removed her hands, she
suggested having a cup of tea with her. At that time David Lee
felt no change; Miss Dott explained that it would take four or
five days before he did feel any improvement in the right eye
and that the left eye would take a little longer—about three
weeks. She added that he would feel a slight sensation of con-
traction in his forehead, as if pulling, when the cure began. As
for his asthma, she said that it was quite a different problem and
she was not certain whether she could do anything about it.
If he could wait about a year, she added, and then see her every
day, she would try whether anything could alleviate it.

David Lee went home; he and his wife were rather amused
by his experience and he became thoroughly resigned to the need
of an operation. But within four or five days his right eye was
completely healed while the left took three weeks. He no longer
had any difficulty with his sight. He wrote to the eye specialist,
telling him what had happened and asked for a re-examination
to see whether the cataracts were still there. Apart from a bill,
he received no answer. The cure was permanent.

Florrie Dott lives in a tiny, very simple house in Hertfordshire.
Her setting, her manner are in complete antithesis to Harry
Edward's elaborate establishment. Right from the start she
created a personal relationship with us—which she seems to do
with everybody who comes to her. She is a devout, sincere woman
who genuinely believes in her own gift of healing—but honest
enough to admit that her powers do not always work. She has
been practising healing for thirty years—though there have been
periods when nothing went right. At such times she has, on
occasion, taken a year off. When we saw her she thought she
might be entering such a period. She said she didn't know why
some people were healed and why others could not be.

"I first found out about my powers one day when I saw a
dog with eczema. Its hair was falling out and it was covered with
scabs. I took it in my hands and said: 'Dear God, make him

well . . .' Healing commenced the following day and the dog was cured within a week."

Her next patient was also canine, with an injured paw; it had an instantaneous cure. She took its paw in her hands, examined it for thorns, cuts or splinters and when she found none, she simply said again: "Dear God, make him well . . ." and the dog moved off, walking on all fours.

In her early sixties, Florrie is a large, stocky woman although not fat but rather sturdy. Her grey hair is simply held back with a band. She dresses plainly in a black woolly jacket and a maroon skirt.

"I have psychic as well as healing powers," she said. "I know when people are ill or in pain. Sometimes I wake up at night and I know that a friend is having pain. Then I say a prayer for him and next day when I telephone I find out I have been right . . ."

She has a strong, unshaken faith in God and believes that her powers are a divine gift. She never asks what somebody's illness is but prefers to establish it through her own system of communication.

She asked one of us to sit in a chair, facing away from her and then put her hands on the visitor's shoulders. First she had washed her hands and said a prayer. She said that the visitor was very tense and had recently gone through a shock. She asked whether she had any vaginal discharge. When the visitor replied, no, she asked the second lady in our party whether she had any—because she "might have been picking up her waves". In fact, there had been a kidney infection recently and the second lady suspected a recurrence and had called her doctor for an appointment that morning.

Miss Dott asked a number of other questions, spending a good ten minutes before she finally announced that she didn't think she was "going to get it". The first visitor then showed her wrist and told about the swelling and pain. Miss Dott laid her hands on her shoulder, massaged her spine and ran her fingers, very lightly, over her face, eyes and hair, continuing for about five minutes. Then she went down on her knees and massaged the spine with her hands, passing on to the arm all the way from the shoulder down to the hand. She held the swollen wrist firmly in her own hand. Her eyes were closed and she stayed on her knees. She then got up and continued the shoulder, face and hair routine for a little longer. When she finished, she suggested that the visitor run the hand under the cold water tap and expect a brighter day tomorrow.

Florrie Dott goes into a state of complete relaxation in order to make her powers work—a technique she learned from a medium in her training days. She has a most comforting and soothing manner which, of course, is a psychological asset. She does not accept any contribution or gift—"my healing powers are a present from God and I feel I must share them with all who need them . . ."

In April 1969 the parish priest of the little village Verniana in the Italian province of Arezzo was sentenced to eighteen months in jail for "misrepresentation and fraud". Don Angelo Fantoni had been charged with practicing medicine without a licence or proper qualifications. His attorneys succeeded in saving him from jail—by lodging an appeal. The higher court has not yet heard the case and it might be indefinitely postponed.

When we went to see him, we found him a strange mixture of a man of the cloth and a healer. The most famous of these was Father Pio in Apulia, in the district of Gargano, who bore stigmata—or at least claimed he did. Don Fantoni maintains that by virtue of his own physical *fluidum* he has been able to diagnose the ailments of *nine thousand people*—and curing them by prescribing appropriate medicines. The village where he lives has only three hundred souls and is very difficult to reach. Yet, as the good Don Antonio claimed, famous politicians, rich industrialists, celebrated sportsmen and filmstars have made the long and arduous journey. Among other "instant diagnoses" the village priest cited the case of Mussolini. When the Duce shook hands with him during a visit to Verniana, he told him immediately : "Your Excellency, you have an abdominal tumor." Surgery confirmed the diagnosis—whereupon the Duce repeatedly consulted the faith healing curate in matters of health. Of course, Don Angelo could not save him from the bullets that finished him off.

Father Fantoni is the son of a poor herbwoman who used to treat the sick with all kinds of home remedies. But the parish priest of Verniana claims a specific gift, a definite spiritual energy.

Though we did not experience it ourselves, some of his visitors maintained firmly that a mere touch by a patient creates a "body-fluid" in Don Angelo which in turn reacts to the various diseases in a clearly marked, different way. For instance, if a man suffering from a liver ailment touches him, Father Fantoni suffers a certain "spasm", while a stomach ulcer produces quite a different reaction. Having studied medical works for many years, he has now every possible therapy at his fingertips—but he mostly suggests appropriate cures as a choice of his "intuition".

Don Angelo claims that he has never broken the law because the prescriptions were made by four physicians whom he trusted —and who became very prosperous indeed in the process. It was because of alleged "unfair professional competition" that other physicians denounced him and the four doctors. Father Fantoni himself never accepts any money—and he has never been censured or disciplined by the Vatican. Those who want to show their gratitude are directed to the poor box and the other collection boxes in the church. With the money he has gathered in this way, Father Fantoni paid for a children's home, renovated the ramshackle edifice and helped the poor in many ways. He himself lives in an unheated room which is furnished with a desk, two chairs and a small chest of drawers—quite insufficient to house the numberless letters of gratitude he receives.

The priest of Verniana is also distinguished by his absolute frankness—both as a man of the cloth and as a healer. When we saw him, he told a Swiss journalist who had joined our party : "I like newspapermen. You have an iron constitution— but you won't live very long."

The Fantoni case caused a considerable sensation in Italy because for the first time a large-scale examination of extra-sensory perception is being undertaken in the country, inspired largely by the Institute of Parapsychology in Freiburg and its head, Professor Bender. Experts of the church are also interested in the critical and experimental investigations—and Don Angelo is a kind of test-case.

In April 1969 a Congress of Parapsychology met in Campione at which telepathy, clairvoyance and telekinesis were the main subjects, with outstanding experts (including clerics) taking part in it. The basic problem was formulated clearly : "Is there a specific psychic energy which cannot yet be measured physically—

comparable to mechanical, electrical and magnetic energy? And if it does exist—for it appears that this is no longer in doubt—what origin and what character, ascertainable by natural law, does it possess?"

Don Angelo Fantoni was quoted as an example of a person equipped (blessed? cursed?) with such extrasensory or "psycho-kinetic" energy. The experts pointed out that mankind has existed for thousands of years without knowing anything about electric energy, at least in a rational and conscious way—and that today we are still groping in the dark concerning the problem of "psycho-kinetic energy", an equally ancient "substance, function or form". All through those thousands of years "magicians", "wizards", founders of religions, political demagogues—and, above all, faith healers—have or may have possessed and exploited, utilized or abused it. And the majority at the Campione meeting decided that every human being is a potential owner of such extrasensory, psycho-kinetic energy; but at the same time only a very few—in most cases with an underdeveloped ego and a disturbed, unbalanced superego—sense these "supernormal psychic powers" in themselves. These may be hysterics, considered in normal relationships as semi-psychopaths—but in the majority of cases they are simply aware of something the vast multitude of humanity does not understand, feel or use.

It is possible that one day we will be able to absorb, receive, measure and study this psychic power with more sensitive electronic apparatus than we possess today. Certainly it is a little-known though startling fact that the general staffs of the great powers devote a good deal of attention (and money) to this problem—above all, the Soviet Union. One of the closest guarded places in Moscow is the Institute of Parapsychology where for decades remarkable experiments have been conducted—involving extra-sensory perception, faith healing (or, if you like, suggestibility, hypnosis, clairvoyance etc.) Professor Henriquez, one of the best-known Italian parapsychologists delivered some time ago a closely-reasoned, highly appreciated lecture in front of high-ranking officers in Rome about the uses of ESP in modern warfare. Not all the generals took it seriously but at least some of them felt that this new "line of defence" must not be ignored. And there have been hints that Don Angelo Fantoni, the faith-healing priest of Verniana, would provide a first-class subject for study—a critical, unbiased, scientific study of the mysterious powers whose existence even conservative science has started to accept.

The United States has the distinction of claiming a husband-and-wife team of faith-healers. The Reverend Ambrose A. Worrall and his wife, Olga N. Worrall, nee Ripich, conduct their healing services at the Mount Washington Methodist Church, Falls Road and Smith Avenue, Baltimore, Maryland, each Thursday from 11 a.m. until noon. This is a rather short time and the Worralls do not receive "patients" at their home. On the other hand, as the Reverend told us:

"There are many names given to this manifestation, such as faith healing, New Thought Healing, Spiritual Healing etc.; but no matter what name may be chosen, we know that the power of God is available and is capable of restoring health, and improving conditions relative to peace and prosperity. We know that this power is able to operate at a distance, therefore it is not necessary to arrange for a physical contact between the patient and the healer. It would not be possible for us to meet personally with the thousands of people who have written to us . . ."

"How do you administer the 'power', then?" we asked.

"We join with all who desire in five minutes of spiritual communion with the Divine Presence, from 9 p.m. to 9.05 p.m. every night on Eastern Standard Time—or Eastern Saving Time when in effect."

We asked what the "spiritual communicants" were expected to do?

"They should pray, either aloud or in silence, immediately before nine p.m. and then, at that hour, all prayer should cease and conscious awareness of the Divine Presence be sought for the five minutes by anticipating in expectancy some revelation, by intuition or sensing, of the actual demonstration of Divine Power."

But the Worralls also want everybody to co-operate with their doctor—and to give thanks regularly in one's chosen place of worship. In their book *The Gift of Healing* (published in paperback as *The Miracle Healers*) they describe themselves as "sensitives"; Mrs. Worrall began to have visions of "people in my room" at the age of twelve; Ambrose, who was born in Barrow-in-Furness, had the same experience at the age of six. Even his father had seen an apparition of his dead brother. Ambrose's first act of healing was performed on his sister Barbara who had suffered an injury to her neck which left her head fixed at an angle; she could only move it with great difficulty and pain. One day some psychic force "grew" out of Ambrose's solar plexus and dragged him to his sister's chair. He touched the sides of Barbara's neck for five or six seconds—and she was healed, permanently and completely. He found out about his own gift from a Methodist lay preacher who was a sensitive himself. His psychic experiences multiplied and expanded and he learned something of the extra-sensory world. Then, in 1922, Worrall emigrated to America. He settled in Cleveland and went to work for the Glenn Miller aircraft factory where he did rather well. It was here that he met his future wife—Cleveland has a large Hungarian colony —and became engaged to her a short time afterwards. He felt he had to tell her about his experiences and gifts; and was startled to discover that she accepted it all as a matter-of-fact because she had similar ones herself. Her father was a Russian who had been educated as a priest of the Orthodox Greek Church; her mother the descendant of a distinguished Magyar family, a Catholic. But Olga was brought up in the Russian Orthodox Church and she and Ambrose were married in St. Theodosius's in June, 1928. The marriage started under some difficulties—their first apartment was haunted by poltergeists— but soon the "psychical forces" provided them with another, cheaper and better one. Before long their healing activities began—and have continued for more than forty years, almost unbroken. It was, however, some time before they established their New Life Clinic, "a blend of faith and practicality" in Baltimore and there were years of apprenticeship, experimentation and "groping" before they both were able to exercise their healing powers in the most efficacious and concentrated way.

In their book Ambrose and Olga Worrall print a number of statements about personal experiences in spiritual healing. These were not meant to be essentially testimonials but examples of the many hundreds of letters which they received during more than thirty-five years of their work.

A physician who, for professional reasons, used only his initials (H.T.C.) described the disappearance of a large abdominal tumour from which a married nurse, living in New Jersey, had suffered. The presence of the tumour had been established by X-rays and she had received orthodox treatment. Visiting Baltimore, she and her husband went to the Mt. Vernon Methodist Church and Olga Worrall "without any type of suggestion, was guided to 'lay hands' upon the nurse's abdomen". This was in May; by November the tumour was completely gone and she was able to return to her normal work.

Charlotte J. Stout visited her doctor in July 1960; his diagnosis was breast cancer. Two days later she called on the Worralls and after spending two hours with Ambrose Worrall in his healing room, she cancelled an operation that was set for early August. The spiritual healing treatments continued for about two months; by early October the lump in her breast had completely disappeared. A medical examination in February 1961 confirmed this fully.

Another physician, Dr. R. K. Adolph examined a colleague who complained of pain in his lower spine which he has had for many years. After Dr. Adolph had diagnosed a rotary scoliosis of the dorsal spine and a compensatory curvature of the lumbar spine, his patient explained that "a lady by the name of Olga Worrall had told him the exact same thing" and had also told him that he had a fall from a swing when he was very young. This was correct; and she had told him where his pain was, when it had happened, how it was caused and what to do to have it corrected. Dr. Adolph treated his colleague from his own physical findings and from the advice of Mrs. Worrall. The treatment was completely successful—and no pain recurred. The doctor declared that he believed Olga Worrall "has a valuable gift to see and detect a person's problem that we as doctors are not always able to do".

There are a good many other "unsolicited testimonials" in the Worrall's book and it is obvious that they practice the kind of spiritual healing which links religion and cures that are not achieved by orthodox medical methods. And while opinions might differ how many of these ailments were psychosomatic, the impressive record of the Baltimore couple cannot be denied.

It is a strange fact that the greatest and most famous centre of faith healing whose very name stood for miraculous cures has faded out of the headlines, receives very rarely a mention in newspapers or other news media. *Lourdes*, about which Zola wrote a magnificent novel and about which there has been recently a sharply critical non-fiction book by the English researcher and writer, Dr. West, has been a place of pilgrimage and a magnet for the lame and the halt for almost a century. Ever since little Bernadette Soubirous met "the Lady" near the bank of the River Gave, the men, women and children in search of help have flocked to it. Bernadette, canonized in 1933, has been dead nearly ninety years; but the miracles of Lourdes have obscured much of the life of this remarkable saint. Now, however, it appears that the miracles are being eclipsed, that faith no longer heals at Lourdes—or if it does, it receives remarkable little attention.

Lourdes had been badly hit by the nation-wide French rail strike of 1968 which forced at least thirty hotels and boarding houses to close temporarily because of lack of guests; yet although this took place during Whitsun when twenty thousand were expected, more than three thousand people still managed to get there. Many of the townspeople, of course, live by selling flagons in which to take home the "healing waters" or other small religious souvenirs—and these were even harder hit by the strike than the hotel people.

Two interesting trends, outgrowths of ecumenism and secularism, seem to emerge in Lourdes. The shrine is becoming more of a Christian than a purely Catholic one. Protestants now visit Lourdes in growing numbers. Secondly, the cost of visiting France has been reduced, mainly by better and cheaper transport. This has put such a journey within reach of the working classes. A new travel agency plan combines holiday and pilgrimage; the tourist can purchase a "package deal" which includes a visit to the shrine and one of several vacation stays at the Cirque de Gavarnie, San Sebastian or Biarritz.

We spoke to Dr. Letitia Fairfield (sister of Dame Rebecca West) a distinguished physician, authoress and psychical researcher who is herself a Catholic and who had been to Lourdes with the express purpose of looking into the medical aspects of the cures. She was particularly on the look-out for psychosomatic conditions; in her view *even when the cures could be explained by entirely natural causes, she felt that they were remarkably speeded up by visits to the place.*

Over half of the "Lourdes miracles" were cures of tuberculosis; only three recorded ones were cancer cures. Four-fifths of the TB cases were women—and hysterical disorders of pulmonary functions are more common in females. No one could really say whether Lourdes had a beneficial effect on cancer or whether the tuberculotic label was used for cases that responded to suggestion. The improvement in subjective symptoms did not always correspond to immediate changes in the physical state. *And yet—*

"There was this nun," Dr. Fairfield told us, "from Northern Italy who had developed a gastric condition. It had been investigated by a good Italian hospital and there was some difficulty in establishing the exact diagnosis—to determine whether it was a form of ulceration or a gross disturbance of the digestion which didn't seem to yield to treatment. She was extremely ill—there wasn't the slightest doubt about the gravity of her condition. She had insisted on coming to Lourdes—with the usual suggestions that she was at death's door and so on. One is never quite sure how much importance to attach to such subjective statements. Anyway, she was about twenty-four, a big, sturdy peasant girl—and her health didn't improve at Lourdes at all. She went into the bath and took part in the processions of the Holy Sacrament—with no change whatsoever. She had to be carried about on a stretcher and she was as weak as one could be. Well, finally she went back to her convent and they put her into her cell—and, I think, within two days—it was almost within hours—she suddenly announced that she was now miraculously cured. She was perfectly well—nothing wrong with her at all. She got up and while before she had never been able for weeks to retain anything but liquid food, she now ate a large meal; after which she never looked back and didn't have the slightest digestive trouble ever. Well, the doctors were very scathing about this, saying that it was all psycho-neurotism—but psycho-neurotic cases as bad as this are very uncommon . . . just as it is very uncommon to achieve this complete and sudden reversal into perfect health. I ventured to speak up and asked if we couldn't have an investigation but was brushed aside completely by the French doctors who staff the permanent medical bureau at Lourdes. Its secretary was quite rude about it. It is only fair to say that the bureau itself is completely honest about these things—but there are some curious attitudes they adopt in their anxiety not to be thought gullible . . ."

"How does this bureau work?" we asked.

"Well, the trouble is, it doesn't. Lourdes is only open for about six months a year and you can't get competent doctors to take off half the year each year just to sit and wait for miracles. Lourdes is not large enough to maintain a permanent hospital staff . . . After the bureau had been running for many years, X-rays were discovered and they provided an entirely new key to diagnosing obscure diseases. Everybody wanted to know whether you'd been X-rayed. And to do the Lourdes Bureau justice again, they did instal X-ray apparatus and they did try to obtain tests before and after the cures. Yet with all the fuss about X-rays and communicating with the hospitals all over the world, the Bureau rarely answers letters, refuses to send plates. I myself was only able to see X-rays before and after the cure in a single case—and these did not support the story of the miracle . . ."

"Is there a foolproof way of testing the claims of faith-healing?"

"It may sound grotesque—but in all these cases the important things are the biological tests, the fine chemical analysis of tissue and excretion. This has altered the whole picture. Let me give you the example of two diseases that for many years were considered practically incurable, a sentence of death. One of them was Addison's Disease—affecting the glands and the kidney; people turn a kind of blackish colour, become thoroughly exhausted, the whole chemistry of the body breaks down—and they die. As far as I know there is no cure for it to this day. The same thing applies to Hodgkins's Disease which is a cancer of the glands of the neck; even early surgery cured it very rarely. But now it's known that with all the classic symptoms of both *there are several varieties* of both diseases that can be distinguished by biological tests and *some of them are perfectly curable*. Not every case is fatal—and you will understand that this makes all the difference in the world. Now, when I was in Lourdes, there was no laboratory that could or did do such tests on people. The X-ray apparatus had broken down because the woman who handled it for many years had died of heart-failure and there was no one to operate the expensive machinery which some American benefactors had contributed. The same thing with the electro-cardiography. A magnificent one they had—donated by overseas Catholics. It hadn't been used for months because it had broken down and there were no Frenchmen to repair it . . .

As with anything to do with the human body and the human mind, there are no simple answers, easy solutions. Faith healing is a flourishing profession and, to some, an excellent business. But until a large-scale and exhaustive series of tests is made of its claims, spread over a decade or longer, both its champions and its denigrators are reduced to name-calling and "terminological inexactitudes". Yet there are thousands who are quite uninterested in this psychological warfare—those whom their own or the healer's faith has helped. And perhaps these are the only ones who matter.

Psychic Surgery

The sixties brought increasing acceptance, by wide circles, of psychic surgery as an important though fairly new branch of faith healing—though a good deal of argument still rages about the authenticity of the recorded cases and the personality of the "surgeons". Unlike faith healers, the practitioners of psychic surgery belong to distant and exotic places—in particular, to Brazil and the Philippines—which makes their exploits both less credible and more suspect. Yet there have been sober and reputable witnesses testifying to the "miracle-cures" these men have effected. On the other hand it is true that no psychic surgeon has yet performed in a proper operating theatre, under medical supervision. But perhaps this is the very requirement of their "talent" —that they should eschew all the orthodox methods.

One of the principal witnesses we interviewed was Miss Ann Dooley, a British journalist who has written copiously about her own experiences—for she has been both patient and observer of the remarkable, half-gipsy Brazilian who bears the romantic name of Lourival de Freitas.

For almost thirty years Ann Dooley has suffered from a crippling ailment called brochiectasis, a lung-disease that often arises when someone contracts pneumonia or pleurisy in infancy, injuring the bronchi, causing a dilation of the bronchial tubes that results in the serious accumulation of mucus in the lungs. In February 1948 she suffered a severe haemorrhage after a dental operation and was taken to St. Bartholomew's Hospital, London, where her condition was properly diagnosed for the first time. The treatment prescribed was "postural drainage"—which meant hanging upside down as long as she could bear the blinding headache that accompanied such a position. Though she continued to work as a newspaperwoman, the doctors warned her that she had only five-sevenths of normal lung capacity, had to take life

slowly and that she was too old to undergo the major operation
a total cure would require.

Bad attacks recurred regularly, especially in winter though she
was coughing all the year round and often had to go to bed.
She lost a good deal of blood in her sputum and the symptoms
were getting worse. In 1959 a chest specialist confirmed her "in-
operable" condition. He told her that she would have to depend
more and more on regular supplies of anti-biotics.

Seven years went by—and on June 10, 1966, she met Lourival
de Freitas.

"I'll never forget that day," Miss Dooley told us. "My editor
had phoned and asked me to see someone who had just flown
in from Rio de Janeiro. He introduced me casually to a man
with greying hair, a long face, deep-set eyes, a toothbrush moustache and said : 'Meet Senhor Lourival de Freitas, one of Brazil's
leading psychic surgeons.' I had just come back from Charing
Cross Hospital because I'd started a haemorrhage although I
had no cold. I didn't feel bad—but the blood-stained sputum
was very heavy. I have had emergency X-rays and was due to
see my doctor at four o'clock. The hospital had told me, in fact,
'you know your trouble, there's nothing we can do . . .'"

"When you met de Freitas, were you a believer in psychic
phenomena?"

"By that time, yes. When I worked in Fleet Street, I had no
interest in these matters at all. If anything, I was an atheist. My
involvement did not begin until after my husband's death."

"Did his loss change your views?"

"Well, I had a strange experience of my own even before he
died and I felt that atheism and agnosticism didn't have the right
answers. I had become interested in yoga. I felt that in the East
they had advanced farther than we had. I was a journalist in a
depressed area and my life turned to politics, industrial and
political journalism."

"So, when you met the Brazilian, you were no longer
a sceptic."

"No. But neither was I a total believer. After I had come
back from the hospital that afternoon, these two men arrived—
Lourival and his friend, a Brazilian businessman. The second
man was a very hard-headed fellow who had become de Freitas's
friend and helped him in many ways—because de Freitas cured

his wife of a spinal ailment. Now though the name of Lourival meant nothing to me, Brazil did. I had spent a good deal of time investigating the claims of spiritualists and psychic phenomena and Brazil cropped up again and again in various reports. I had heard so many stories about psychic healers in that country that I had realized it was rich in such prodigies—in spite of the fact that it is illegal for an unqualified person to practice surgery. So that evening after I had interviewed both men, I expressed great interest. They asked me whether I would like to accompany them that night—not as a journalist but as a private person. They were going to try and help a young girl, the godchild of Lourival's companion."

In the course of the interview Anne Dooley had learned some facts about De Freitas. The psychic surgeon was born in 1929 in the fishing hamlet of Coroa Grande, a village famous for its great waterfall which provided a popular centre for weekend psychic festivals. As a young boy, orphaned almost at birth (his parents died in a fire) he earned badly-needed cash as a water-carrier for the weekly trainloads of city folk making a pilgrimage to Coroa Grande. He was brought up by his grandmother, a gipsy and well-known as a local healer. She taught him herbal lore and he was only nine when he first practiced healing himself, ridding a visitor of a stubborn stomach-ulcer. By the age of twenty he was internationally known.

"The fascinating thing for me," Miss Dooley continued, "about the little girl who was operated on that night in a Wimbledon house was the fact that she, too, had been diagnosed as a bronchiectic case, in addition to a heart murmur. Intensive treatment had failed to clear her lungs and the doctors spoke of a lobectomy as the ultimate attempt to cure her—the removal of the lower right lobe of her lung. She was pitifully thin and pale and her parents had been advised to move from London to the south coast as she needed sea air . . . That night I saw her being operated on—the first operation I ever saw performed with nothing but a crystal tumbler."

"A crystal tumbler? How was it applied?"

"Lourival plaited some very thin wisps of cotton wool around this heavy and expensive tumbler—the type you use for whisky. I think he did this just to soften the edge of the glass because he used tremendous pressure. There were eight adults in the drawing room. The child was held in her mother's arms; I stood quite close to Lourival and there was no dousing of lights, no screen or any other cover. There could be simply no question of trickery. I never took my eyes off the edge of this glass. I could see it all the time as he was holding it, except at one point when he called the child's grandfather—who was very sceptical, almost antagonistic—to press his hand on top of the tumbler. But even then, the base was never obscured. At first I thought I must have blinked at the wrong moment—I was furious with myself because I didn't see the flesh open. There was the little girl's flesh, you see, surrounded by the glass; you could see it very plainly through the base. One moment it was just like that—and the next moment, literally in slow motion, like a surrealist nightmare, this tissue started to grow slowly out of the flesh, growing and emerging right before our eyes—without a drop of blood, just a clump of putty-coloured tissue."

"No chance of de Freitas having anything concealed in his hands?"

"None at all. You see, his hands were on the outside of the glass. It was a very broad-based type of cut-off tumbler. You and I could have hardly clasped it in our hands."

"And this putty-coloured stuff? what was it?"

"All I could see it grew out of the skin. Some tissue . . ."

"Was it ever examined?"

"No, it dropped into the tumbler. There was no trace of any scar on the skin. The bit of tissue just dropped off; it was covered with surgical spirit and the glass was put on the table. There it remained throughout the time I stayed in the house. We could all see it. When we left—the child had been put to bed and had gone to sleep long before—it was taken away by the medium because it is his custom to destroy such substances in some extraordinary ritual . . ."

"You called him the 'medium'. Was he a medium in the spiritualist sense?"

"Well, he does go into a trance whenever he operates, a state of complete, self-induced mental withdrawal. This he achieves very quickly, without any effort, just by bending forward and letting his head drop. His breathing changes markedly, you clearly hear him gasp. He says he is merely the instrument with which a team of healers carries out the work of God."

"Who are the members of this team?"

"All through the operations he performed at Wimbledon, he told me was successively controlled by very contrasting personages. The first claimed to be Nero, the Roman Emperor—the second a nameless woman, supposed to be a member of Nero's court."

Miss Dooley went on to explain that Lourival performed a second operation in the same Wimbledon home, on the same evening. The little girl's father, having seen him operate on his child, told him about the discomfort and occasional pain he suffered at the back of his head. Though she was out of the room when it took place, Miss Dooley was shown upon her return a second tumbler, containing a mass of what was described to her as "diseased cerebral tissue" drawn from the back of her host's head.

Nine months later she visited the new home of the Wimbledon family at the seaside. She found the little girl completely changed with excellent appetite, high spirits, restored vitality. And her father told Miss Dooley: "Our daughter made an immediate and dramatic recovery. On the very next day she raided the refrigerator and would not stop eating. This was totally unlike her previous attitude towards food. Her cheeks had a better colour and she was more relaxed and cheerful. From that day to this she just hasn't looked back. A later medical examination showed that her lungs were clear, there was no more blockage or congealed phlegm and her heart murmur has also gone . . ."

Some months afterwards Anne Dooley herself underwent psychic surgery.

"At a later demonstration," she told us, "there was some controversy and I felt that this man had been treated very injustly, was misjudged completely. When I had seen and watched him that night in Wimbledon, I knew that I had met my psychic master, that this was something totally beyond my experience and knowledge. In the autumn of 1966 I was invited to go and visit him in Brazil. I accepted and arrived in Rio in November, staying with a friend and taking some trips with an interpreter."

"Were you still suffering from your bronchial trouble?"

"Oh yes. I had an attack the moment I set foot ashore. It was the wet season. I didn't expect an operation—but after I'd been

c

there about three weeks, Lourival asked me one day through the interpreter whether I'd like to have one. He told me that it wouldn't be a cure but he thought he could improve my condition by 40 to 70 per cent. And of course I said yes. It was very interesting—about a week before the operation De Freitas decided to find out whether the whole thing could be done or not. We'd gone to visit his birthplace, about two hours' drive from Rio, a village in the mountains. As we drove through the countryside, he stopped near a waterfall. He promptly went into a trance and climbed down to the bank of the river where he plucked one of the long, razor-sharp reeds growing in the fast-flowing water . . ."

"How did he look when he did that?"

"The same as he did in that Wimbledon drawing-room."

"He didn't take any drug or drink to prepare himself?"

"No. Normally he doesn't drink—which is a most interesting fact. But during his operations I've seen him drink on one occasion two large bottles of spirit."

"Does he smoke?"

"He's a chain-smoker. He says it helps him with the trances."

"Does he smoke ordinary tobacco? or some narcotic or stimulating substance like pot?"

"Only quite normal cigarettes—and he will offer them around. But as for drink—the only time I saw him accept one when they pressed it upon him at a party, he became sick, he had to get up and leave the room. In a trance, however, it's different. I feel it's one of the supernormal aspects of his mediumship—"

"Does he go into trance before or after he drinks a whole bottle?"

"Let me think . . . No, not before. He's already entranced when he drinks. I've seen him drink whisky and I saw him drink surgical spirit—and on this occasion I've been telling you about, he drank a bottle of cassarta, a Brazilian brandy, the strongest I have ever tasted. It's distilled from corn. Once, while in England, when I sat with Lourival, there was a doctor next to him and Lourival picked up a bottle of whisky which had been bought by his hosts—he couldn't have possibly tampered with it, watered it down or something—and he just poured it down his gullet. You could almost hear it going down, gurgling. The doctor said he couldn't believe his eyes—for if the strongest man had drunk even three-fourths of that amount within such a short time, he'd have collapsed in a coma and, most likely, would have died. But however much he drinks while in trance, his hand remains steady as a rock—and although I haven't carried out this test myself, those who have smelled his breath said that there wasn't the slightest trace of alcohol in it . . ."

Miss Dooley went on to describe how, after de Freitas had plucked the razor-edged reed, he asked her to unzip the back of her sun dress. He drew the reed across her back, below her right shoulder blade and she felt it scarring her skin. He explained that he was marking the outline of the operation area. Later that day he examined the cut and told her that "the way it had taken" ensured it would be possible to perform the operation in six days.

During the interval he asked her to cut down her heavy smoking and made her drink daily four wine glasses of a syrupy mixture he had prepared. It was a lemon-mint concoction which lessened her usually severe bronchial catarrh. In addition she had to drink every day several tumblers of herbal "tea", a brown liquid with a nauseating flavour. This was supposed to clear excess fluid from her kidneys.

At last, unexpectedly, the moment of the operation arrived.

"I thought it was going to be a glass operation," Miss Dooley told us, "like the one I saw performed on the little girl in Wimbledon and I wasn't at all alarmed. I also thought that I was to be alone with him. But when it happened, I found myself in a derelict farmhouse in the mountains which had two large rooms linked by a wide archway. There was the harsh light of unshaded electric bulbs—and there were other patients and lots of other people, maybe twenty at different times, crowded around it. This was most peculiar, an aspect of Lourival's mediumship very different from anything we know in Europe. He likes to operate with people in the room, often friends he knows and other patients. But on this occasion there was great tension in the air and it seemed as if he could tap this psychic power by the means of anger. When he went into trance, he was in a harsh mood and he virtually attacked me in fury. Whether this served to draw extra power or to make *me* tense in some way, I just don't know. I became very nervous. He was scolding and abusing me without any apparent reason, quite unjustly. I didn't really know what he was saying—which was just as well because I've got an Irish temper and I might have exploded—but I felt very uneasy and at one point, to be frank, I would have run away if I could. I went out of the farmhouse and stood on the steps outside, trying to regain my composure and I thought, well, this is ridiculous. I said to myself that I was a journalist, here to do a job. I had a responsibility, having travelled all that way. I felt that Lourival was an honest man, a genuine healer—and I had a chance of proving it on my own body. He was risking his freedom in order to help. Having marshalled all these arguments, I went back inside, took a glass of water—and then the operation began."

This time it wasn't one of Lourival's usual "controls" that took charge but a Japanese doctor named Sheka. And, as Ann Dooley remarked, judging from the way he worked through De Freitas, he must have been a pretty bad-tempered man while in the world of the living. Lourival made her open her mouth and he said (this was translated later to her): "Oh, my God, we'll have to take out your tonsils first."

"He had a pair of kitchen scissors," Miss Dooley continued her story, "which he proceeded to put into my mouth, digging away at the back of the palate. Of course, I was terrified."

"How did it feel?"

"Very painful and also, of course, when you have bronchiectasis, you don't breathe very well. At the same time he was half-dragging me across the room to get into the maximum light. I thought I was screaming—but evidently it was a sort of interior scream, for a spectator, a South American journalist who later wrote an account of it, said that I just sort of grunted. But he also said that it was the most brutal psychic operation on the throat he had seen Lourival do. It lasted about a minute and a half or two minutes; then, I remember, somebody handed me a glass and I was told not to cough, just spit with all my might. Some tissue came out—about the size of a baby's fist."

"Could you feel it coming up?"

"It just seemed to emerge so rapidly—all I know I was spitting blood into the glass and it filled about a third of it and it was photographed in my hand as I held it . . ."

"You didn't feel it coming from the chest?"

"Well, no. You see, I was in a panic. All I remember was

thinking that I must keep conscious, I must stand on my feet, I mustn't fall—and it seemed to be all in a rush and this stuff was all in the glass and I was spitting out this extra sutff . . ."

"Do you feel he could have dropped something into your mouth?"

"No. There was no question of that. The scissors were just in my mouth, you see, and the glass was put straight into my hand, not by Lourival but by somebody standing near. Also, when it came into the glass, whilst I don't remember the actual lump coming out from the back of my throat, I was spitting mucus and blood from that lump. I had a great job clearing my mouth. There is no doubt about it, it couldn't have been introduced into my mouth in any way . . . Well, that was the first part of the operation and doctors who later examined me found that my tonsils were actually removed. Whether it was something else beside the tonsils, I just don't know. It was just one big lump."

"What happened next?"

"I just had to stand there and he operated on my back. He used the original scar of the wound he had made with the reed. But now he used a razor blade, cutting it at right angles, opening up the flesh. Of course, I could feel that . . . The whole thing lasted about thirty-three minutes. I know because a picture was taken of this operation at the rate of one a minute . . ."

"An ordinary lung operation wouldn't involve opening your back, would it?"

"No. The doctors I consulted since say that Lourival's operation couldn't be compared at all with surgery for bronchiectasis because in the latter they have to remove part of the ribs, there is complete anaesthesia, it takes about two or three hours and naturally you are prone on the operating table. He cut my flesh in that Brazilian farmhouse as I stood upright—but it was a very superficial cut—and then he sucked something out of it. I could feel his teeth gripping my flesh with very great pressure . . . I was hoping it wouldn't last too long . . . He sucked out a huge black clot . . ."

"Could you feel it coming out?"

"Yes. I felt the pressure of the teeth drawing it out, the very strong pressure on my back, I prayed it would end soon. It was as much as I could take . . . and then it did end. He lifted it, he put it with a knife into the palm of an observer—and then I was asked to hold it in my hand and it was photographed there and whatever it was . . ."

"What was it?"

"He said it was virus from the base of the bone. Then I was stitched up with cotton wool and a sewing needle, ten stitches. . ."

"Did he sterilize the area?"

"No, nothing of the sort. Later the stitches were cut. Well, all I know is that whatever happened in that operation—either the first or the second part—helped me to breathe very much more deeply than I've ever been able to do. I won't say I am cured but I feel infinitely better."

"Have you had any haemorrhages since the operation?"

"Nothing. My whole general health is much improved."

"Do you think that your illness might have been psychosomatic and therefore the improvement purely psychological?"

"Oh no. It was very physical. Too physical for my liking. I endured considerable pain. I've still got the scar on my back. There is no question about it not being physical . . ."

Lourival de Freitas performed several other operations in Britain and on British patients in his native Brazil; we tracked down several of them and interviewed a number of eyewitnesses of these extraordinary operations.

Neville Armstrong, managing director of Neville Spearman Publishers has known the psychic surgeon for a number of years and saw him in 1969 perform two extraordinary operations; one of the patients was a personal friend.

"One concerned the eyes," Mr. Armstrong explained, "on which a penknife, nail scissors and the handle of a coffee spoon were used to extract a piece of foreign matter. To an onlooker—me—who stood next to Lourival it appeared brutal and really rough, and there was indeed some pain (the knife blade was pushed into the forehead through the eye). The other operation was on the back of a young dancer who had decided to abandon her career because of pain and inability of the doctors to diagnose the cause. Once again the operation was crude—just a razor blade to cut a three-inch incision, an inverted glass and a needle and cotton to sew up the wound. And no pain. Twenty minutes later there was hardly a scar and the girl was dancing and jiving and happier than she had been for years."

We saw another young lady who claimed that she was cured by Lourival: Miss Mona Lisa Boyarson whose mother is a highly-respected Reikian therapist and certainly not a particularly credulous person. We saw her and her two daughters in their home in Kensington. Mona Lisa, a beautiful girl of twenty-four, had suffered from a slipped disc for over two years and though sometimes the intervals between the bouts of pain were as long as two or three days, she was practically permanently incapacitated. She visited doctor after doctor and spent time in a large medical centre in Denmark undergoing a series of tests but no one was able to do anything for her. Her mother and her sister both told us that her face was drawn with pain and she was unable usually even to visit the movies with them. She could not read for half an hour without suffering discomfort. Sometimes she began to scream and when she did so, she felt better—but as soon as she stopped, the pain returned and "I couldn't spend my life screaming". She told her mother that if she had no relief by Christmas 1969, she was going to commit suicide.

In September 1969 she went to the home of Francis Huxley, the distinguished scientist and writer to meet Lourival. She felt sceptical and certain that she would not allow him to touch her. There were about thirty or forty people present and it was "quite nice. The atmosphere was calm." She felt comfortable and she began to feel that she trusted him. She found herself approaching him when he asked if there was anyone who needed help and she told him her story. He asked her if he could see her back and she undid her dress. He looked at her back and said he thought he *could* help her. She knelt down and held the hands of a woman friend, looking into her eyes. Lourival took a razor blade and made some small scratches on her back, as if looking for the spot to make an incision. All of a sudden, with a sharp movement, he did make the cut. It didn't hurt but felt as if someone had scratched her. Miss Boyarson demonstrated the sensation by scratching the wrist of one of us with a fingernail.

He then made her bend over, with her head down. She was on her knees and Lourival made a woman stand next to her—someone "he had selected from the audience for her special energy". She stayed this way for about five minutes while Lourival encouraged the other people to sing and the woman danced. During this time Mona Lisa felt quite ill and nauseated—as if some transformation were taking place in her body. Then De Freitas took a pair of scissors and rooted around inside the incision with the sharp end. He was digging and probing and the young girl was bleeding—but did not feel very much pain nor was the bleeding uncontrollable. After he had rooted around, he took from her back a "mass of material", about the size of a circle formed by one's thumb and forefinger. He put this into a tumbler and then proceeded to stitch up the wound with needle and cotton. As usual, there had been no sterilization and the tissue was neither examined under a microscope nor submitted for any testing. Lourival kept it—"to dispose of it in his ritual manner".

Miss Boyarson went home and her back felt stiff and sore for two or three days. She found that she was afraid to move—but miraculously, there was no pain. For about two weeks she was afraid to raise her arm for fear she would wrench her back or do something to make the pain return. Nothing happened. By February 1970 when we saw her, she had no recurrence of pain or difficulty. She dances and works at her sculpture and lives a normal active life.

She pulled up the back of her dress to show us her back and in the spot where the incision was supposed to have been made, there was a small scar—a hair-thin red line one would never notice unless looking for it. There was no sign of stitches. Yet it all happened and there are pictures to prove the actual operation.

We asked Mona Lisa whether she thought that her trouble could have been psychosomatic—in which case her belief's could have brought about the cure subconsciously. She said, no— though she also added that the X-rays of her spine are exactly the same as they were before the operation.

The Boyarsons, mother and daughter, subscribe to the tenet that repressed energy is the cause of a great deal of psychological unhappiness; the same repressed energy, residing in various parts of the body, can cause physical disturbances as well. They believe that Lourival gathered up this energy and removed it in the shape of the tissue he took from Mona Lisa's back. It was this transformation of energy into matter, they say, that effected her cure.

The other Lourival patient to whom we talked had already provided us with some material about George Chapman and his "spirit partner", Dr. Lang. Gordon Creighton had been treated by Lang for chronic sinusitis and had earlier sought help from De Freitas for the same trouble. But Freitas told him : "You've got a bad infection there. I can make it a bit better but it's a chronic thing and I can't really help . . ." Then he added, suddenly : "You've got something much more important . . . much worse," And he operated on the spot.

"Did you know that you had this condition?" we asked Creighton.

"No. No. He operated on me—and the year before he operated on my son and he also did something quite extraordinary to help my wife."

"When did you meet him first?"

"On his first visit to England. I speak Portuguese because my wife and I spent some time in Brazil with the Foreign Service. Maurice Barbanell's secretary suggested that we should come along with Anne Dooley because Lourival doesn't speak any English. We were at that gathering in Wimbledon and later at another in Belgrave Square. Here the atmosphere was most curious—because the behaviour of the entity controlling Lourival was imperious and bad-tempered. People got frightened; De Freitas himself panicked and things went off the rails. I do know that the man who was operated on that night was dying of cancer; he had reached the terminal state and that was why he was brought to Lourival. Suddenly cancerous substances were extracted from him—I have talked to doctors and they have agreed that they *were* cancerous tissues. My wife was holding the basin—but then I heard Lourival say in Portuguese : "I haven't finished" and there was an interruption which broke the current. He wasn't able to continue and I think as a result this man died. I think it quite possible that Lourival might have done all that was necessary and this chap might have lived . . ."

"Can you explain the motives of Lourival's behaviour?"

"I know him in his ordinary state when he's quite a different person—but when he goes into this trance, he has to be reintroduced to everybody in the room. He really doesn't know who you are. He's very modest, diffident, shy . . . used to be a taxi-driver in Rio. He writes a very strange language, a kind of private doggerel, in this queer script . . . and when the power comes over him, he drinks a bottle of whisky—just like that . . ."

c*

(We had, of course, heard Ann Dooley describe this phenomenon but here was Creighton confirming it.)

"Does he do that before he goes into trance?"

"Just after it. He doesn't drink in his normal state at all;
but I've stood beside him and heard that whisky running down
his throat like water down a drain-pipe. It's claimed that this
alcohol is used as fuel, as in a car . . . There is no smell of drink
on his breath and when he comes out of the trance, he is not
tight. He isn't drunk at any stage of doing it though an ordinary
person would be killed by drinking a bottle of whisky. It's nonsense to say it's a fake. My wife was there and we both noticed
that it was an ordinary, well-known brand of whisky. He probably likes that particular one because it is one of the brands
sold in Brazil. I think it's true that it is used in some uncanny
way as a source of energy."

"When he goes into trance, does he change?"

"Yes, from a diffident, shy man he turns into an extremely
dominant, imperious one. Sometimes we are told that he adopts
the personality of the Emperor Nero—which is absolute nonsense. At other times he is identified with Ambrose Paré who was
a fourteenth-century surgeon; but a whole number of other
entities are supposed to work through Lourival . . ."

"To get back to the cancer operation—what type of cancer was
it?"

"I had a long talk with the doctor both before and after the
operation. Lourival took the cancer-tissues from the throat. The
doctor said the cancer was not in the throat at all—but Lourival
got a pair of sharp scissors and rummaged around in there . . ."

"How did the patient react?"

"Oh well, he was pretty ill, of course. He had to be propped
up. The doctor said that Lourival dematerializes the cancerous
growths. I spoke to Hallowell, the British businessman whose wife
was miraculously cured, the next day. He has devoted his life
to Lourival and he said roughly the same thing—only the other
way round. He said that Lourival assembles all the cancerous
growths in one place and then he dematerializes the flesh above
and around them and brings them out. Afterwards he closes the
openings. So it's really the same thing the doctor said but the
other way round . . ."

"What do you mean by dematerialization?"

"Well, I believe there is such a phenomenon as dematerialization. If you study the evidence in psychical research you will find overwhelming indications that under certain paranormal conditions matter can pass through matter without leaving a hole—which indicates that there has been an atomic change. I suppose the atoms are taken apart and are pushed through the apertures between the atoms of the walls because no atoms can touch each other."

"There was a British physician present at this operation? Who was he?"

"I cannot name him without his permission; but I can tell you that he's a most distinguished medical man."

"And he did confirm that the material which Lourival removed was a cancerous growth?"

"Yes."

"And it came from inside the body?"

"Yes. Now, it is true that the man died later and the sceptics claim that Lourival was a washout—but he probably would have been successful if it had not been for the panic, fear and hostility that threw him completely off balance. The entity became extremely bad-tempered and started throwing knives about. He threw one on the floor near me and one on the walls. My wife and I weren't so worried about it but the others thought he was insane doing this. That's why I said that we were dealing with something that's imperious . . ."

"Did the man who was operated on feel any pain?"

"I don't think so. I don't know of any people who've been operated on by de Freitas who felt pain. And they don't feel much fear and this I think is because they're obviously in some kind of trance. It's quite clear that they're in a special condition. Anyhow, these were my experiences at the Spiritualist Association. Then, a most distressing thing happened, my son, a teenage boy about to go to university, just ready to do his A-levels, was attacked by hoodlums. The unknown assailants left him for dead, fractured his skull. It was touch-and-go for a while and he lost his hearing in one ear for life. As he wants to be a doctor, this is a great handicap. So when Lourival came back in the summer of 1968, we went down to Brighton where he was staying with some people called Phipps. I wrote and told him we were coming and explained that the doctors had said my son couldn't be

helped—the inner ear was smashed. The usual thing happened
Lourival sat there and drank a bottle of whisky. A certain atmosphere has to be established. Time is important. He likes to operate
late at night. And I'm perfectly certain that this 'group-field'
which is created in the audience is very important."

"He seems to like to have people around him when he
operates?"

"I think he *has* to have people around because I believe something is taken from them. Power is probably drawn from them,
too. I remember on one occasion he made one person sit close to
him and he said he was drawing ectoplasm from her—so this may
well be true. Anyhow, he said about my son that he probably won't
be able to cure him because the inner ear was practically smashed
—but he said there was something else, something that could
create very serious conditions. This could become very grave—
so now I will deal with it, he said. 'Because you are people with
good hearts and good will, I will do this for you and I will help
this boy.' He asked for a pair of scissors; the only ones within
reach were a pair of embroidery scissors belonging to Mrs.
Phipps. He took them and suddenly plunged them into my son's
neck. I should say, however, that first he made a slight incision
above the spot with a razor blade. I don't really understand why
he does that . . ."

"He did it with Anne Dooley, too, as you will remember."

"Well, anyhow, he plunged the scissors in very deeply and then
he began to bring out stuff, tissue, obviously diseased tissue,
the colour of blood, rather dark, and the boy was just sitting there. When we were allowed to look at it a quarter of
an hour later, there was no bleeding or hardly any bleeding
at all. One of the people present was Francis Huxley and I
know that he was astonished the next morning when he saw
the boy."

"Was the tissue examined?"

"There were doctors present. Whether they examined it with
Lourival or not, I don't know."

"Does he not destroy such tissues in some ritual ceremony?"

"Yes, he does. By the way, I have photographs of my son's
operation, taken by a doctor—by Andrew's own physician who
was so impressed by the change in the boy that when Lourival
was at Brighton he went down to see him."

"Did you obtain any medical opinion as to what would have happened if this tissue had not been removed?"

"No—medically there was no agreement that there was anything wrong there. My wife and I think that his body had encapsulated a very large area of diseased tissue and this might have been all right for a number of years but later might have caused trouble."

"Was there any noticeable improvement in your boy's hearing?"

"None at all. But we noticed immense improvement in his general health . . . Now let me tell you about myself. This happened in 1969. As I told you, I had suffered from chronic sinusitis all my life. I spent many years in China and didn't have it properly treated early in my life. These last two years I had a particularly bad time so I wrote to Francis Hallowell and asked him to let me know when Lourival came back so that I could find out whether he would do something—because this sinus was really dreadful. And so we gathered at the home of Francis Huxley and as the evening went on, there was a feeling of calm and relaxation—but after a while there was a change and we were told that 'Nero had arrived'. There was a little girl present who was partially deaf and Lourival said, I'll deal with the catarrh first and then I'll put her to sleep. But he added that she had not been brought by her parents and he was 'blocked off' as it were from obtaining proper knowledge about her as her real parents were not present. Then he turned to me and said: 'I understand you wanted to speak to me?' I said, yes, I wanted him to look at my sinus—so he said, well, come and let me have a look—and he started. It was incredible. By our standards the things he does are perfectly ridiculous. He got a tumbler and looked at my eyes through the bottom of it which to me seemed a totally ridiculous thing. He said, there's something very wrong here . . . I can't do much about the sinuses, I can ameliorate the condition a little but there's something much more important which could be fatal. He started scrabbling around my eye and I wasn't worried because by then I had total confidence in him. I knew he wouldn't harm me. He called for a knife and he stuck the knife in above the eye. Then he wiggled and squeezed and said, come into the other room . . . He always insists on letting everybody see what he's doing, he calls for doctors, for cameras, let everybody watch. There's never any attempt to hide anything. He can't possibly use any sleight of hand. It's nonsense to say that he does. He took me into the other room . . . and there I was photographed. Here they are . . ."

He showed us some photographs. These were of a hand holding a piece of tissue about the size of a large marble. In the photographs it looked soft and spongy with some tendrils hanging from it.

Creighton told us that he was not authorized to let us use them—and of course we have his word that these were the actual photographs taken of his "psychic surgery". He added:

"They say he removed a growth from my optic nerve. And the wife of the cultural attaché wrote an article about it in a Brazilian newspaper . . ."

"Was this tissue examined?" we posed the regular question.

"I don't know if the doctors examined it or not."

"Did he say what would have happened to you if this tissue wouldn't have been removed?"

"He told me it would have been fatal."

"He believed that it may have been cancerous?"

"Something like that. Then, a few days later at Mrs. Boyarson's house, he looked into my other eye to check, and confirmed that it was all right. My boy, by the way, pointed out the extraordinary speed with which these men operate and the sureness of touch. They do it at an incredible rate."

"You said that Lourival also helped your wife?"

"Yes. She was there, holding the basin, right at the centre of things; and she was also present on the other occasions. When we were in Brazil, she was pregnant. It was hot and it was quite a weight for her to carry so she developed varicose veins. They have been a bit troublesome at times; and last year, during the very hot summer, one of them popped out and she was bruised and in pain. Well, she was sitting there and I think Lourival said: has anybody got any complaints? So half-jokingly my wife said: here, have a look at this. And he looked at it and said: 'Oh, not possible, I can't do that . . .' and as he was saying it, he was rubbing it. Next day it was totally gone. He said he couldn't do anything—and it was all gone. She has some of the marks from earlier ones and when Lourival comes back next, she's going to ask him to rub his hands over those. I'm perfectly sure he's going to remove them . . ."

What does orthodox medicine think about psychic surgery? When it does not ignore the whole field, it denounces its practitioners as dangerous quacks to be put behind bars lest they do incalculable harm. We discussed the case of Anne Dooley and the others with one of them, an eminent woman physician who has also spent a good deal of her time in psychical research and who has seen the film which was taken during an operation performed by another Brazilian psychic surgeon.

"It was technically poor," she told us, "and details were difficult to make out—but what I saw certainly laid them open to the charge of faking . . . more than anything I've ever seen on the screen. For example there was a pillow well in sight and they produced some tissue from under it—at least as far as I could make it out. It was as crude as that. In the film the entire proceedings were so muddled and obscured that it was perfectly possible to introduce fake blood or fake tissues or what-have-you. You could do any kind of palming."

Our medical expert insisted on remaining anonymous. She pointed out that Anne Dooley was given a good deal of herbal tea to drink before her operation "to clear her kidneys". This, the doctor said, was one of the standard opening moves of a quack. They always gave people drugs to "clear out" any orthodox medicine which they called "unnatural". Nor did Miss Dooley, it seems, have had the normal urinary tests and she had previously no idea that there had been anything wrong with her kidneys.

"As far as Miss Dooley's operation is concerned," the doctor summed up, "there is nothing to investigate . . . She made a good deal of her tonsils being taken out with a pair of kitchen scissors . . . But I have seen children held down on a table by a farm servant while a doctor simply chopped their tonsils out with a pair of roughly sterilized scissors. Miss Dooley was given anti-biotics and had the normal amount of pain. As far as the 'tissue' extracted from her back is concerned, I have no idea what it was—but it could have been easily concealed in De Freita's mouth. And bronchiectasis, of course, is never treated by removing tissue . . ."

We asked Miss Dooley whether the tissue was subsequently examined by a pathologist. She said, no, it couldn't be, because these operations were illegal. Would she have chosen to have such an examination?

"Oh, it would have been the ideal thing and the medium would have liked it, too—but you see, as it is, you cannot get these ideal conditions. He wants very much to have such examinations."

"He would have permitted you to take it and have it examined—but he was afraid that he might be later prosecuted because of it?"

"Well, there was no doctor to take it to, you see. We had no laboratory or doctor available—and there were other patients present that night, about six all told, it would have been impractical . . ."

All these might be perfectly legitimate excuses—but of course, they do weaken the case. What is left is the subjective feeling of Miss Dooley that she is better; and indeed, three years after the operation her condition appears to have considerably improved. Of course, the *cause* of this improvement is open to argument. However, she has cited other cases in support of her unshaken and unshakeable belief in Lourival de Freitas. One was that of the Brazilian opera singer, Cleusa de Penaforte who had watched the psychic surgeon perform a spinal operation on a woman while the patient kept up a lively conversation, feeling apparently no pain during the process and "able to do immediately afterwards violent gymnastics without discomfort". Impressed by this, Senhora de Penaforte asked Lourival a week before she was to sing at an international festival to remove her "spongy tonsils". She told Miss Dooley: "After operating on my throat—I felt no pain whatsoever—he commanded me to sing a resounding song. I found that I was able to sing with the greatest of ease the fourth act of 'Aida'."

Anne Dooley also spoke to two Brazilian doctors who had both undergone psychic operations at the hands of Lourival. The first had an intestinal one and testified that he hadn't felt anything either during the cutting or during the subsequent stitching. The scar healed within twenty-four hours.

We asked Anne Dooley about *her* scar. Hers, she said, had lasted though it had gone "very thin and faint".

The second doctor she interviewed was Dr. Cavalcanti Bandeira, a busy Rio de Janeiro specialist in tropical medicine. He is also a well-known psychical researcher and lectures to audiences that include student-priests and nuns. He, too, underwent an operation for a septic appendix without feeling any pain; after three days there was no trace of a scar. Dr. Bandeira had his own theories about psychic surgery. He believed that the spirit controls who directed the surgeon during trances were able "to bring about a temporary disintegration of diseased tissue within the patient's body. This enables them to be brought to the skin surface where they re-integrate and can be 'lifted out'." And if this sounds a somewhat outlandish interpretation, at least it explains the alleged results.

Dr. Bandeira declared that he had personal knowledge of nearly a dozen psychic surgeons in Brazil, still unfamiliar to the public. Most of them were highly respected and included a woman, a university professor, a magistrate, an army officer and a millionaire—certainly a wide enough range. "In Brazil such gifted psychics have to operate in secrecy and at considerable personal risk," he said. "I think that a more enlightened science will regard it tomorrow as a privilege to investigate their achievements."

One of these psychic surgeons who has been both investigated and has run afoul of the law is José Arigo who runs a healing centre in the tin-mining town of Congonhas de Campo. (It was about him that the Brazilian journalist and TV producer George Rizzini, whose headquarters are in Sao Paulo, made his controversial film which our British medical expert saw.) Arigo had been twice sentenced to jail for illegal operations but he still seems to function in the backwoods of the vast country.

His work was the subject of an investigation by a team of United States doctors headed by Dr. Andrija Puharich, a New York neurologist.

Fifteen researchers spent a week in Congonhas de Campo, subjecting the medium to a seven-hour physical and mental examination. Arigo claimed that he was only the instrument of Dr. Adolf Fritz, a German doctor who died in the First World War. "He is the one who works through me, and it is Jesus who does the healing."

According to *Psychic News*, the leading spiritualist weekly of London, after exhaustive testing of the patients, the team as well as Arigo remained "mystified" as to how he "operates".

Dr. Puharich himself underwent an operation by Arigo for the extraction of an arm tumour. Apparently such an operation usually takes at least fifteen minutes—while Arigo performed it in fifteen seconds! Afterwards Dr. Puharich said: "The mystery is not only in the absence of anaesthesia but in the whole surgical process employed by Arigo. Some of his diagnoses would normally be possible only by X-rays."

When Anne Dooley returned to England, she began a determined campaign to win recognition for Lourival de Freitas and other Brazilian psychic surgeons. She wrote a series of articles, delivered a number of lectures and tried hard, though as yet without success, to organize a British medical team to go to Brazil for a thorough examination of their work.

"I feel that the importance of this extraordinary breakthrough," she told us, "lies in the fact that it does two things in a most remarkable manner which I think is a direct challenge to the whole medical profession. We can die under the knife. I was later told by a doctor that even under anaesthetic tonsilectomy creates a free-flowing blood area and I could have choked on a haemorrhage, especially because my lungs were in such a bad state. The other thing is that I have met only one other person who experienced pain as I did. I've seen more than a score of operations, some of them very painful but of all the people to whom I've ever talked only one felt pain. The majority do not feel a thing . . . ."

She added that Lourival never accepted a fee and that the majority of psychic surgeons work without any remuneration. And she hoped that the Brazilian *Sanatorias Espiritas*, Spiritual Hospitals, would be introduced to Britain and help countless suffereres whom orthodox medicine would not treat effectively.

The Filipino psychic surgeon's name is Agpaoa though he is more commonly known as "Dr. Tony". Ian Stevenson who visited him several times gave a detailed report in December 1966 at the ninth annual convention of the Parapsychological Association. According to him "Dr. Tony" operated (like several of his colleagues) within the framework of Christian Spiritualism, made incisions, opened the abdominal cavity, removed tissues without knives, with no infection, with little or no bleeding and with instantaneous or very rapid healing of the wounds or openings. However, the circumstances of observation were determined by the natural sites at which these healers worked and so did not permit adequate control. Stevenson suggested that the alleged phenomena were interesting and important enough to warrant further examination under better control. Until then no valid judgment could be made on "Dr. Tony" or other Filipino psychic surgeons.

Harold Sherman devoted a whole book to the "wonder healers of the Philippines" and came to very positive conclusions about them. Other observers were more critical and pointed out that many cases offered little or no evidence that the "patient" was in any need of an operation. It had happened repeatedly that mere onlookers at these operations were told by "Dr. Tony" that they needed psychic surgery. In other cases no subsequent medical examination was made to prove that any operations had actually taken place; and in still others the people involved stated that after psychic surgery they were still afflicted by the growth "removed" by "Dr. Tony". It seems that a good deal of work still needs to be done in this field to decide whether the believers or the sceptics hold the balance of truth.

Mrs. K. M. Goldney, the noted psychical researcher of vast experience and an enquiring though open mind, pointed out the basic difference between faith healing and spirit healing. "The first," she told us, "demands conscious or unconscious faith in the mind of the person to be cured. This was clearly demonstrated by the work of Coué in the Nancy School of Medicine where the originator of couéism ('every day and every way I feel better and better') practised suggestion and auto-suggestion. Charcot with whom Freud studied for a while also worked on the same lines at the Salpetriere Hospital in Paris.

"Spirit healing involved either Christianity or magic, Lourdes certainly *did* produce cures and so did similar places when the Harley Street school of orthodox medicine failed. Why? Because from an evolutionary point of view the appeal to magic has sometimes a much greater effect. Orthodox medicine appeals to the rational mind—which is a much later evolutionary development than human belief in spirits and magic."

Just like faith healing, psychic surgery is likely to figure as an important field of research in the future. In our tense and sceptical age the belief in unorthodox and unusual methods is likely to grow rather than diminish and this is a fact psychical research cannot ignore in the seventies.

The Invisible Eye

Of all the psychic phenomena, real or alleged, orthodox science considers clairvoyance and telepathy the "most respectable" or, perhaps more modestly, the "least fraudulent"—perhaps because under the collective name of extra-sensory perception they have been the subject of long academic investigations. Precognition, the various forms of forecasting or sensing future events, has also had its share of attention and is sometimes difficult to separate from the first two disciplines.

Not that ESP experiments have remained unchallenged or unassailed; Professor Rhine of Duke University and Dr. Soal of London have both been attacked by die-hard sceptics. At a symposium held by the American Psychological Association in 1938 Rhine's work and the experiments of Dr. J. Gaither Pratt (treasurer of the American Parapsychological Association and President of the Psychical Research Foundation of Durham, North Carolina) were strongly attacked. When, in the early 1960's, Dr. Rhine wanted to continue and expand his studies at Duke, the university officials found scientific opinion firmly opposed to the idea. In 1965 Dr. Rhine retired and set up, off the campus, his Foundation for Research on the Nature of Man which still survives. Yet even the Soviet Union's hardbitten materialists have been experimenting at the Moscow Institute of Psychology with hyperaesthesia and have produced tantalizing reports about people being able to see with their skin and hear with their hair.

Almost fifty years ago, the Psychological Society of Berlin, headed by Dr. Albert Moll, posed the basic questions:

(1) Is there a clairvoyance involving space or time?
(2) Does telepathy exist—that is, thought-transference without any means of the generally accepted channels of communication?

77

Dr. Waldemar von Wasielewski, a highly-respected authority in this field claimed that telepathy and clairvoyance were only different branches of the same psychical talent. He defined them under the collective names of "direct perception" or "panaesthesia". Another expert, Dr. Ubald Tartaruga who combined the functions of a high police official in Vienna with psychical research, classified these two under "supranormal psychology".

Dr. Pratt believes that there are three kinds of ESP—clairvoyance which he defines as "being able to see some object or situation that physically one shouldn't be able to see"; telepathy "being able to read another person's mind" and precognition, the ability of foretelling a future event. According to the veteran North Carolina researcher, if these three divisions of extra-sensory perception are rated on a scale of one to a hundred, using one hundred to represent conclusive evidence, clairvoyance and telepathy could be rated at eighty and precognition at fifty-five. Clairvoyance and telepathy, Dr. Pratt explained, were hard to separate in scientific tests and as most ESP experiences were a combination of the two, he would rate the combination one hundred. In other words, he was a hundred per cent satisfied that it had been proved to exist.

But the questions posed forty-eight years ago in Berlin still haven't been answered. So we undertook a quest to discover how close clairvoyants and telepaths, precognitive individuals and the scientists themselves were to a clear and definite answer in the 1960's

Maurice Barbanell has been a Spiritualist for fifty years. In 1932 he founded and has since then edited *Psychic News*, a bright and combative organ of his faith. However, he has also discovered at a very early stage that he was a trance medium himself. At that time he was an agnostic who had been originally an atheist; as a businessman, he decided to investigate matters for himself and before long he was both a believer and a crusader for Spiritualism. He has written many books and thousands of articles on the subject.

"How many clairvoyants would you say are functioning in Great Britain today?" we began our interview with Mr. Barbanell.

"Hundreds."

"You couldn't give a more exact estimate?"

"No—it's impossible because we've got so many of them."

"And how many of them are legitimate in your view?"

"Hundreds."

"How can you be sure of that?"

"Because we have national organizations, with churches holding regular services at which the demonstration of clairvoyance is a normal feature. In London and elsewhere there are meetings on Sunday evenings and weekdays. The largest is in Belgrave Square. They have a list of mediums as long as your arm. In fact, if I show you a diary published by one of our organizations and you'd take a good look at the London churches alone, you'd find it a real eye-opener!"

"Does the same thing apply to America?"

"Indeed it does. I can show you reams of advertisements for Spirtualist churches throughout the States . . ."

"Is there any region where they are particularly strong? For instance, the South?"

"No. The difficulty in the United States is one of distance which doesn't exist in Britain. If you wanted to get mediums or clairvoyants travelling across the States it would be quite a job because of the enormous distances. In our compact little country one can travel the length and breadth of the land in three or four hours by plane, so that's not such a problem. Besides, with great respect to America and the Statue of Liberty, there is more freedom and tolerance in Britain than in any other country in the world. We have reached the stage where Spiritualism is a recognized religion; we have our own ministers who can sign any documents that ordained priests can sign and these are accepted by the Government authorities."

"What criteria would you use to establish the legitimacy of a clairvoyant? For instance, when we visited one, she said many things which were right on the target. She also said many things which to us were nonsense."

"You must judge the evidence on its authenticity. If it's rubbish, dismiss it. If she's right, that's fine. I think the best thing I can do is to quote the Bible text which says, 'by their fruits shall you know them'. If they can deliver the goods, they're genuine."

"Is there anything you would accept as being a very good percentage of accuracy?"

"That's hard—because the success of clairvoyance or any form of mediumship depends on certain imponderables—conditions about which we know practically nothing. I mean, a medium can be feeling on top of the world and the sitter feels lousy, so they don't click. Or they may not be on the same vibration . . ."

"You mean—there is some sort of wave-length?"

"Oh yes, the whole thing is wave-lengths. A vibration or radiation that determines the reception."

"In other words the medium could be right on the target with some people and completely miss out with others?"

"I have sent two people to sit with the same medium, one appointment following the other. One called me and said it was marvellous and the other phoned and said, it was rotten. It's not the fault of the sitter but of some imponderable thing that could explain it. I don't know the answer myself. It's similar to entering a room full of strangers. You may be okay with A, possibly with B but you're sure you won't hit it off with C. It's just a *rapport* that establishes itself and there is a natural sympathy that emerges with some and not with others. This is what I call the imponderable—something that cannot be measured. I've had some of the best results spontaneously—say, with a medium who'd come to tea. It's just bang! She feels there's something and she has to say it."

"Do you think then that when a medium knows she is being tested . . ."

". . . it's immediately inhibiting. A medium, you see, by the very meaning of the word, is an intermediary for higher or subtler forces than the purely physical ones. You mustn't treat a medium with suspicion or wild scepticism—and I don't mean open-minded criticism—because that will close him or her down at once and they cannot tune in as easily. But if you go and say, well, do the best you can, we'll judge the results by what you did—that opens them up. So when you consult a medium, don't ever tell her you're a journalist or writer. Tell her you're an enquirer. Mediums have had, generally speaking, rough treatment at the hand of journalists and so tend to shut up. But if you are sympathetic—I mean, no one wants an over-credulous person but if you radiate warmth and sympathy while still retaining your critical faculties, you'll get the best results. But if you face them with the attitude: 'you're a fraud unless you can prove to me that you aren't one!' that's obviously not conducive to getting good results. And you're dealing with a delicate plant, a sensitive being, highly responsible to vibrations others cannot normally perceive."

"Do you think an average person has the same equipment as a medium but that it generally remains undeveloped?"

"We all have to pay a price for civilization that takes us farther and farther away from nature. We live in smog and pollution, away from the countryside; we have to accept that the originally natural faculties have become dormant. You go out among primitive peoples and you'll find it's still a natural thing for them to be telepathic like the aborigines of Australia and others that practice thought-transference and similar things. Now, if you have an emotional link with a person, it creates a vibration between the two of you—and if there's trouble, you can pick it up . . ."

"Are there any special physical or emotional characteristics a clairvoyant might have?"

"Not physical. Certainly, they are sensitive. It's the ability to feel, to respond, to pick up and transmit vibrations—something you and I can't do normally. It's like a TV set. Why can't you pick up with your eyes the waves of light and sound which the TV tube does? Only because it's tuned in to receive more delicate sights and sounds than your eyes and ears can pick up. And that's what the medium is. She's a human TV and radio set."

"What kind of people go to a clairvoyant? Could they be classified?"

"Well, all sorts. You have those who simply want to know the future—what tomorrow will bring. Then there are the people in real trouble who seek guidance. There are the grief-stricken, looking for comfort, hoping to get evidence that their beloved have survived. And the sick ones who go to a healer because the doctors told them nothing more can be done. There's great variety . . ."

"Do you think that people who are clairvoyant are able to do other things—just as faith healing?"

"Oh yes, because there's another faculty related to clairvoyance which is called clair-audience, super-sensitive hearing. That means they are able to tune in with the equivalent of their ears just as they can tune in with the equivalent of their eyes . . ."

"They hear voices?"

"The word 'hear' is rather a misnomer because they are not seeing with their eyes and not hearing with their ears. It's an inner sight and hearing, an invisible eye—"

"Something 'just comes' to them?"

"It's a little more complex than that because in addition to our physical body we also have a spiritual body, one that we'll use after death. And this has the counterpart of our other organs—so there are spiritual eyes and ears etc.—and it is these the mediums use. They don't see through their eyes and don't hear through their ears. If they close their eyes, they can see just as clearly. It's not a physical thing."

"Is that how most of the clairvoyants you know function?"

"It's how *all* the clairvoyants function. If they use a crystal ball, it's only an object of concentration. The seeing is mental, not physical."

"What about fraud in mediumship? Do you claim that all the clairvoyants are genuine?"

"Of course there's fraud in mediumship as there's fraud in every human activity—but no more than in any other aspect of life. I mean, there are no more fraudulent mediums than shyster lawyers or quack doctors. It so happens that I've exposed more fake mediums than any person alive today. I know the difference between the genuine and the fraudulent, having seen it operate for almost fifty years. Psychical researchers use a scientific approach—and my quarrel as a Spiritualist with so many of them is that their approach to mediums is wrong. There's always the test of their attitude: they think that a medium is fraudulent until they can prove that she or he isn't. Obviously you aren't going to get results that way. I sit on a committee which has now been meeting for six years, composed jointly of Spiritualists and psychical researchers; we conduct experiments together. It's no longer true that there is hostility between us. There are certain dyed-in-the-wool researchers who refuse to believe in phenomena because they've closed minds—just as we have got some ridiculously credulous Spiritualists ready to believe anything. I'm all for the psychical researcher making his scientific contribution. There's no quarrel with that. All we ask is that the medium should be treated with honest scepticism and not with this stubbornly negative approach that 'you're all a lot of frauds unless you can come up with something genuine'!"

We explained that when we visited some mediums we were captivated by their personalities and found ourselves wanting *to tell them* things. Was this a general inclination? Did many people tell a medium facts which helped them?

"Maybe," the editor of *Psychic News* said. "But you know, the moment you start telling them things, the top mediums will ask you to shut up—*they* want to tell *you*. In fact, mediums prefer to sit with strangers rather with people they know."

We took Mr. Barbanell's advice and went to see the Spiritualist Association of Great Britain. We found that it was doing very well, indeed. The reception desk, on the right of the entrance, was closely besieged by people and clerks were making the cash registers ring with obvious enjoyment and zeal. The bookshop— also conveniently located in the hall or lobby—was selling everything from Billy Graham's sermons to *Pilgrim's Progress*.

We had arranged to participate in a small group sitting with Mrs. Rose Harley at 3 p.m. These are announced as taking place in a room about 5 feet by 8; apart from the clairvoyant, only three or four people are supposed to attend. The charge is 8s. 6d. (a little over a dollar) per head and 5s (sixty cents) for a day's membership in the Association. This works out at something like £7.—or $18. a month—but then, you are more likely to take a 'season ticket' if you want to use the 'facilities' every day.

Except for ourselves no one arrived so we had what amounted virtually to a private sitting. We found Mrs. Harley to be an elderly lady in her late sixties or early seventies—perhaps even older. Her hair was snow-white, her features somewhat heavy, her figure short and plump. She began by explaining to us that usually the sittings were better attended but since the weather hadn't turned warm enough for people to come to London for shopping, ours would not be crowded. (We wondered, inevitably, whether and when a clairvoyant knows that she need not turn up herself because she won't have any 'clients'?)

Before she gave us any information about ourselves, the medium covered her face with her hands and rocked back and forth a little. Then she covered her nose with a handkerchief and said she suspected we did not have money problems. As one of us was wearing a mink coat and Gucci boots, we did not find this a particularly convincing proof of her powers. (Of course, we could have bought both on the never-never.) She then went on to say that the wearer of the mink-coat wasn't married (she had no visible wedding ring), whereupon we corrected her and said that it wasn't quite right, the lady was only separated from her husband.

Mrs. Harley immediately grasped this promising lead and said that there was no other woman in the picture (which was untrue) and that the lady had no children (which was equally off the mark.) We put her right, gently, and she went on to offer the lady in the mink consolation. She was assured that the "patient" felt perfectly fine.

"I cannot understand," Mrs. Harley said, "how a man who had children could do such a thing." She then predicted the errant husband's return, repeating the lady's earlier comment who had said she wasn't at all sure whether she would have him back. "Something would happen possibly in two years . . ." Mrs. Harley added.

We reminded her that two years was the time needed for a divorce to be completed and suggested that she might see another marriage in the lady's future. This she quite happily agreed to do—and we left it at that.

The same evening we attended a large group demonstration of clairvoyance conducted by Mr. Stanley Poultney. A tall, handsome, well-dressed man with considerable charm, he was in his late thirties or early forties.

The meeting was held in a large chapel painted a soft grey, with navy-blue carpeting and velvet drapes. It began with a recital of organ music—the programme included, a little frothily, some Strauss waltzes—after which Mr. Poultney, having been duly introduced, offered a prayer.

There were about twenty-five people in the chapel with a platform in front from which the medium worked. He spoke to various people in the audience and gave them messages "both from the spirit world and the world of the flesh". He told us that he could only get messages from the spirit world "when pure love existed."

He pointed to one woman and said he had a message from someone he thought was her father. She said, yes. People were told to to answer either "yes" or "no"—however, most of them appeared to be quite anxious to help. Mr. Poultney informed this particular woman that he was trying to help her and influence the minds of the other five (of which she was one). He did not specify whether these "other five" were brothers or sisters or mixed siblings. He continued emphasizing that it was impossible to bring three of the five together, referred to Germany and the Iron Curtain and added that the father wanted to know: he was trying to influence "the sister". The woman said "yes" to all this—without any questions or comment.

Mr. Poultney told another woman that she was having problems now because of another person's illness but there would be "a clearance" in a month or two. He said she had broken every link she had made but implied that this wasn't her fault.

He spoke to one man about business associates he named as Campbell, Cooper and Alan. To a third woman he mentioned someone called "Steve". For the most part people agreed with him though he did get several negative replies. His statements all tended to be general, easily amended—but we found his demonstration far more convincing than the one we had attended during the afternoon.

The third clairvoyant was Miss Nora Blackwood and because we wanted to make the confrontation personal and foolproof, only the female half of our team went to see her. This is her report:

Miss Blackwood lives in Colindale. I had telephoned her for an appointment, telling her nothing but my name. She asked me who had recommended me and I mentioned Maurice Barbanell.

I was about twenty-five minutes late—I had been out the night before and hadn't had much sleep for several nights running so I had trouble dragging myself out of bed that morning. Nora Blackwood said it was too bad and my loss because she had another sitter coming in and wouldn't be able to give me a full session. I apologized but she repeated: "it's just your loss" and all I could do was to agree with her. She was right.

She met me at the side door of the semi-detached house, a pretty woman, about forty-eight or fifty, in a sleeveless two-piece silk print pastel dress that reached just below her knees. A few pieces of genuine jewellery. Her lipstick was pink, her eyeshadow blue, her mascara black. Her hair was red—a colour that came from the beauty parlour and not just from an ordinary hairdresser. Her get-up was part of her mediumship. A mini skirt or ciré trousers wouldn't have been fitting. She had the true redhead's complexion, with pale skin and freckles.

We sat down in her small room she uses for her sessions and she drew the curtains. There were several tweed chairs and a sofa and a wine-coloured carpet with yellow, white and green scroll leaves on it—like those in the movie theatres of my girlhood. She was straightforward, with a businesslike attitude; she asked me for something of my own to hold—her way of making contact. I gave her my linked three-part silver ring I bought in King's Road, Chelsea. She rolled it around in her fingers, stared at it for a brief moment, then she stood up and clasped the back of a hard chair and said a prayer, invoking the spirits to reveal themselves to me, their daughter, and help me out a bit. It was all rather pragmatic and right to the point—as if she knew exactly what to ask for. I didn't get the feeling she was the kind of lady to fool around with crystal balls or tarot cards.

Then she sat down, faced me and began: "You've recently had a break in your life, a strong break."

I nodded.

"You've been married." Another nod. "But you aren't any longer." Nod again. "Both your parents are alive but I have a Granny here who says she is your mother's mother."

This didn't strike me as too unusual because all these clairvoyants seem to drag in grandmothers and grandfathers. All this is generally meaningless to me because they show this enormous concern for me after they are dead—while when they were alive they could barely manage to remember my name. In fact both my maternal and my paternal grandmothers were literally senile when they died. Miss Blackwood, however, went on to say: this Granny was telling her that the deed of agreement would be settled in late September and that I was going to move into a new place and that my furniture was being shipped from the States. All true. The deed of agreement was that of my legal separation. I was beginning to feel some respect for her accuracy because she didn't ask me if these things were true—which is an old trick—but making statements. On the other hand she was also picking various things that would concern any old grandma, not only mine. Any break-up of a marriage involves these things : legal position, home and furniture.

Up to this point I had been just nodding but now she asked me to speak out loud, because "they like to hear you". It was like recitation time back in school. I felt like a little girl again. "Speak up, speak up, child, they can't hear you at the back of the room." Then Nora Blackwood said : "I have a man who says he's your husband's father."

This was a bit of a shock and I sat up and took notice. My father-in-law had "passed over" as mediums put it—but she couldn't have known that. He was the only one of my own kin or my in-laws who hadn't "dropped in" on any of the other clairvoyants that I've visited. Those others all produced Grannies, Gramps and great-Grannies and Gramps but none of them "called up" my father-in-law. Yet here he was now, "on the line".

Actually, it was far more logical for him to show up than any of the grandparents because at least I had a relationship with him, such as it was—and I really didn't have with the previous generation. Besides, he was likely to care about what was going on because his grandchildren were involved.

Nora Blackwood went on to say that my husband was in the entertainment industry and that his father was telling her : there was a "link with music". She saw an orchestra. "Right !" I answered, loud and clear. My father-in-law had been a bass player in the New York Philharmonic for seventeen years—"link" enough. Then Miss Blackwood reeled off the names of my husband's aunts—although she didn't know they were aunts but just said : "I'm getting the names Ann, Leah, Lee . . ." and I think she hit "Clara" too. She said that he had a sister and she mentioned the name Joe. Now, Joe is the husband of my sister-in-law. Then she gave me my husband's initials, *R* and *C* but she somehow missed out on the middle one. She said *M*—actually, it's *I*.

At this point, I began to feel strange and other-wordly. There was really no logical explanation for her possibly knowing all this. I hadn't even given her my name nor told her a single thing about myself. In fact, even my yeas and nays she had to coax out of me. I thought briefly of Maurice Barbanell as the source of all this information—but I hadn't told *him* anything about myself or my husband either.

The ladies and gentlemen we had seen before had given nothing like this impressive performance. Usually we could figure out that they *had* to get something right by simple guesswork—under the law of averages. Also, most of them had been at it for a long time, getting to be good judges of character so that they could make highly educated guesses as to what was on one's mind. If they were able to extract from you your religion, national origin and social background, they could produce half a dozen names and somewhere among them one was bound to recognize a couple. We all helped them by remembering an old lover with the initial *A* if they produced *A*—because basically one *wants* them to be right. Any answer beyond a yes or no unwittingly provides information which they later throw back at you, convincing you further of what you want to believe, anyhow. Sometimes they ask: "is it true that recently you've had a shock?" Well, most people do have one fairly frequently. Then you say: "why, yes" and tell her what it was—and even if it was only getting out of bed that morning when you thought you never would, it gives her something to go on. Or if you say *no*, she can turn the whole thing into an act of precognition, and say she hopes she isn't wrong and no shock is coming.

But Nora Blackwood did none of this. What she produced was correct and commendable. Of course, the nagging question always remained: why should someone take all the trouble to return from the dead, stop off in Colindale and then tell *me* the names of members of the family and a few initials? Do the dead lose their wits beside their bodies? Or is there some sort of law that keeps them to trivialities?

In addition I became a little resentful because all this involved my husband's family. Nora looked rather like *his* mother and she had brought back *his* father—who, incidentally, had nothing but admiration for his son. I wasn't getting very much sympathy myself. Then she said: "He's not a promiscuous man. He never ran around with a lot of women". I began to suspect that Miss Blackwood was not a clairvoyant but a propagandist or apologist for errant husbands. "You never got on with his mother," she added. "You just tolerated her and she just tolerated you." Well, if my father-in-law wanted to bring that one up, he might as well remember that *he* never got along with her either!

At this point the tables began to turn—symbolically, that is, not literally. "Living with him wasn't easy," Nora Blackwood told me. "It was like living on top of a volcano. You never knew when the eruption would come." Then she laughed and jerked her thumb over her shoulder. "That other girl he has . . . *he* says, she's a tart. That's what he's called her." So my father-in-law knew. Maybe the dead were not so witless, after all. *I* hadn't told him. "*He* believes in family unity and he wants to protect the children. He says your husband loves the children very much but he is infatuated with this girl and he doesn't know what's happening to him now. He's going around saying that it's your fault. It isn't your fault, his father says." Vindicated in the eyes of the Great Beyond! I was beginning to feel distinctly better. "I can't see a reconciliaton. I'm sorry to have to tell you that— but I just can't see it and I have to be honest. She's going to leave him, though and it will be through a job. She's an actress, isn't she? She's going to find another man. Her name should be 'I-want'. Honestly, she wants everything, that one. She didn't care about breaking up a home and when she feels like leaving him, she won't care about him either!"

The spirits and Nora Blackwood had her number!

So she went on to say that "he" was going to suffer and be left high and dry. Eventually he'd be back because I was the only friend he had and he would need me . . . "But . . . are you ready for this? There'll be a happy ending because someone's going to come along who's really going to love you for what you are."

That was the sentence that brought me back to earth—and sanity. I felt as if I had indeed come home again and listened to my parents. And even though it was my father-in-law speaking through someone who looked a lot like my mother-in-law, it was the same thing. Nora Blackwood and the "spirit visitor" had drawn a picture of me as the wronged woman and I had enjoyed every moment of that coddling and sympathy for poor little me. Home is the only place where you can get this—because things are not so simple in reality and even if our parents don't know it, we ought to by the time we grow up.

Yet I couldn't deny that Nora Blackwood had given me some tangible proof of her powers, hard to explain in human terms and certainly worth further investigation. It was the closest to a psychic experience I had ever been. But beneath her homely,

D

matter-of-fact exterior she was sensitive enough to know exactly what I needed—so she dispensed with the spiritualism and provided me with some commonsense morality disguised as "coming attraction".

But I wasn't blameless, either. I had helped her turn the whole thing into a soap opera because she was telling me exactly what I wanted to hear—and I hadn't done anything to stop her. So now I had her sympathy and her word that a couple of spirits felt the same way she did. Perhaps this was the sort of reason why people visited clairvoyants?

She indicated that the time was up and said that when I met "that man" who was going to love me for myself, I would have to make a decision. "When you do, come back to me." She gave me back my ring and asked me for two guineas. Her next sitter was exactly on time.

The next clairvoyant we saw was Mrs Mary Rogers, a lady abundantly endowed by nature and full of good will. When we met her, she was wearing a scoop-necked, sleeveless dress and a large carved crucifix hung between her breasts. The dress was hot pink, her hair was white blonde and fluffed around her face. Her eyebrows were very thin and she was carefully made up. She reminded us a little of Miss Mae West.

Her home in Wivelsfield Green has a lovely big garden, lots of cats and a friend who was apparently recovering from a very serious illness. Her future daughter-in-law who looked like a young carbon copy of Mrs. Rogers served us tea and we met her son and her husband, Mr. George Rogers who was a distinguished Labour Member of Parliament. It was a cosy, family atmosphere with nothing spooky or unearthly about it.

We retired with her to a small room which serves as her office or seance room. A cross made of two twigs marked the door. There was a small shrine with candles, statues of Christ, crucifixes, a painting of a Cross and other religious articles; but the room also contained a studio sofa, several chairs and a desk.

She told us immediately that her real interest lay in healing. She used clairvoyance mainly to diagnose her patients.

We found her extremely jolly and easy to get along with; so much so that it didn't seem to matter if she slipped up and missed the target nor that she could have drawn most of what she said from information provided by ourselves. She also made a good many predictions—most of them long-term so that only time could tell how correct these were.

She claimed that her powers came from God. She did not know how or why she was chosen for this particular task—but she was. It all began one day when she was a child of five or six and she was upstairs in her home, being ill. She wanted to go downstairs—and suddenly a nun in a grey habit appeared at her bedside and asked her whether she would like to be carried down. She said yes, and the nun did carry her downstairs. She could feel the stairs under her and the solid body carrying her. Her mother said there wasn't a nun in the house nor was there any way one could have entered without her, the mother, knowing it. It was her first psychic experience and "it left a mark".

Mrs. Rogers had a firm belief in reincarnation. Human beings came back "in a different shell but the life force remains the same". She told us that one of us was "an old soul" and had been around for quite a long time in different incarnations. She added that she had the ability "to go backwards and forwards along the life-lines of people" and see what they were.

As a child she was frail—"this being often the case with psychic people". No one believed her story about the nun though she repeated it to members of her family and friends. Then, about twenty years later, she was staying with a couple in Cornwall. The wife was a Spiritualist and she said to Mary Rogers: "Do you remember being carried downstairs by a nun when you were a child?" Now, she had never told this story to these people nor had she known them before that weekend. The woman went on to tell her that the nun "was standing right there, next to her and had just told her about carrying her downstairs twenty years earlier . . ."

"You function as a clairvoyant," we asked, "so if we came to you and had recently a great misfortune and were in need of comfort, would you be able to sense it clairvoyantly?"

"Yes, I can do that," Mrs. Rogers replied. "I'm unusual in that I am also a healer. Because as a rule clairvoyants are clairvoyants and healers are healers and never the twain shall meet. But I've got both. I do my own diagnosis . . ."

She gave us some examples of her faith healing successes and explained why she really preferred that branch of psychical activity. But when we asked whether she agreed that the body could sometimes get sick for purely psychological reasons, she nodded. "So if you could by your clairvoyance discover what ails a person . . ." we suggested. And again she said, yes, she has often done that.

Mrs. Rogers has appeared on the Alan Serk TV show in New York and has done similar work on the B.B.C. She said that in New York she had been able to "diagnose the whole studio audience". And by and large she was more interested in describing her past successes, her "cures" and "clairvoyant diagnoses" than to give us a demonstration of her powers. This was understandable enough for our visit was not in search of help but of information.

The last British clairvoyant we saw was Miss Jessie Nason whose handbill announces that she PROVES SURVIVAL OF LIFE AFTER DEATH. She holds regular meetings at the Dulwich Library, Lordship Lane, London on every Wednesday evening where "a wonderful band of healers is available"; but she is also available for private appointments—which is what we sought.

We visited her in her large flat in Clapham, South London. She is a big woman with a practical no-nonsense attitude about her. Her hair is short and reddish-brown and she wears Harlequin eyeglasses. She is very direct and comes right to the point. She asks few questions and appears to be quite convinced that everything she says is right—very much unlike some other mediums we visited. Her charge is £2.12.6. per sitting; a brisk businesswoman for whom clairvoyance is like any other job or profession.

She received us in her sitting-room which had grey tweed sofas and gold-coloured rugs. She told us that she would be pleased to give an interview but no clairvoyant reading. She had been working hard all night and during most of the week and she wasn't sure she felt up to it. We said we were sorry but we did not press her. Then she sat down—and proceeded to give a clairvoyance demonstration.

Before and after this display she told us that she had known she possessed such powers ever since she was four or five years old. It was then her grandmother died and several nights later when she went to bed, she found Granny standing at its foot. She was frightened and cried out. Now her mother who had passed over is with her all the time, instructs and advises her.

As a child she used to press an imaginary button located in her navel—whereupon a beautiful lady dressed in gossamer green appeared. Now she no longer has to press the button but this lady is her spirit guide and comes whenever she needs to talk to her.

She said she believed it was very comforting to people to know that those they have lost can be reached in the spirit world—and she was proud to be able to perform this service for humanity. Like Mary Rogers, she was also a firm believer in reincarnation. She explained that whenever she was unable to make contact with the spirit world for some clients who came to her, she would tell them directly rather than string them along—for that would be very wrong.

After which her questions began. First she wanted to know if anyone in our families had ever been married twice? No, we told her.

"Well, I'm getting two marriages . . ." Miss Nason said and added : "Don't either of you come from what I call a churchy background? People who were rather narrow, orthodox in their conception of life? And you were the first one to break out?"

We said that was right. "Because in this breaking-out," she continued, "you say, Oh, I can't take that, you see and you had to come right away from the whole thing, you understand . . . Tell me, please why do I get an influence of the Catholic faith? Your people weren't Catholic but there was somebody in Catholic conditions . . ."

We admitted that there were very devout people in our families but . . .

"I never bend messages," Jessie Nason declared. "It's either right or chuck it out . . ."

She went on talking about "Catholic influence in the background" which could be something to do with ancestors. "I don't know," she admitted, "but there is a Catholic influence . . ."

We denied the existence of any such thing and she veered off on another tack :

"Tell me . . . who is Mary? I don't mean Mary Rogers, obviously. Who is Mary, connected with the family?"

There was no one we could dig up to suit her. Then she concentrated on one of us and fired a whole barrage of questions:
   "Would you know anything about the name of Nelson? . . .
This is not the job you've always done, is it? Because I get you
at some time connected with an office . . ."
   No Nelson—not even Lady Hamilton—could be produced:
but we admitted that at one time or other *we* were connected
with an office. (Who wasn't?) Jessie wanted to know whether
we ever had anything to do with the medical profession or allied
to the medical field, whether we have ever worn a white overall,
done any receptionist work or anything like that—to all of which
we had to return a negative answer. But, being an insistent lady,
she pleaded with us: "Will you bear it in mind and see if you
can think of it?" This we promised to do.
   After that it was a matter of hit-and-miss—though more
miss than hit. Apparently a doctor's white coat led her to an
artist's smock—for she wanted to know whether we had anything
to do with art "because I see all pictures around you". One of us
confessed to having painted. Then she turned to the female
member of our partnership:
   "You know your marriage was wrong from the word go,"
she declared, "but you couldn't see it. But you woke up in three
months."
   "I was married for a long time."
   "Yes, I know. But I would say within three months you began
to get funny feelings. Then gradually after a period of time the
gap became wider and wider and wider . . . Why am I getting
two children, please?"
   "I have more than two," the lady admitted cautiously.
   Jessie Nason risked a desperate gamble and declared that two
of the children were girls (correct) and that there was something
wrong with their teeth—a safe enough guess with growing young
'uns. When it was admitted that this was correct, she crowed:
"*They* know what they're talking about. It's the truth that they're
talking about!"
   She went on about visits to the Continent, mentioning France
and Germany. We said that we always tried to stay out of Germany, but Miss Nason insisted that there was a link. (Some
six months after the interview, one of us did pay a short visit
to Berlin.) She then rapidly referred to the Jewish faith (saying

that she herself was proud to be Jewish), to "two places" in America (New York and California, which was logical enough as one of our team had lived in both places); then the conversation became a little more personal, always on the feminine line:

"Someone just said to me: 'ask her what she's done with her hair?'" Jessie Nason said. The lady had had very long hair which she cut off about eight months before the visit to Jessie Nason. "It used to be so pretty!" she added and then suddenly sprang a question: "And tell me, please, who is Lilly?"

This was apparently a bull's eye. "Lilly is my friend. My good friend."

"They told me to ask you who Lilly is. They know about Lilly. They said she's confused, too. They said you make a proper pair together. Do you understand this?"

"Yes."

"I don't know why but they said I'm to talk to you about a flat tyre."

"I can't think why."

"I often get things which I am not meant . . . I'm only a transmitter . . . it may only mean something to you. I'm sorry but I'm in a car and something's happened to you which has something to do with a flat tyre . . . You'll have to think about it. Sometimes you can't think of it at first. *I* don't know what it means. You see, every medium is only a transmitter. And we often get things we don't have to know. And who would be Evelyn?"

"My aunt. But she's not close to me."

"Doesn't matter. They're mentioning the names of the family. And isn't there someone called Joe?"

"Can't think of anyone . . ."

"Tell me, were you involved with people who were drugging?"

"You mean, taking drugs?"

"I don't know where it is or what it's all about but they tell me there was an involvement with you and the people who were taking drugs . . . And I don't know why but I'm going to the Earl's Court area of London . . ."

"Well, I nearly took a flat there . . ."

"Thank you. Because they know about this part of London . . . And tell me, who in the family is called Ann?"

"I don't know anybody."

"Have you a grandmother who passed over?"

"One of my grandmothers died a few months ago."

"Because I have got a Granny here on the line and she sends her love to you and she is trying to help you. She says you are a bit impulsive. She thinks she's got you just right and then you are up and off. Sitting down one minute and up and gone the next. Now where would Granny connect with your phone number?"

"I don't know."

"Well, check it . . . She's now giving me the name of Sara."

"I have a friend named Sara."

"I want someone who belongs to the family. They may have called her Sadie, I don't know. I think the original name was Sara but they may have called her Sadie."

"I have an aunt named Sadie."

"That may be the one they're talking about . . . Tell me, who walks with a limp?"

"I don't know."

"Because she's telling me she even knows about this. Tell me, who walks with a limp?"

"A man I go out with broke his toe . . ."

"Because your grandmother says would I tell you she knows about the man who walks with a limp. And would the name Miriam mean anything? No? And is there a John?"

We admitted we knew a John. Who doesn't?

After the somewhat inconclusive demonstration of her powers, Miss Nason agreed to answer some general questions. We asked her how she got her messages? What exactly did happen?

"Well, first of all, it depends," she replied. "Sometimes, more often than not, I hear voices telling me things. There have been other occasions when I'm, as it were, impressed. And if they want to show me something, it's as if there were a television screen," she pointed to her head, "right here and I see it in the mind . . . Then sometimes all three are going on. Sometimes I will go on to the platform and say, what's your name and she'll say Margaret H. Smith and then I will get a clairvoyant picture of what this person looks like and I will describe her. Sometimes they give me a sensing of the condition they died of and I know that this person has had a stroke, I get the name, I describe as much as I can what they look like. They say this man had a coronary . . .

But I have got all the lot going in order to get this person over and get the message through. I rely on the spirit to feed me the information. I don't look at you and do it. I do it with *them*."

"Where do you think this gift comes from?"

"Well, I'm not anybody special. I was born with it."

"Do you think it comes from God? Are you a religious woman?"

"Not in the ordinary sense but if you say I have a belief in a great power or in a great source of power . . . I know that I am nothing without this source of power. I know that this gift was not given to me for myself but to help others and I think the greatest thing that it teaches you is a belief in the brotherhood of men.

"What kind of people come to mediums?"

"Get it out of your mind that the people who come to mediums are emotional. There are some very shrewd people who come to mediums. They know the score. But I can't say that I get more of one kind of person than another."

Unlike Jessie Nason, Jeane Dixon, perhaps the most famous American clairvoyant, definitely claims that her power comes from God. This creates certain difficulties for she has refused any scientific examination—she feels there is no need for it. And though parapsychology researchers are willing to admit that she has some ability, they are not convinced about it's extent and total genuineness because they had no chance of studying it adequately.

Jeanie Dixon does not read peoples' minds and does not pretend to bring messages from those who have "passed over". Her particular clairvoyant field is precognition—and she has claimed, publicly and repeatedly, remarkable powers of prophecy. By now her claims have been widely accepted—if not by the scientists, by the public. Her books about prophecy have sold more than three million copies. A prosperous real-estate broker who lives in Washington, D.C., she has refused to accept any money for her forecasts of the future—though, of course, she has had a very large income from the indirect exploitation of her prophecies.

It would take too long to tabulate Jeane Dixon's successes and set them against her failures; and in precognition, unlike in ESP tests, statistics prove very little. Certainly her followers who

D*

believe unhesitatingly in her powers amount to tens of thousands. She has a large circle of personal friends and is constantly besieged by people who want their fortunes told. She has foretold the future of presidents and politicians and has made something of a speciality of the field of international affairs.

Certainly the most celebrated prediction she ever made was that a young, blue-eyed President of America elected in 1960 would be assassinated while serving his term of office. Then in 1963 she begged the President not to go to Dallas. She told others that she had a vision of the White House with a dark, forbidding cloud hanging over it. She phoned Kennedy's aides several times, insisted that her prophecy would be fulfilled—and, of course, it was. Presidents receive such warnings—as indeed, people in high offices do—fairly regularly and if they paid attention to them, their work and activities would be severely curtailed. But Jeane Dixon's "precognition", whether coincidence or real prophetic vision, made her famous and she has been since consulted by a surprising number of V.I.P.'s. Her career actually stretches back quite a few years for she had even gained the attention of President Roosevelt shortly before his death. Evidently he had heard of her Delphic powers and asked her how long he had to live. She said, several months. He consulted her later and then she told him he would not live much longer. Roosevelt's death came as a traumatic shock to the world—because to outsiders it was so sudden. In a sense it was as unthinkable as an assassination.

One of the main characteristics of Jeane Dixon's powers is this ability to foresee deaths in the families of people who come to see her. Apparently her forecasts come through in a large number of cases—which, in turn, reinforces the faith people have in her. Whenever she fails—as her "precognition" usually entails a tragedy, her friends and clients happily forget and forgive. But many responsible people in America claim that she has been extremely accurate in forecasting the future. As the Ladies' Home Journal reported in November 1965 :

> In the midst of a discussion about coutouriers, her eyes suddenly clouded, she touched her long, slender fingers to her forehead and she said to her companion, ex-Congresswoman Coya Knutson, now a Pentagon official. 'Coya, I just picked

up the vibrations from outer space. The astronauts will not complete all of their scheduled revolutions of the earth on this space mission. They will fall one or two short.'

Mrs. Knutson reacted with no surprise to this prophecy, nor even eight days later, to the now recorded fact that Cooper and Conrad indeed had to terminate their flight after the 120th instead of the 121st orbit. Mrs. Knutson says, 'I have long since learned that when Jeane Dixon foresees an occurrence, it is going to occur. Jeane has the God-given gift of prophecy.'

The business about a single orbit may not appear to be particularly world-shattering—but at least the facts about it are indisputable.

Jeane Dixon claims that her powers of prediction are a divine gift. Many of the "spiritual messages" are relayed to her "by the Power of the Lord" while she is in church. A report in the August 10, 1966 issue of the *Christian Century Magazine* contained an eyewitness account according to which she dematerialized—"disappeared tracelessly"—during morning mass in St. Matthews Cathedral, Washington. However, she turned up at her home, apparently little worse for wear after what must have been a unique experience. The divine messages are, however, not the only source of her prophetic powers. She uses a crystal ball which was given to her by a gipsy when she was a small girl. "Vibrations from outer space" bring her news of the future. She also relies upon astrology, numerology and a deck of cards.

Miss Dixon's supporters proudly list her successes. They claim that she accurately forecast the rise of Communist China when the vast sub-continent still seemed to be firmly in the grip of Chiang Kai-shek; she described the first Sputnik (even giving its size as "about as big as a basketball") years before it made its first historic orbit; she predicted the downfall, far in advance, of a great many statesmen, including Nikita Khrushchev, Sir Winston Churchill and Thomas E. Dewey. Her most frequent prophecies refer to assorted public and personal calamities—including the devastating Alaskan earthquake of 1964; the airplane disasters which killed Dag Hammerskjold and maimed Senator Edward Kennedy; President Eisenhower's first heart attack and Marilyn Monroe's suicide were also forecast by her.

She seems to have slipped up on Jacqueline Kennedy for she confidently asserted that she would never marry again.

The failures are on record—but they are seldom remembered. Her partisans gloss them over and she herself has made it quite clear that she is not perfect. "You know, I'm not infallible," she said, referring to a prediction concerning Red China's admission to the United Nations in 1959—an event still far in the future. "I will get my timing wrong when I read my symbols wrong," she told an interviewer in September 1965. "There have been inevitable mistakes . . ." In 1958 she foresaw war with Red China over the off-shore islands Quemoy and Matsu. She said that the labour-leader Walter Reuther would seek presidential nomination in 1964. (She did not foretell his tragic death in a plane accident in May 1970.) She picked the Conservatives to win the British General Election of 1966.

The *Christian Century* and other American publications have denied her any religious powers and scoffed at her assumption of "communication with God".

"One morning at St. Matthew's," the magazine wrote, "someone saw her disappear. Remarkable! Also remarkable is the fact that the visions she sees at St. Matthew's and elsewhere are often visions of elephants and donkeys and other religio-political symbols!" (The two animals, as we know, represent the Democratic and Republican parties of the United States.) Equal scepticism has been expressed by other critics, while at the same time, Dr. Daniel A. Foling, the former editor of the *Christian Herald* called Ruth Montgomery's book about Jeane Dixon (*A Gift of Prophecy*) "perhaps the most important volume that has appeared in the field of prophecy since the Biblical prophets".

The more balanced commentators admit that Miss Dixon has been a failure at times but agree that her successes far outweigh her failures. They play down her minor mistakes and point only to her totally wrong forecast about Nixon winning the presidential election in 1960. However, Miss Dixon has a ready answer to this—she says that Cook County, Illinois, a democratic stronghold, "stole the election—so Nixon really did win". And she actually predicted a possible win for Kennedy (who *did* triumph), thereby hedging her bets.

None of this has lessened her popularity which is still increasing. She offers her prophecies free of charge and she has been able to gather considerable support from people in Washington, especially among the politicians. Since she gives her advice gratis, there is no doubt that gossip provides her with valuable resources. She circulates in the social gatherings that are such an essential part of the Washington scene. And she feels it a duty to offer her knowledge to those whom it will affect either directly or indirectly.

Jeane Dixon is in her forties and she has a long life ahead of her. Perhaps she will even live to see the fulfilment of her most recent prophecy which is, indeed, a long-term and ambitious one. She said recently : "A child born somewhere in the Middle East, shortly after 7 a.m. (Eastern Standard time), on February 5, 1962, will revolutionize the world . . . He will bring together all mankind in one embracing faith . . . This person . . . is a descendant of Queen Nefertiti and her Pharaoh husband; of this I am sure."

Queen Nefertiti was the consort of Amenhotep IV who abolished the cult of Amun and the worship of all the old Egyptian gods, replacing them with Aton, the only god, whose symbol was the disc which sent out rays ending in hands. It was a strange and valiant attempt at monotheism which lasted less than twenty years. She and Nefertiti had many children—all girls—and their descendants must number hundreds of millions. But Jeane Dixon is not really concerned with history—the past, after all, is the field of historians and she is only interested in the future.

Britain's answer to Jeane Dixon is called Maurice Woodruff—though more recently he has invaded her home territory and has become, among many other things, resident astrologer of McCall's Magazine in which he was described as "astrology's brightest star". In Britain he became famous through his regular television appearances, his newspaper columns and his much-publicized predictions. These seem to be based less on precognition than on the reading of the stars and their courses in the heavens. Son of Vera Woodruff, the favourite clairvoyant of British society in the twenties and thirties, he was brought up in an atmosphere of "prophecy" and when at seventeen he struck out on his own, he billed himself "clairvoyant astrologer, readings by appointment" which certainly brings him into our orbit. And his autobiography, published in the spring of 1970 in New York, is simply called *Clairvoyant*. It seems that the invisible eye finds nourishment in various sources—inspiration, crystal balls, the

Zodiac or extra-sensory perception—and Woodruff's grandmother was a Romany gipsy from Suffolk so he can claim to
have digested and absorbed all the various elements of his craft.

He, too, had his successes and failures. Early in March 1970,
however, he really stuck his neck out and made a whole series
of predictions for the coming year. By the time you read this
book, you might be able to check them against your daily newspaper (though one or two are rather long-range) and find out
how the score of Maurice Woodruff stands. But before you do,
you might like to hear Woodruff's definition of a clairvoyant;
according to him he or she is a person "who can see where others
are blind. He can see backward and forward. Everybody has been
one at some time in his life. Surely you have said, 'I knew darned
well that was going to happen,' and you couldn't have told why.
But you were right. All you needed was confidence in your
instinct. Men call it a hunch. Women call it intuition. I think
it is extrasensory perception."

And here are Mr. Woodruff's 1970 predictions:

The cure for cancer will be discovered, probably in September,
in two countries at the same time—in America and in Europe.
There will be a massive breakthrough in optical surgery.

The war in Vietnam will peter out late in the year. At the
same time another will flare up in Korea. The Chinese will have
a real go at the Russians *twice*—so it will take the Russians'
minds off other places.

There will be quite a business depression about April. The
Canadian dollar will be worth more than the American, although
normally it is about ten cents less. Europe, however, will be
all right, the pound will be stronger because a general election
will bring a new Prime Minister to power. The franc might
slide a little. American business conditions will not improve until
late summer or early autumn.

The mini-skirt will disappear early in the year. Skirts will be
just below the knee, flared and quite full. Formal evening gowns
will have a little train. Men will go back to knickers and Beau
Brummel type clothes, with fitted lines, longer sleeves and frilled
cuffs. Colour will dominate men's fashions.

No Kennedy in the White House in the foreseeable future.
John F. Kennedy's son will be a scientist. Ethel Kennedy, Bobby's
widow, will go into politics. Jackie Kennedy Onassis will have a

son but her present marriage won't last more than another year and a half or two years. It will be Ari Onassis who will break it up. Her sister, Princess Lee Radziwill, will be divorced sometime in 1970, possibly in England.

Ronald Reagan will not be re-elected governor in next autumn's election. John Lindsay will give up the mayor's job in New York and will run for the United States Senate. Senator Jacob Javits may reach Presidential level in politics, with Nixon offering him a Cabinet post when the Vietnam war has ended. Spiro Agnew will not serve his full time in office. If he does, he will not stand for re-election, Richard Nixon will gain great popularity in 1970. When the time of re-election comes in 1972, I guarantee that he will be almost unopposed.

Well—by the time these words are in print, you will be able to decide the score of Mr. Woodruff's hits and misses.

In *Children of the Supernatural* Robert Tralins gathered a remarkable collection of well-documented cases demonstrating the inexplicable powers of clairvoyance and precognition recorded in the young. While no original sources are provided and sceptics might very well ask for further examination, some examples are certainly worth mentioning as part of the rich and still not fully explored psychical world of the sixties.

There was five-year-old Michael Hall of Norfolk Virginia who woke on the night of January 17, 1965, screaming at the top of his lungs. When his parents managed to calm him down at last and asked what had frightened him into a nightmare, he told them that he saw "Uncle Joe and Aunt Marthy and Cousin Frankie burning to death in a big fire . . ." He gave further details. adding that the whole downstairs part of their house was burning up and they were trapped, unable to get to the telephone.

At first his parents were sceptical but the little boy insisted so frantically, that his father called the firemen and hurried over to his brother's house. He found that everything had happened exactly as Michael described it and the three people were saved just in the nick of time.

On July 16 of the same year Michael had another nightmare. This time it was his mother, his grandfather and grandmother whom he saw being "real sick. Mommy is gonna die if somebody don't save her right now!"

Mrs. Hart was staying at her mother's that night, nursing her after a minor operation. He telephoned, heard a feeble voice gasp at the other end—then there was a thud and deep silence. Walter Hall called the police and drove with Michael over to his in-laws house. He found that all three of them were seriously ill with food-poisoning. They were rushed to hospital and recovered—but the odds were that except for the little boy's telepathic dream they would have not survived the night.

Up to 1969 Michael Hart had no other prophetic nightmares; but if he ever has one again, it is hardly likely that his parents would not act on them promptly.

A little London girl, Kathy Hodson, saved the life of another child in December 1963. Kathy, like many other eight-year-old girls had an invisible playmate who was called "Alice" and who, like her name-sake, was linked to a mirror—she "lived" in it. That night Kathy heard her calling and, for the first time, "Alice" actually emerged from the glass which was glowing with a strange glow. It wasn't, however, in order to have a romp—she had a message for Kathy. "Your friend Gracie is very sick and you must help her!" she told the little girl. "She didn't listen to her mommy and took too many pills the doctor left for her chills and fever. If you don't help her she will die."

Kathy went to her mother and told her about "Alice" and the message. Of course she was promptly sent back to bed. But instead she slipped into the kitchen and dialled Gracie's number. Mrs. Sennett, too, was sceptical and hung up in the midst of Katy's explanation. At this point Kathy's mother caught her and when the girl told her what she had done, scolded her and insisted that she should immediately apologize to Mrs. Sennett. But when they telephoned for the second time, the voice at the other end was full of gratitude and excited thanks. It was Kathy's first call that made Gracie's mother go and check on Gracie—whom she found in a coma. She *had* taken a whole bottle of pills and if the doctor had not arrived in time with a stomach pump, she would have, indeed, died. But— "however did Kathie know?" A question only "Alice" could have answered.

In March 1961 Opal Wynne, aged six, was offered a cookie (biscuit) in a bakery store in Charlotte, North Carolina. She refused it, saying: "I don't want that—it's *poisoned*!"

The shop was full and the clear, high-pitched voice of the

little girl caused an understandable sensation. The woman who served at the counter protested but Opal repeated that the cookies *were* poisoned. "The baker man," she added "accidentally spilled some poison on them before he brought them out and put them in the case."

Everybody tried to silence her but she stood her ground. Finally the assistant took the customers into the bake shop at the rear of the store. There the baker proudly displayed his work, insisting that only the best ingredients were used. And as he demonstrated this, he discovered to his horror that someone had accidentally placed a can of deadly roach powder on the same shelf with the confectioner's sugar and that the powder had been mistakenly used on the sheets of cookies. It was Opal Wynne's clairvoyance that had prevented a tragedy.

Opal had been involved in several similar incidents. On Christmas 1960 she woke up in the middle of the night to tell her mother that the Christmas decorations were about to catch fire from a short circuit. Within a few minutes this was actually taking place. At five she refused to go for a ride in her uncle's car—and the car was involved in an accident within an hour. A few months after the episode in the bakery she foretold that her grandmother would be taken to hospital—and she was, though luckily only for observation.

Tralins reports similar cases in Addis Ababa (where clairvoyant twins were involved), in the Philippines (a little girl who, going into a trance, revealed things she could not have possibly known), in Rome (a small boy whose clairvoyance was centred on animals), in various states of America, in Cairo, Madrid and half-a-dozen other places scattered over the globe. It would be a most interesting and rewarding task to investigate what happened (or is going to happen) to these children when they grow up. Would their powers wane? Would they persist and develop? Only when a large-scale research project is undertaken, however costly, can the questions about the "children of the supernatural" be answered with a minimum of certainty.

Clairvoyance in the last third of the twentieth century is, roughly speaking, working in two disciplines, trying to fulfil two, perhaps mutually exclusive functions. The first is connected with Spiritualism and the clairvoyant acts as a voice medium trans-

mitting messages from the dead—and these messages, as we have
seen, are often of monumental banality and ordinariness. It may
be a proof of psychic powers to tell somebody the name of her
husband's aunts but it is hardly likely to change her life or open
up new philosophical or religious heights. A classic example was
the clairvoyant lady who appeared on a popular television show
and delivered the vitally important message from the dear departed mother of a man in the studio audience, warning him
not to hurry painting his kitchen because he had to watch his
weak back. It turned out that the man had no intention of
painting the kitchen at all—though his wife had fell designs
on him in this respect. Whether this sort of activity, whether
connected or not with fortune-telling, forecasting the future or
simply lay psychoanalysis, can be called clairvoyance in the strict
sense of the word, is a difficult question to answer.

The other form of clairvoyance appears to have nothing to do
with the spirit world. It is based on extra-sensory perception—or
perhaps on a sense we have neither named nor explored as yet.
It does not claim to transmit messages from the other world or
be based on supernatural powers. It is, by and large, a function
of the brain that has developed in certain human beings and may
be present in all of us—comparable, on a much higher plane,
to perfect musical pitch or the palate of a professional wine-
taster.

In the last decade, though Professor Rhine's pioneering experiments have been violently attacked and the frame-work of
his activities has changed, more and more scientists have become
interested in this field. We have spoken of Dr. J. Gaither Pratt
whose American Parapsychological Association has over 200
members. He believes that scientific interest in his specialty is
growing; credit courses are being offered on several campuses in
California and Colorado; graduate students at the College of the
City of New York can earn master's degrees in psychology for
work in parapsychology. At the University of Pittsburgh, at Saint
Joseph College Philadelphia, at the University of Virginia
serious and devoted research is continuing. It is both a pity and
somewhat characteristic that certain mediums are shy of submit-
ting themselves to scientific tests—such as Arthur Ford, the
medium through whom the late Bishop James Pike claimed he
talked to his dead son. Ford has been invited repeatedly to the

Duke University parapsychology laboratory—but never accepted the invitation.

Dr. Pratt worked with the Czech clairvoyant Pavel Stepanek, testing him both in Prague and later in Charlottesville. The tests were completely foolproof : Dr. Pratt slipped four-by-six-inch cards, green on one side and white on the other, into grey cardboard envelopes which would be put into larger grey envelopes and finally into even larger biege manila file envelopes.

Then he flipped the envelopes, asking Stepanek to tell him whether the green or the white side was up. Thousands of cards were flipped; in one test, when the card was used 250 times, it came up green 143 times and Stepanek called it correctly 131 times—a proportion far above any statistical average for accidental guesswork. Later, however, the Czech clairvoyant's powers seemed to wane—as it happens more than once in similar experiments. But his impressive record still stands.

Clairvoyants have also been employed by police headquarters all over the world or have offered their own services. In recent years it seems they crop up whenever a spectacular crime has occurred—volunteering or being called in by some baffled police chief. Ubald Tartaruga, whom we have quoted before, worked for years with the clairvoyant medium Megaris and claimed to have solved a number of cases with her help. Peter Herkos, the Dutch clairvoyant, has made several trips to the United States. He is a considerable showman—but Dr. Pratt and other researchers maintain that there is no record indicating that he actually solved a crime. And, indeed, neither the massacre of beautiful Sharon Tate and her house-guests nor the identity of the Boston Strangler were revealed through the clairvoyants who were consulted or volunteered their services. But clairvoyants are working with various psychology departments of Western and Eastern universities, are collaborating in a number of still unfinished experiments and it is certain that in the coming decades they will be more and more accepted even by orthodox science. Perhaps we are on the threshold of a breakthrough that will link the hallucinatory drugs with clairvoyance under strict test conditions and also plunge into the exciting and slowly unfolding depths of dream, sleep and clairvoyance which now occupy both physiologists and psychiatrists.

The Companions of Bridey Murphy

Dr. Ian Stevenson, formerly head of the department of psychiatry at the University of Virginia, spent several years investigating one of the most ancient dreams of mankind: the dream of immortality through reincarnation.

Dr. Stevenson studied hundreds of reports from people who claimed to recall a previous life. In his preliminary writings, he reached no firm conclusions about reincarnation—but at least some of his colleagues (among them Dr. Pratt whom we have quoted before) suspect that he would probably bet for its possibility rather than against it. Others are more sceptical.

In 1970 an anonymous patient wrote to Dr. Loriene Chase, a clinical psychologist who has a private practice in Beverly Hills, California and conducts a widely-syndicated column of psychological advice.

"I consider myself an intelligent person with a college education," the man, seeking help, wrote, "but I have an unbelievable feeling about my own reincarnation. Examining everything that I have studied does not begin to explain why I should even consider such a thing. But I do. How does a person just out of the blue start accepting such a belief?"

Dr. Chase asked him whether he had any particular experience which he thought might have some connection to a life before?

"One afternoon," the nameless advice-seeker explained, "I was very tired and decided to lie down and rest. It seemed as though, as soon as I closed my eyes, I was in a very familiar city. By the way the people were dressed, I could tell it was in the early eighteen-hundreds and the place was in the South. When a person spoke to me, I opened my eyes to see who it was, and then I realized it had taken place in what you would call a dream. Since then, the more I think about it the more I am convinced it was not a dream but an experience of my own past from maybe the collective consciousness, as Carl Jung would call it. This doesn't seem like enough to make me feel as sure as I do about my own reincarnation, so I thought you could help enlighten me. Do you think it is dangerous to think such a thing is true?"

The lady-psychologist's answer was highly characteristic of the modern, American attitude. She said that the danger depended on how a person handled such a belief—it was one thing to accept it and another to allow one's life to be affected in a negative way. Then she added :

"Close to one half of the world's population believes in this philosophy and many use it as an assist in understanding what is happening to them today. They feel it gives them answers to their present life that they find in no other philosophy. Many feel it gives reasons behind some of the unanswered questions about hardships in life and thereby they are more able to cope with adversity. Satisfactorily understanding the concept of reincarnation is something each person seems to do for himself."

Dr. Chase inclines to the Jungian teachings in dream interpretation. "Among the many types of dreams, there are those dealing with current problems, symbolisms, with fulfilment, prophesy and diagnosis . . . We consider the dream process as a problem-solving device, embracing direct communications with the unconscious. What you experienced could be a symbolic dream in which an attempt was made to help you on some level to understand an area in your life that may be puzzling you. However, this is only one explanation among many . . ."

The belief in reincarnation is both ancient and wide-spread though Dr. Chase's estimate of "close to one-half of the world's population" is a somewhat vague figure. It is, in a way, a reversed faith in survival after death, the deepest and most universal longing of mankind. But survival whether through your actual, single identity or through an infinite series of reincarnations, is senseless unless it is *conscious*—unless we are able to remember our previous lives or are able to link our "spirit existence" with the physical being. This, of course, entails memory. If when we are reborn, the slate is wiped clean and nothing remains of the knowledge, emotions, impulses of the past, the new beginning has no meaning.

Those who believe in reincarnation have been seeking for untold centuries to establish this consciousness, to prove the survival of memory. It has also been the favourite subject of novelists and playwrights, of science fiction and gothic mysticism. Whenever it looks that such proof is forthcoming—that a human being, under the influence of strong emotion, waking or sleeping or in a hypnotic state actually recalls a previous existence of which he or she could have had no knowledge,—there is tremendous interest and acclaim. And, almost immediately, there is the attack by sceptical sicentists who seek to prove (and, alas, succeed in most cases) that the information *was* available to the subject; that what he produced was simply thrown up by his subconscious, embellished and rounded off—and that reincarnation is still a hopeless wishdream, a convenient delusion and self-deception.

In the last twenty years there has been an increased interest, a new avidity in the search for proof, for certainty in this vast and ancient field. We have spoken of Professor Ian Stevenson whose *Twenty Cases Suggestive of Reincarnation* was published in the series of the Proceedings of the American Society for Psychical Research in September 1966. The book represented long years of research but it included several fairly recent cases.

It was in the middle of March 1966 that Dr. Stevenson arrived in the village of Kornayel in Lebanon, some fifteen miles east of Beirut, carrying a letter of introduction in Arabic to a resident who was said to be able to provide information about cases of reincarnation "that were said to occur frequently there". He found that his hoped-for link was spending the winter in Beirut; but in the course of making enquiries and explaining the reason for his visit, he was told of a five-year-old child in the village named Imad Elawar who had been making claims about an earlier life he had lived in another town. He went to see the boy's family and they told him their recollections of Imad's statements over the past three years of what he remembered about that preceding life. Though no clear distinction was made by the parents during the first interview between what their son had *said* and what they *inferred* from some of his statements in the effort to make sense of them, Dr. Stevenson found it all interesting enough to prepare a written record.

Imad claimed to have been a member of a Bouhamzy family that lived in Khriby, a village about twenty miles southeast of Beirut. Kornayel and Khriby are about fifteen miles apart but connected only by a winding, precipitous mountain road with a driving distance of twenty-five miles; there is little traffic between the two villages. The boy made frequent references to a woman called Jamile and mentioned a given name, Mahmoud. Jamile was described as beautiful, well-dressed, wearing high-heeled shoes and preferring red clothes which Imad often bought for her. The boy also claimed to have had a sister called Huda and he mentioned several other names without specifying blood relationships but referring to each one (as is the custom in the native culture) as "brother". These names included Amin, Mehibe, Adil, Talil (or Talal), Said, Toufic, Dalim, Kamel and a friend, Yousef el Halibi. The parents assumed that Imad was claiming to have been Mahmoud Bouhamzy, that his wife was named Jamile and that he had four sons (Adil, Talil, Salim and Kamel). They also assumed that the other names used by Imad were a sister and brothers in his family.

From other statements made by Imad the parents deduced other circumstances regarding the life and death of the boy in his former existence. Imad spoke of an accident in which a man was run over by a truck and received serious injuries; both his legs were broken and later he died of the consequences of the mishap. The parents assumed that this was the manner in which Mahmoud Bouhamzy had met his death. There were a number of other references to specific details related to the earlier existence.

On the second day of his visit, Dr. Stevenson made a trip by car to Khriby, accompanied by Imad, his father and an interpreter. During this journey, before reaching Khriby or before any check of the earlier statements were attempted, Imad added ten further "facts" about his former life.

A scientist must use statistics—so Dr. Stevenson recorded that the claims made by Imad regarding a former life consisted of 57 details, 47 older claims or incidents reported by the parents or other adult members of the boy's family and 10 new ones which Dr. Stevenson heard directly from Imad on the journey to Khriby. Analysing and tabulating all this, the American researcher came to the conclusion that 51 details were found to be correct—a strikingly large proportion. What was, however, both surprising and disconcerting was the fact that the statements did not apply to the person whom the parents assumed Imad claimed to have been in a previous existence. While there *was* a man named Mahoud Bouhamzy in Khriby he was very much alive.

There was, however, another person, *Said* Bouhamzy to whom the facts applied to a certain degree. He had died due to an accident in which he was run over by a truck and had received the injuries Imad has described. But there were difficulties about squaring most of the details from Imad's collected statements with the circumstances of Said Bouhamzy. Up to this point the positive results appeared to consist of a small nucleus of facts which was cancelled out by a mass of inaccurate imagined relationships and circumstances.

On a second visit to Khriby Dr. Stevenson spent most of his time with Haffez, the son of Said Bouhamzy, who had been absent on the previous occasion. The interpretations by Imad's parents of the boy's claims were shown to be even more inaccurate. But then Haffez Bouhamzy pointed out that the facts applied with remarkable accuracy to the life of one Ibrahim Bouhamzy, a cousin who had lived with his uncle in a house located only 300 feet from Said's house. Ibrahim was a bachelor —but he had a mistress, Jamile. He had died at the age of about twenty-five—of tuberculosis. Imad's statements seemed to refer to the circumstances of Ibrahim's life, including the names and outstanding experiences of his close relatives and associates. The reason why Dr. Stevenson had difficulty in verification was the incorrect inferences Imad's parents had attributed to his meanings, going beyond the things he had actually said. This they now admitted readily.

The American scientist wanted to go beyond the young boy's verbal statements and wished to test his ability of recognizing the people and the places he claimed he knew from his previous existence. The first such recognition of a person actually occurred in Kornayel. When he was four, Imad was once on the street with his grandmother, when he suddenly went up to a stranger and embraced him.

"Do you know me?" the man asked, startled.

"Yes, you were my neighbour," answered Imad.

As it turned out, the man lived in Khriby where he had been a neighbour of Ibrahim Bouhamzy. His first name was among those Imad claimed to remember. It was this event which led the boy's parents to take his claims more seriously. (Until it happened, his father had scolded him for lying about his "previous life" and threatened to thrash him if he continued.)

On the visits when Imad was taken to Khriby he did not do particularly well in the identification of buildings and directions in the town. He did point across towards the house where he said he lived but at the same time called attention to a nearby house which was not the correct one. But he correctly pointed in the direction of the village where Jamile had lived. He did not recognize houses in the immediate neighbourhood where Ibrahim lived; but the people of Khriby said the appearances had changed considerably over the years. The more important aspect of the test was whether Imad would know people Ibrahim had known and details about the interior of "his" house.

Dr. Stevenson listed sixteen correct statements or identifications made by Imad when he was taken through Ibrahim's house by the latter's mother and sister, Huda. This was the first time the boy had seen these two ladies and they appeared unexpectedly at the house when the tour of the premises was about to begin. But they gave the child no clue, their questions were direct and non-leading and yet the accuracy of the sixteen items was totally independent from any possible inference from things that could be seen inside. (The house itself had been closed up for a number of years.) This, according to the critics and examiners of Dr. Stevenson's work, added greatly to the serious evidence of the case as a whole. The researcher paid three visits to Khriby in March, 1964 and then went back in August of the same year. Stevenson's material provides a strong argument for a real relationship between the "memories" of Imad and the experiences of Ibrahim Bouhamzy. But of course, sceptics are bound to raise the question whether the statements and correct recognitions made by the boy really fit the circumstances of Ibrahim's life to a degree that is beyond reasonable chance correspondences? This, at least to a certain extent, is a matter of personal judgment. Dr. J. G. Pratt who reviewed the Stevenson book for *Theta*, the newsletter of the Psychical Research Foundation of Durham, North Carolina, believes the answer to be clearly in the affirmative. However, there is still the problem of whether all this could have been the result of a hoax or fraud? Here, again, there is a serious absence of motive. Dr. Stevenson's visit was totally unexpected; and at least some aspects of the case, if it were fraudulent, would have required careful coaching and considerable dramatic ability on the part of those concerned, including five-year-old Imad. Finally, there is always the possibility that information could have been normally acquired and then forgotten— to be produced by Imad after a suitable period of incubation in scattered statements. But Dr. Stevenson affirms that the two villages were not "on visiting terms" and any such information could not have reached Imad to become the basis through cryptomnesia ("false memory", or memories from one source unconciously disguised so as to be wrongly attributed to another source).

We have dealt at some length with one of the twenty cases Dr. Stevenson chose to illustrate the kind of evidence he encountered and the different facets of evidence relevant to the problem of reincarnation. The cases could be grouped, roughly, into three main varieties. In the first a child behaved in a manner that was consistent with the life and personality of the individual it claimed to have been—showing special tastes which the former person had, expressing nostalgia for his former home and family; showing proper recognitions and emotional reactions in their presence. The second class demonstrated special skills or technical knowledge which the former individual possessed and which the later individual had no opportunity to learn; and in the third the body of the later person showed birthmarks similar to those carried by the former person or a scar, such as would have been caused by the wound from which the former person died.

It is not easy to investigate such cases; but Dr. Stevenson has gone himself to the scene of those he presented and made every effort to establish the facts by interviewing the available and most directly involved people. When he needed interpreters, he often used different ones in separate interviews in order to check the consistency of the information.

He established a few general facts—though here, too, exceptions often prove the rule. The occurrence of reincarnation cases is apparently linked with cultural differences in some way. Cases are more likely to be found among people who traditionally accept it on religious grounds—while in the United States where, by and large, there is little belief in the idea, the incidence is very low. In many instances the distances involved, the difficulties of communication between villages, castes and other groups and the early age at which a child began "remembering" his previous life make it even more difficult to discount the validity of the cases. Nor do fraud or cryptomnesia account satisfactorily for the facts. The explanation might very well be something quite different from reincarnation—but we have not yet found it. And while the concept of reincarnation seems to be repulsive to most educated people in the Western world, such a strong prejudice does not disprove its possibility. Certainly Dr. Stevenson who studied some 600 instances of claimed memories of previous lives and travelled to India, Ceylon, Brazil, Lebanon and Alaska to investigate and evaluate the suggestive evidence, has gone far to open up entirely new horizons in this world.

One of the most interesting champions of reincarnation was the late Edgar Cayce whose work and memory are kept alive by the Association for Research and Enlightenment with headquarters in Virginia Beach, Virginia. Though Cayce died in 1945 at the age of 67, the ARE continues research and the dissemination of information on this extraordinary man about whom Noel Langley has written a highly eulogistic book, stressing his work on reincarnation.

Cayce, born in 1877, in Hopkinsville, Kentucky, of an old Kentucky family, was an unschooled though by no means an unintelligent man. His childhood was normal "except for a vision he had when he was seven years old". He was asked what he wanted to do with his life. He replied that he wanted to help others, especially children.

He was twenty-four when he lost his voice and during an attempt at a cure through hypnotic suggestion he discovered that he could go to sleep and answer questions put to him. He just lay down and entered a sleep-like state during which he talked; he spoke on any subject he was questioned about, at any length necessary to answer the query. This wasn't easy for him to accept—for, as the A.R.E. publication put it :

. . . the fact that he seemed to have contact with a river of infinite wisdom—much of which was in conflict with his upbringing and beliefs—was even more disturbing. The fact that the information, known as *readings*, proved correct time and time again did not make the problem easier.

Cayce himself never heard a word he said in his trance nor remembered anything when he woke up; and he freely admitted that he could not explain his "psychic powers" which he seemed to have used both for diagnosing illnesses and forecasting future events. Much of the latter was tied up with astrology and again and again he spoke to his "subjects" about earlier lives, previous reincarnations.

For most of the next forty-odd years he lay down and entered into this sleep state at least twice a day. "The Work", as he called it, came before everything else and he sacrificed privacy and all the hopes for financial security.

The American press soon took up Cayce.

PSYCHIST DIAGNOSES AND CURES PATIENTS—IGNORANT OF MEDICINE, TURNS HEALER IN TRANCE—headlined the Chicago *Examiner*. PUZZLES MEDICAL SCIENCE. CAYCE HIMSELF CANNOT EXPLAIN PSYCHIC POWER. REMARKABLE PSYCHIC DIAGNOSTICION [*sic!*] IN CITY. PHYSICIAN IN COMA : PHOTOGRAPHER AWAKE—the others followed suit. Cayce was a psychic healer who based his subconscious activities on reincarnation, claiming that it was his own past lives—and those of his patients—that enabled him to help the sick and the handicapped. For several years he lived in a pleasant house near a quiet lake at Virginia Beach where many of his readings were given; on the small dock at one end of the property he found relaxation in the style of the archetypal fishermen. One of his dreams was the establishment of a hospital where people could come and be treated according to the recommendations of his "readings". (He himself restricted himself to diagnosis, leaving the treatment to qualified doctors.) A hospital *was* established but became a casualty of the 1929 Depression. It changed hands several times and after Cayce's death was repurchased by the A.R.E. which now uses it as its national headquarters. The A.R.E. itself disseminates information on the thousands of readings, organizes lectures and conferences, small groups throughout the world for further study and continues research into the recorded texts Cayce left behind. These total over 16,000 though no systematic records were kept for the first twenty-two years. Since 1923, until Cayce gave up his work in 1944, a total of 14,249 have been indexed and filed. Some 2,500 of them form the group in which Cayce began to introduce his concept of reincarnation. The A.R.E. publications include more than twenty books and pamphlets on the subject, ranging from *All Things to Your Remembrance* to *Panorama of Rebirth*. In one of his readings Cayce dealt with the strongest argument against reincarnation, declaring :

> There's the law of cause and effect in *material* things. But the strongest argument against reincarnation is also, turned over, the strongest argument for it; as in *any* principle, when reduced to its essence. For the *law* is set—and it happens! though a soul may will itself *never* to reincarnate, but must burn and burn and burn—or suffer and suffer and suffer! For, the heaven and hell is built by the soul!

There are strong echoes of Swedenborg here. In one of his readings (made in 1927) Cayce traced back an "entity" to the court of Louis XIII of France, to Salonica some centuries earlier, to Persia where the "soul" was reincarnated in a physician, to ancient Egypt "during the period when there was a division in the kingdom" and to Atlantis when "the floods came and when destruction ruled in that land".

Cayce's theories and so-called proofs of reincarnation do not matter a great deal; like so many "seers" he was apt to pour out vague generalities and homilies though in matters of practical difficulty he could be surprisingly concrete and forceful. What matters is the organization he left behind, still flourishing almost a quarter of a century after his death—whose members, following his precepts, are firm believers in rebirth and the continuity of memory and identity.

Certainly the most widely-publicized claim to the establishment of proven reincarnation was the case of Bridey Murphy. Its story began in 1953 and, spanning almost twenty years, it is still far from being ended—for controversy still rages around the almost "total recall" of the Pueblo, Colorado housewife.

The book called *The Search for Bridey Murphy* was written by a Colorado businessman called Morey Bernstein who became interested in trance phenomena when he witnessed a casual demonstration of hypnotism in 1942. (There is a parallel here with Cayce's start.) It must have been impressive enough for, as he put it, "I gobbled up every book on it I could find." Eventually he became an amateur hypnotist in his own right and performed a number of "age regressions"—taking the subject back to various earlier stages of his or her life—before he met Virginia Tighe with whom he went a giant step further into the past, into pre-natal life, that is, previous existences.

Bernstein is a graduate of the University of Pennsylvania's Wharton School of Finance and a successful business executive—he still runs The Wholesale Supply Co. selling equipment and appliances in Pueblo—and these facts have been cited as proof of his rationalist and materialistic attitude; the hard-headed man of affairs who became convinced much against his original in-clinations of the truth of reincarnation. He studied therapeutic hypnosis and worked with qualified physicians in a number of medical cases. Then he proceeded to explore the problems of parapsychological research and extrasensory phenomena. He attended a conference conducted by Professor Rhine at Duke University's Institute of Parapsychology. He felt that it was both a logical and comparatively minor step from the study of the paranormal to the exploration of "discarnate survival" and the principle of reincarnation. So he looked around for a suitable subject to "regress to a previous existence".

He found her in Virginia Burns Tighe, a casual acquaintance. (In the subsequent book he disguised her as "Ruth Simmons".) In some earlier experiments Mrs. Tighe had proved exceptionally susceptible to hypnosis. Bernstein knew that for his new and unusual experiment he would need such an exceptionally pliable medium. Virginia Tighe was born in April 1923, the daughter of Mr. and Mrs. George Burns of Madison, Wisconsin. Her parents' marriage failed and she was only three when she was sent to live with Mrs. Myrtle Grung, her maternal aunt, in Chicago. There she grew up as a completely normal child, attended North-western University for a year and a half, married a young man who was killed in the Second World War, and eventually moved to Denver. It was there that she met and married Hugh Brian Tighe. When *The Search for Bridey Murphy* was published and became a sensational bestseller—in two months, between January and March 1956 it went through nine printings and sold 170,000 hardcover copies, remaining for many weeks on the top of the non-fiction bestseller lists—she was living in Pueblo with her husband and her three children. To avoid the blaring and demanding publicity, the Burnses have since then moved from the city.

The first references to the Bridey Murphy experiments appeared in the September 12, 19 and 26, 1954 issues of *Empire*, the Sunday supplement of the highly respectable Denver *Post*, in the form of three articles entitled *The Strange Search for Bridey Murphy* written by William J. Barker who was on the magazine's staff. A follow-up called *More About Bridey* appeared in the December 5, 1954 issue of the same publication.

The book itself was published in January 1956 by Doubleday. The best summary of the case was given by C. J. Ducasse four years later in the *Journal* of the American Society for Psychical Research. Ducasse wrote :

Although neither Virginia nor Bernstein had ever visited Ireland, as soon as she had in deep hypnosis been regressed first to the years of her childhood and then instructed to go back to a time anterior to her present life and to report what she perceived, she began to describe episodes in a life in which she was Bridey (Bridget) Kathleen Murphy, an Irish girl born in Cork in 1798, daughter of a Protestant barrister, Duncan Murphy, and his wife Kathleen. She said she attended a school run by Mrs. Strayne, and had a brother, Duncan Blane Murphy, who eventually married Mrs. Strayne's daughter, Aimee. She had another brother who died while still an infant. At the age of twenty Bridey was married in a Protestant ceremony to a Catholic, Sean Brian Joseph McCarthy, son of a Cork barrister. Brian and Bridey moved to Belfast where he attended school and where, Bridey said, he eventually taught law at Queen's University. A second marriage ceremony was performed by a Catholic priest, Father John Joseph Gorman, of St. Theresa's church; they had no children. She lived to the age of sixty-six and was—to use her own expression— "ditched", i.e. buried, in Belfast in 1864. Many of her other statements referred to things which it seemed highly improbable Virginia could have come to know in any normal manner, but which might possibly be verified or disproved, and "the search" for Bridey Murphy is the search that was made for facts that would do one or the other.

If Bernstein's book had been largely unnoticed, if there had not been a very successful film based on it, starring Teresa Wright and Louis Heyward, if the record made from the tape of the seances had not sold hundreds of thousands, the "search" would have also remained within modest proportions. But Bridey became a national, even a world figure—the book was translated into a dozen or more languages—and this fierce limelight led to a violent controversy in religious and scientific circles alike. For it was construed by many as circumstantial proof of the principle of reincarnation—though Bernstein himself carefully refrained from making pronouncements one way or other; he merely suggested that further study was indicated. But both orthodox religion and science attacked him and his book with open hostility and the battle still rages though there have been several periods of cease-fire.

Two months after the appearance of the book the Denver *Post* published a twelve page supplement, the result of a three-week fact-finding mission by Barker to Ireland. Eight days later *Life* ran the first of two articles on the Bridey Murphy case; the first was called *Here are the Facts about Bridey That Reporters Found in Ireland* and credited to Barker with co-authors Ernie Hill of the Chicago *Daily News* and *Life* correspondent Ruth Lynam. The second article, entitled *Here Are the Opinions of Scientists about Bridey's 'Reincarnation'*, was written by Dr. J. Schneck and Dr. L. Wolberg, both expert medical hypnotists. All these pieces were sympathetic or at least "open-minded". But in May and June 1956 the Chicago *American* ran a series of articles (syndicated in all Hearst papers), setting out to show that "Bridey Murphy" was nothing but a product of Virginia Tighe's subconscious remembrance of her childhood. Within a couple of weeks the Denver *Post* printed a rebuttal to the *American* which called the Chicago newspaper's charges unfounded. In the same month *Life* seemed to swing to the *American's* side of the controversy. In June, 1956, too, Lancer Books published a revised paperback edition of *The Search for Bridey Murphy* which carried a new chapter, *The Case for Bridey in Ireland*, by the Denver Post Reporter, William J. Barker. About the same time the completely negative *A Scientific Report on the Search for Bridey Murphy* (edited by M. V. Kline) appeared—the consensus of its contributors appeared to be that Bernstein was (at the best) a fool or (at the worst) a fraud. By October 1956 the identity of "Ruth Simmons" was revealed when the Denver *Post* published a six-part article, based on a long interview with Virgina Tighe. Many national magazines and newspapers carried reviews of the book and added critical comment.

Dr. Ian Stevenson of whose work we have spoken before did the long review for the *Journal* of the American Society for Psychical Research. This was a triumph for the Bridey Murphy-ites for the learned expert in reincarnation cases declared that the criticisms of the Bridey case were unwarranted and did not stand up to the facts. Ducasse's article appeared in the same *Journal* three years later and was later added as a chapter in his *A Critical Evaluation of the Belief in Life After Death*; it is the most comprehensive evaluation up to date. Stevenson's recent *Twenty Cases Suggestive of Reincarnation* also refers to Bridey Murphy and he agrees that much about the case has yet to be explained and concludes that the reincarnation hypothesis "is as likely an explanation as any yet advanced".

It must be pointed out at this stage that no psychiatrist or psychoanalyst ever had the chance of examining Mrs. Tighe—nor is it likely that such a chance will be given. The age-regression experiments were discontinued at the request of Virginia and her husband even though Bernstein was eager to go on. Thus any corroboration or refutation of the reincarnation hypothesis must depend on—secondary sources. This is extremely unlikely. While even if it were possible to prove that a Bridey Murphy did live in Cork at the actual time, it would have to show that Mrs. Tighe had not acquired her knowledge through normal or para-normal means—and the only *conclusive* proof that Virginia Tighe is *not* a reincarnation of Bridey Murphy would necessitate an explanation of every bit of relevant information her regressed personality produced. Nor is psychoanalysis and hypnotism suffi-ciently advanced (whatever its practitioners claim) to pass final judgment on this subject. It has been claimed that if Morey Bernstein and Virginia Tighe were professionally analysed, the case for reincarnation would be totally demolished. This appears to be a particularly silly argument—saying, in effect, that if one knew everything about Virginia Tighe, one would know everything about Bridey Murphy. This is hardly scientific logic.

E

There were three fronts on which the Bridey Murphy claims were attacked. First, they were said to be incompatible with contemporary religious dogma—though this, of course, would hardly constitute a valid argument against them. Next, it was maintained that the information Virginia Tighe gave under hypnosis about Ireland was wrong. And finally—perhaps the most important—there were serious objections to Bernstein's methods and techniques.

Life and the Chicago *American* recruited a host of "experts" on early nineteenth-century Irish life. As it turned out, virtually every objection they raised was easily and clearly refuted. Bridey Murphy's first statement was that "she scratched the paint off the metal bed" as a small child. *Life* challenged this on the grounds that there were no metal beds in Cork at the time. According to Dr. E. J. Dingwall, the veteran British psychical researcher, however, metal beds were advertised by the Hive Iron Works in Cork by 1830. Furthermore, the tape made of Bridey's story, due to her rather indistinct speech, might with greater probability be read as "scratched the paint off the *little* bed".

The Chicago *American* claimed that the aunt who raised Virginia Tighe could remember a similar paint-scratching episode when Virginia was six or seven. But the lady denied all knowledge of this.

Life claimed that Bridey said she lived in a "wood" house which she called *The Meadows*; the magazine pointed out that, due to a timber shortage, there were very few wooden houses left in Ireland at that time. A closer study of the tapes, however, revealed, that she said *good* house, not *wood* house. She did not say that she lived in a house called *Meadows* but in an area known as *The Meadows*. An 1801 map of Cork revealed an area in the western suburbs called *Mardike Meadows* with several buildings on it.

According to the Chicago *American*, Virginia Burns Tighe had a brother who, like Bridey's, died when he was very small—stillborn, as a matter of fact. Virginia categorically denied this. This claim was later deleted from the *American* story before it was syndicated for other Heast publications. Bridey said that her brother died of "something black . . .", by inference, the bubonic plague, the Black Death. Although there were no reported cases of the plague in Cork at the time, the symptoms could easily apply to several other diseases, especially advanced diphtheria, small pox, bacilliary dysentery and cholera.

Life claimed that a book reputedly read by Bridey, *The Sorrows of Deirdre*, did not appear until Synge wrote it in 1905. Barker, however, cited a "cheap paperback" published by Bolton in 1808, entitled *The Sorrows of Deirdre and the Death of the Sons of Usnach*. *Life* also challenged the various Irish expressions used by Bridey, such as *tup*—an uncomplimentary reference to the male, *linen*, for handkerchief and *brate*, a small drinking cup. Barker's research revealed all of these being in use in Cork in the early eighteen-eighties.

The *American*'s most "sensational revelation" was the discovery of the existence of a Bridie [*sic!*] Murphy Corkell who lived across the street from Virginia's home in Chicago. Later research revealed that this was true—but also that Virginia never spoke to her. Nor has it been established that her first name was Bridie or her maiden name Murphy. She refused to see reporters and later turned out to be the mother of the editor of the Sunday edition of the Chicago *American*.

All these were trivial enough facts and arguments; but the amount of information relevant to the Bridey Murphy story that has been checked and found valid was undeniably impressive—if not completely conclusive.

She correctly identified by name (Farr's and Carrigan's) the *only two* shopkeepers who sold food in the neighbourhood at the time of her death; she also named a rope company, tobacco concern and dry-goods store. She correctly identified the currency used at the time and mentioned in passing a two-penny coin that was in circulation *only* between 1795 and 1850. In spite of allegations that there was no Queens University as such, it was established that such a university was founded in Belfast in 1850. Referring to her own burial, she said that she was *ditched* in 1864. *Life* asserted that no such synonym for burial was used at the time. Seamus Kavanaugh, Professor of Linguistics at University College, Cork, stated that the expression came into wide circulation following the Great Famine of 1854-56 and was kept as a variant of the verb *to bury*. Bridey referred to the Protestant Irish as *Orangers*. Richard Hayward, writing in *Life*, claimed the only correct expression being *Orangemen*. Barker, exploring this in Ireland, found *Oranger* still accepted without question.

It must be remembered that no documentary evidence directly referring either to a Bridget Kathleen Murphy McCarthy or any of her family was ever found. A clerk named John McCarthy was traced at Queens University but there was no conclusive proof that he was the husband of Bridey Murphy. It must also be remembered, however, that no proper registers were kept in Ireland until 1864—the year of Bridey's death. Family records, as Bridey pointed out in one of the taped sessions, were entered in the household Bible. The existence of Bridey's parish priest in Belfast, "Father John Gorman" as well as his parish church St. Theresa's, remain a mystery.

Psychologically one could draw a number of interesting conclusions from the coverage of the Bridey Murphy story by the mass media. The reincarnation hypothesis and its possible "proofs" always provide a good and marketable story. At the same time it seems to shake and infuriate so many people—among them journalists—that there is an instant urge to find ways of refuting it. For whatever reason, our humanity wants to toy with the idea, seek a refuge in it from the universal terror of death—and yet no one really wants to accept the consequences and follow them to their logical end. Because of the devastating though inaccurate and in many ways distorted attacks in *Life,* *Time* and the Chicago *American* the general public—as opposed to the specialists and experts—considers the case closed. And certainly, because of the firm refusal of Virginia Tighe Burns to submit to any more experiments of the same or of any different kind. The *corpus* of evidence is thus limited—but that does not mean that science has finished with it.

The scientific opponents of the Bridey Murphy claims argued that all the information provided by her was or could be traced to suppressed or repressed information acquired by Virginia Tighe in her childhood. This, of course, is just as much a theoretical conclusion as those drawn from the Bridey Murphy tapes in support of the reincarnation possibility. The guide-lines for *A Scientific Report on the Search for Bridey Murphy* were laid down by Dr. Milton V. Kline who asked six authorities in the fields of psychiatry, hypnotherapy and psychology to give their impressions of the techniques used by Bernstein in his age-regression experiments.

Bernard M. Raginsky, President of the Society for Clinical and

Experimental Hypnosis, dismissed the entire phenomenon as "the product of an insecure and goal-less individual's attempt to assign meaning to his life through exercising 'omnipotent' control over the hypnotized individual". Not having met Bernstein at any time, he psychoanalyses him on the basis of the book alone. Whatever such a long-distance analysis may be worth, it does still not explain the factual information Bridey certainly provided. Dr. Raginsky makes no attempt to hazard a guess as to how or where Bernstein or Mrs. Tighe could have gathered the facts of Bridey's life. And, quoting Bennett Cerf, the celebrated publisher and wit (not exactly an accepted expert in the field of psychoanalysis or hypnosis), Dr. Raginsky argues that even if Bridey's "repetitious revelations" are true, they are incredibly dull and trivial. This is a universal complaint about "spirit messages" or communications, however elaborate, from "the other side" but dullness and ordinariness in themselves do not invalidate the claim as to their genuineness.

Dr. F. L. Marcuse, a member of the Society for Clinical and Experimental Hypnotism, weakened his own case by misquoting Bernstein on several points—accusing him of implying that those who do not believe in reincarnation are ignorant of the facts, something which the amateur hypnotist never said; charging him with the claim that there are no dangers involved in the use of hypnosis—again, there was no truth in this; and finally that Bernstein asserted that hypnosis was always instrumental in producing a rapid and unfailing cure.

Marcuse added : "All the information Ruth Simmons might have picked up if her aunt had told her any of the folklore of Ireland, or her husband had ever been there, or even if she had merely attended a play, seen a film or read a book about Ireland." But William Barker's investigations on the spot showed that only laborious research could have provided such recondite information as Mrs. Tighe produced—and neither she nor her husband nor her aunt nor Bernstein had ever been to Ireland.

Dr. Margareta K. Bowers, a former resident of the New York State Psychiatric Institute and also a member of the Society for Clinical and Experimental Hypnosis, examined the Bridey Murphy phenomena in terms of Bernstein's age-regression technique. She, like Dr. Raginsky, made one valid point—Bernstein did not guard against hypnotic suggestibility. In many instances he actually steered Virginia Tighe toward particular, definite answers. Ian Stevenson agreed with Mrs. Bowers that this vitiated any claims Bernstein might have made for considering the six sessions a *critical* experiment—though the amateur hypnotist never actually made such a claim. This lack of control became the principal reason why scientific interest was never very strong in the case. The vast majority of alleged reincarnation cases under investigation did not involve hypnosis and so were easier to research.

Dr. Kline, the editor of the book, accused Bernstein of a deliberate hoax; in 1965 the Colorado businessman was still considering whether to sue for libel but has not done so up to this moment. Kline's particular interest was to defend the use of therapeutic hypnosis against its possible misuse by such '"rank amateurs" as Bernstein.

Ian Stevenson who reviewed both the original Bernstein book and the scientific report, summed up the latter :

Despite its failure to encounter the basic issues of the Bridey Murphy material, the book has some merits. It correctly points out that Mr. Bernstein failed to provide adequate controls against the influence of suggestion . . . The authors also discuss the utterances by hypnotized subjects of foreign and ancient languages, so-called xenoglossy. They rightly cite cases in which such linguistic ability was traced to earlier exposure to the language perhaps unknown or forgotten by the subject. Unfortunately, these wise and cogent criticisms cannot compensate for the more fundamental errors of the book. Of the firm believers on both sides it will please and outrage others, just as did *The Search for Bridey Murphy*. But to the dispassionate scientist it was merely disappointing. In proclaiming science the authors have only succeeded in defending orthodoxy.

The major criticisms of the Bernstein experiments were answered to a considerable extent by C. J. Ducasse's article, published in 1964 which was later reprinted in Martin Ebon's *Reincarnation in the Twentieth Century* under the title *Bridey Murphy Revisited*. This has done much to dispel the mistaken popular notion that all the facts of the case had been explained. Gina Cerminara in her *Many Lives Many Loves* (1965) discussed briefly the attack of Dr. Kline and his companions and arrived at the same conclusions as Ducasse. In 1966 Dr. Stevenson repeated his own earlier views.

In January 1970 Morey Bernstein's secretary wrote to us: Mr. Bernstein is still intensely interested in parapsychology. But age regression is old hat.

It is precisely "old hat" because an amateur hypnotist and a hard-headed businessman made it a world-wide sensation through his work with Virginia Tighe. Others before him have worked in this field and similar experiments are going on in many parts of the work but he, wittingly or unwittingly, dramatized and focused attention upon their possibilities. Bridey Murphy is still alive in the seventies and perhaps her example will lead to other, similar or more complete and rounded cases to be discovered and explored.

A similar case, though unconnected with hypnotism, was recorded by Robert Tralins as recently as August 1967. Richard and Maude Berger, a young married couple of Pennsylvania, Philadelphia, took a short trip to Washington, D.C. in the month of August. On their way home they decided to see something of the beautiful countryside north of Baltimore. As they drove toward Pikesville, Maryland, their nine-year-old daughter Patty cried out suddenly: "Gee, everything's changed! I used to live around here, Daddy. Look there, I used to go to school way down that road."

The parents shrugged, taking it for a joke or a childish fancy. But Patty insisted that they follow the road until her father pulled off and parked at the bottom of a hill. Then he taxed his daughter: "Patty, you know you've never been in Maryland before. What are you talking about it?"

But the little girl ignored him. She pointed and cried: "I used to play way over there, Daddy. If you'll turn right at the next road, you'll come to the railroad tracks. I wasn't allowed to play there but I was allowed to play in the woods near the cornfields."

Mrs. Berger persuaded her husband to humour Patty—to prove that she was mistaken. But as he wrove up the hill, he found at the crest a narrow road and, turning right, after several hundred yards, reached a bend—and, just past it, a railroad track. Patty, her excitement growing, gave further instructions from the back seat:

"Go down there for about half a mile, Daddy, and then you'll

come to another road. That road will take you back to Reiters-
town Road. When you go across you will come to this spooky
cemetery. I wasn't allowed to play there but once we kids went
there, it was real scary . . ."

Once again Patty proved to be right. This was too much and
Richard Berger demanded to know of Patty how she knew this,
whether she had seen a map in a book or had seen it on some
television show. But Patty just nodded and said: "I told you,
Daddy, I used to live here."

"When?"

"Long ago, before I became yours and Mummy's little girl."

Mrs. Berger told Patty that she mustn't talk such nonsense but
the child protested: "No, it isn't. I'm telling the truth. I can
prove it. If you drive in that cemetery, I'll show you where I'm
buried."

At this Berger started the engine and drove away quickly. But
beyond Pikesville, on a secondary road, Patty again foretold
that they would come to a cross roads, with a small pond, a
stream and ducks swimming. The rural scene was exactly as she
had described.

The Bergers drove home as quickly as they could. Later they
consulted an amateur psychical researcher and he and Richard
Berger went to Pikesville. In the meantime the Bergers had tact-
fully drawn some more details from their daughter. When he
returned, they decided to drop the matter once and for all. He
was afraid that if it were pursued, Patty would become subject
to the same harrassment and abuse which Virginia Tighe had
to suffer when it became known that she was "Ruth Simmons".

And he had good reason to be afraid. For in the graveyard
which Patty wanted them to visit he found the name she had
given as her "previous" name, plainly engraved on one of the
headstones of almost a century before.

The End of Rosalie?

One of the most intriguing riddles of twentieth-century psychical research is beyond doubt the case of Rosalie, the mystery of the spirit child. Its investigation has covered more than thirty years and while it seems that the basic secret has been revealed, there are still a few nagging doubts, unanswered questions. The final denouement is very much part of the sixties and its details have never been published before.

It was on Wednesday, December 8, 1937 that Harry Price, founder and director of the National Laboratory for Psychical Research in London received a telephone call from a lady.

By that date Price, originally a businessman, had spent almost twenty years and a considerable part of his private fortune on his experiments and investigations. Though he was self-trained and largely self-educated, he had been able to attract many noted scientists, psychologists and philosophers to the various organizations and research groups which he had founded or of which he was the moving spirit. He was neither a hardened sceptic nor a spiritualist; he described himself as a man with an open mind. Somewhat addicted to publicity, his various cases had always aroused considerable interest in England and on the Continent; for some years he also held the position of European Research Officer to the American Society for Psychical Research. Among the distinguished men of science who had been associated with him at one time or another were Sir Julian Huxley, Professor R. J. Tillyard, Baron Schrenck-Notzing, Sir Richard Gregory and several others. During his lifetime—he died in 1948—he published fifteen books on various aspects of occult phenomena and contributed to a large number of newspapers and magazines. He left a seventeen thousand volume library to London University.

The caller—whose voice sounded "educated and cultured"—said that its owner had read an article Price had written in *The*

Listener which appeared on November 10, 1937. It dealt with haunted houses and Price used a phrase which struck the lady as significant—he said that he could "guarantee a ghost" in a particular house. The anonymous caller claimed that she, too, could "guarantee a ghost" if Harry Price cared to join a circle that met every Wednesday in her home. In this family circle, she said, a little girl called Rosalie materialized every time without fail.

Price who received such invitations almost weekly and found that ninety-nine per cent of them led nowhere was somewhat reserved but interested. The lady continued by explaining that his participation in the seance depended on his acceptance of certain, fairly stringent conditions. The identity of the participants or the actual locality of the house must not be revealed. There was no objection to his publishing a report of the investigation; but Price was not to press for "scientific enquiry". The main reason for this was that the mother of "Rosalie" (who attended each sitting) was terrified that the "girl might be frightened away". Price also had to undertake not to use a torch or touch the "materialized spirit" or apply any tests without first asking permission to do so. These conditions were to constitute a verbal "gentleman's agreement". However, if Price accepted them, he would be given full control in the preparation of the proposed seance, he could seal the windows and doors and use any of the methods he had imposed on his previous investigations.

Price told the unknown caller that he would consider her proposals and give his final decision in writing. (This meant, of course, that she gave him her name and address). Five days later, on December 13, he wrote to her, accepting the invitation and the conditions—but asked for permission to bring with him Mr. R. S. Lambert, then editor of *The Listener*, with whom he had been associated in a number of investigations—notably, the bizarre and fantastic Talking Mongoose case. He had discussed the matter with Lambert that day at lunch and Lambert had also agreed to observe the conditions the lady had set. Price asked her to telephone him if the idea of an extra witness was acceptable. But apparently it wasn't. Price had to tell Lambert that the invitation was for him alone.

Two day's later, on December 15, Price made his solo trip to the house in a place he only identified by the initial "M".

He reached it just after seven o'clock. It was a large, double-fronted, detached house in a good-class road, with a flight of twelve stone steps leading to the front door, on each side of which was a large room with a bay window. It stood on the corner of another road and had an area. There were three entrances—or rather four, if one included the French window leading to the garden—the other three being the front door, an area entrance (seldom used except for the delivery of coal as the cellar was under the front steps), approached by a flight of steps and, finally, a door at the back of the house that was reached by a path running parallel with the side road. There were seven windows facing the main road; two on ground level, two above two small attic windows at the top and a small one (guarded by iron bars) in the area room. At the back of the house were four windows and a French window opening on to the long, narrow garden which was reached by iron steps. On the side of the house, facing the transverse road, there were two smallish windows and a lavatory one; in the wall opposite the next-door house two more, a bathroom and another lavatory window. It was a typical late Victorian home, largish, suburban, like tens of thousands of others.

Price rang the front door bell and was admitted by a trim parlour maid. The lady of the house—it was she who had made the telephone call originally—received him and introduced him to the other members of the circle. There was her husband, a "well-known City businessman", then in his mid-forties (his wife was a few years younger) and their daughter—aged seventeen. Price described his host and hostess as charming people interested in psychical research but not Spiritualists—though they had studied the standard literature.

Two other people were in the drawing-room: Madame Z. and a young man named "Jim". Madame Z., a Frenchwoman, had been a nurse who married an English officer early in the first world war. He died in action some eighteen months later, leaving his wife and a baby girl named Rosalie. Rosalie was a delicate child; at the age of six she contracted diptheria and, after a few day's illness, died in her mother's arms.

In the spring of 1925, some four years after her daughter's death—so the story was told to Price—Madame Z. was awakened during the night by the voice of her dead child, calling "Mother"

—at least she was convinced it was Rosalie's voice. This was repeated so frequently that she began to lie awake at night, listening for it. Gradually she began to see in the dark the dim outline of her daughter—until finally one night she put out her arm and felt herself clasped by the hand of the little girl.

Madame Z. had very few friends in England but she had met Mr. and Mrs. X to whom she told her story. They were sympathetic and suggested that because her modest home was unsuitable for seances, these should be held in their house. Perhaps, they said, this would encourage the visits of Rosalie.

The sittings started near the end of 1928. After six months, in the spring of 1929, Rosalie suddenly and completely materialized—though in total darkness—making her presence known by clasping her mother's hand. Very gradually light was introduced in the shape of four cheap mirrors covered with luminous paint. Finally Rosalie began to speak—starting with monosyllables and progressing to very simple phrases; though most of her "conversation" consisted in answering yes or no to questions. Later on a very occasional visitor was invited, among them the young man identified by Price as "Jim", a bank clerk and apparently the boy-friend of young Miss X.

The only two other occupants of the house were two servants—the parlour maid who admitted Price into the house and the cook he met later when he prepared the room for the seance. The two servants had been told about the sittings but were given no details about Rosalie. They were instructed that they must not answer any knock or ring at the front door during the seances; telephone callers were asked to ring later.

The final inmate of the house was an Airedale terrier who apparently slept through the proceedings.

Having listened to Madame Z.'s story—and showing, of course, not the slightest sign of scepticism which would have antagonized her and his hosts—Price asked permission to search the house. He met the two servants but did not mention anything to them about the purpose of his presence. He sealed and initialled every window; even in the case of the two dormer types he twisted tape around the fasteners. He did the same with the doors, both those leading outside and those connecting the various rooms of the house with the corridors and staircase. Finally he turned his attention to the seance room itself. He examined every piece of furniture, removing ornaments like clocks, pictures, vases in the process. He emptied every drawer and moved the large settee with the help of Mr. X. to see if there was a trapdoor underneath. (There wasn't.) Then he removed the floor rugs and minutely went over the boards for any similar possibility. He sealed the windows and the single door and initialled the tape. The chimney presented a problem which he overcame by placing a sheet of newspaper flat on top of the bar of the low grate, then sprinkled starch powder on the paper and drew his initials in it. No one could have tampered with the grate or the chimney without disturbing this.

Price had been told that he could examine the sitters before the seance if he wished. Being an Englishman (and a staunch member of the Church of England) he hesitated about the ladies. He first removed the outer clothing of the two men, frisking them until he was satisfied that they did not conceal anything that could produce fake phenomena. The older ladies—no doubt sympathising with Price's predicament!—compromised by sitting on either side of him so that he could more closely control them. Miss X., without waiting to be asked, lifted up her skirt and revealed a pair of tight-fitting knickers underneath. She had just attended a "health and beauty" class and was still wearing her gym-suit.

When the examination was completed, Price directed the sitters to their respective seats. He sat with his back to the fireplace, Madame Z. was on his left and Mrs. X. on his right. Next to Madame Z., was Miss X., then followed Jim and Mr. X., sitting next to his wife, completed the circle. The Airedale was still settled in front of the electric fire.

Having finished these arrangements, Price sprinkled starch in front of the door and the chimney. Then he switched off the lights.

It was ten minutes past nine. They sat in complete darkness, without the usual spiritualist prayer or hymn-singing. Quiet conversation, however, was permitted and Price was able to determine accurately where a voice was coming from and whose voice it was. He could even hear the breathing of the group when they were silent. After about twenty minutes Mr. X. said he would switch on the radio and left his seat, groping his way to the right of Price. When the instrument panel began to glow, all the participants could be seen distinctly. After about five minutes' music, Mr. X. switched off the wireless and returned to his seat. Soon Madame Z. began to whisper: "Rosalie . . . Rosalie . . ." repeating the name at short intervals for about twenty minutes. Sometimes Mrs. X. joined her, also calling out softly the child's name. It was now a few minutes past ten o'clock.

Suddenly Madame Z. gave a choking sob and whispered again: "Rosalie!" Price had been warned not to speak but now he sensed that something was close to him—it was his sense of smell that warned him; he inhaled, very near, a fresh spring-like odour like freshly-mown hay or the smell of rain on bracken. He heard the sound of shuffling feet and something touched the back of his left hand which rested on his knee. (The circle sat with hands unclasped.) As he had promised, Price made no attempt to find out what had touched him. A few minutes later Mrs. X. asked permission from the mother—who had been fondling her child all this time—for Price to touch the "presence". This was granted. Price reached out with his left hand—and, to his amazement, came in contact with the nude body of a little girl. Slowly his hand covered every part of her naked body, first placing his palm on her chest, then working upwards to her face. He felt that her flesh was warm but apparently "colder than that of a human child". Placing his hand on her chest again, he felt it rising and falling as if it breathed; then he continued to feel her thighs, buttocks and finally her legs and feet. He estimated her height about 3 feet 7 inches with the limbs of an average six-year-old. He felt her hair which he described as long and soft, falling over her shoulders. All this made him extremely perplexed—he analysed his own feelings as "supreme scientific interest coupled with absolute incredulity". He asked permission to hold the child. Madame Z. agreed and so he moved his chair closer to the "apparition".

Now he was able to use both his hands, covering again every inch of this "form that seemed as real and human as any normal being". Then the puzzling question rose in his mind: "Why does this solid form, claiming to be a spirit, have the same body as any living six-year-old girl?" With his right hand he lifted "Rosalie's" right arm and felt her wrist. He estimated her pulse rate to be ninety per minute. Now he put his ear against her chest and could quite distinctly hear her heart-beat. As a test, he took hold of both her hands and requested Mr. X., Miss X. and Jim to speak in turn. When they did so, he was convinced by direction of their voices that they were all seated in their respective places. Because he himself sat between Madame Z. and Mrs. X., he did not consider it necessary to apply the same test to them.

But he asked permission to use the light from the luminous plaques he had brought with him—these were small discs coated with fluoride paint. There was a little discussion between Madame Z. and the others—but in the end he was granted his request. He moved the plaques—he held one in each hand—from the feet of the child upwards over the rest of her body. The soft fluorescent glow showed the feet to be perfectly normal. Mrs. X. helped in this examination by holding and raising a third plaque which illuminated the left side of Rosalie while Price now concentrated on her front. Fascinated, he stared at the soft texture of the little girl's flesh which appeared to be without blemish. Her face had classic, regular features—although "she looked rather older than six" as Price remarked. The fluorescent light could not give an accurate idea of her complexion but she seemed pale. Her eyes were bright and intelligent, their colour apparently dark blue; her lips were set in a determined expression. At this point Madame Z. declared that the examination must end. As a special favour Price asked whether he could speak to her—and though he was told it was most unlikely she would answer, he went ahead.

"What would you do if you were suddenly faced with an alleged spirit?" Price wrote in his *Fifty Years of Psychical Research*. "What sort of questions would you ask it?"

He imagined, when faced with the problem, that he was addressing a real child, capable of at least some simple conversation. He asked her: "Where do you live, Rosalie?" "What do you do there?" "Do you play with other children?" "Have you any toys there?" "Are there any animal pets?"

There was no answer to any of these questions though Price deliberately paused between each of them. The little girl just stared at him with a set expression (the luminous plaques were directed at her face) and did not seem to understand his words. Finally he asked: "Rosalie, do you love your mummy?" Her expression changed and she answered in a soft whisper: "Yes."

Madame Z. cried out and caught the "spirit girl" in her arms. Mrs. X. now placed all the luminous plaques on the floor and asked for silence. Price could hear the three women sobbing quietly; in his own account he confessed that he himself was affected by the pathetic scene.

Fifteen minutes later Rosalie disappeared—although he neither heard nor felt anything to mark her departure. The hall clock struck eleven. Mrs. X. declared that the seance was over. The lights were switched on. Price examined every part of the room, checking the furniture, sideboard, settee etc, and found everything normal. All his seals were intact and finally he removed the seal of the seance room. Jim accompanied him as he made a complete inspection of the rest of the house; again, he was completely satisfied that everything was undisturbed.

Drinks and sandwiches were served and he remained with his hosts until midnight. He thanked them for what he called "an extraordinary, interesting and puzzling evening" and drove back to the Royal Societies Club where he usually stayed if he could not return to his own home in Pulborough. But his day was not yet finished. Sitting up in bed, he drafted an immediate report of his recent experiences while the vivid impressions were still fresh in his mind. It was much harder work than he had expected—for some reaction had set in and he was dissatisfied with the phrasing of his report. A host of questions rose in his mind. Was Rosalie a hoax? Was she a genuine spirit-child? If it was a hoax, then it had to be a rather elaborate one to fool him—and whom would it benefit? Was Madame Z. playacting? If she was, she must have been a consummate artist—and the others, too, had to be in the plot.

Price felt sorry about opportunities he had missed. He could have taken Rosalie's fingerprints; perhaps he could have tried photography—but he had not provided for the necessary equipment. He was also puzzled by the fact that there seemed to have been no medium at the seance—and yet he had never heard of any so-called materialization without one. Was Madame Z. the medium? She had denied having any psychic powers. The more he thought about the evening he had spent with the X.'s, the more unanswered questions appeared.

The day after the seance Price wrote to R. S. Lambert whom he had tried to take with him as an extra witness and whose presence had not been acceptable to his hosts:

Dear Lambert,

Herewith is the "Rosalie" report, which I am sure you will read with great interest. I have added a foreword to the report, in case I use it as a chapter of my new book. I am hoping that some day I may be able to add additional matter, should I be fortunate enough to get another sitting.

Will you kindly let me have the report back, when finished with, as I have said, it is part of the MS "Fifty Years of Psychical Research."

Trusting to see you soon, and with kind regards etc.

Harry Price.

Price was no great stylist but the clumsiness of the phrasing of the letter showed that he was under a considerable emotional strain. There was, however, a more personal and immediate witness to his state of mind on the day following his introduction to the "spirit child".

Mrs. K. M. (Mollie) Goldney whom we have quoted before, was a very old friend and associate, herself a veteran psychical investigator and (since 1942) a member of the Council of the conservative and sceptical Society for Psychical Research. It was her custom, as an intimate friend, to drop in at Price's office to find out "what was going on". This is what she did on the morning of December 16, 1937. She was received by Miss Ethel Beenham, Price's secretary who appeared to be greatly worried about her employer. "You'd better go in and see him," she said. "He's in a rare state! I have never seen him so upset in all my time with him . . ."

Mrs. Goldney found Price looking haggard and perturbed. He gave her a full account of the events at the X. house—a detailed though plainly agitated and occasionally hesitant report. When he had finished, Mrs. Goldney said to him; "If you think, Harry, that you had witnessed a genuine materialization and if Rosalie's mother refused to give you more than this one sitting, you must insist that she should change her mind—even if you have to take the Archbishop of Canterbury to her to make her see her duty . . ."

It was a joke, as Mrs. Goldney later admitted—"I might just as well have said instead of the Archbishop 'the King of England' or 'the Pope' for that matter. Naturally, I didn't expect Harry to take it seriously." But it showed how impressed and intrigued she was by Price's tale.

One of the principal reasons why psychical investigators and ghost-hunters fall out so easily is the very human desire to share someone else's experiences, benefit by someone else's discoveries— to "see and hear" for themselves. Mediums are precious possessions (especially if never shown up as fraudulent) to be guarded much as a jealous husband would guard a beautiful wife. Mrs. Goldney, naturally, thought that Price should share this shattering and wonderful discovery with others—or at least with one person, herself. But Price was not ready to do that; as a matter of fact, he couldn't have done so even if he had wished to.

The day after he wrote to Lambert, he received a reply in which his friend thanked him for the Rosalie Report which he promised to read with great interest and expressed his hope that "later on you will get another sitting and be able to reach a conclusion about the phenomena . . ."

But Price never obtained another sitting.

He tried very hard, appealing to the X.'s and above all to Madame Z. But the Frenchwoman felt that there was one great risk : any further investigation might break her link with her dead child, put an end to the appearances of Rosalie. This was a thoroughly valid reason from her point of view; and whether Rosalie was her "materialized child" or not, did not really matter; these seances were her only source of happiness. As it happens so often when someone loses a parent or a child, a husband or wife, the authenticity or fraudulence of the "spirit" make precious little difference; it is the consolation, the comfort of belief, that matter.

Mrs. Goldney who felt very strongly about it, tried to persuade Price to force the issue before it was too late. But Price had accepted the conditions which the X.'s had imposed and he felt he could not break his word; he could not approach them directly, however strongly tempted he must have been. Nor did he want to betray the trust by revealing the identity of the people involved or the actual place where the seance had been held.

Though in his letter to Lambert Price had referred to the possibility of including the Rosalie case in his forthcoming book, he was now reluctant to do so. More than a year passed before he wrote to Frank Whitaker, editor of the literary magazine *John o'London's Weekly* to which he was an occasional contributor. Whitaker was a sort of literary mentor to Price on whose advice he often relied. This is the letter :

26th January 1939

Dear Mr. Whitaker,

As promised, I am herewith delivering, by hand, the complete MS of my next book. I shall be grateful if you will make any alterations in the preliminary remarks to the "Rosalie" chapter, as you suggested. I think you know my real views about the matter, but probably I have not expressed these very well, or have not made them strong enough. But I know that you realize my attitude in the matter. As I told you yesterday morning, it was never my intention to include the chapter in the book, though Mr. Potter of Longmans thought it should go in.

You will see on Page 385 of the MS that I have again referred to the "Rosalie" sitting.

It is very good of you to glance through the MS, and I shall be much interested to hear what you think of it. Of course, the "Rosalie" chapter should be read in conjunction with other chapters dealing with "materialization".

Five days later Whitaker replied; but his answer simply pointed out the need for a slight clarification in the topography of the X. house; Price had not established quite clearly that the two rooms with bay windows to which he referred were on two floors, one above the other, rather than on the same storey.

Price's reluctance was well justified. He had published many accounts of alleged paranormal phenomena, had unmasked a good many fraudulent mediums—but this was the first and practically only case in his experience when he had no independent witnesses to support his statements and when it was a single seance on which he had to depend. At the same time what he believed he had experienced during those few hours was so shatteringly inexplicable, so contrary to most of his beliefs and convictions that if it *was* genuine, he would have to revise his entire thinking. No wonder that he hesitated and even argued with his publishers. In the end he overcame his own resistance and in-

cluded the Rosalie case in the book. However, he ended his
account on an extremely cautious note, warning his readers that
he was *suspending judgment* as to the nature of this "materialization" until he had a chance for further investigation.

This chance never came. In a later chapter of the same book,
Price wrote about materializations in general and stated that : "I
have observed in the past experiments even under perfect control
of all concerned . . . materialized pseudopods (limb-like shapes),
limbs and hands and have been satisfied that this was a fact . . ."
He added that twelve months had now passed since the Rosalie
seance held "under conditions that not one materialization
medium in a thousand would accept". He reported on his numerous unsuccessful attempts to persuade Madame Z. to consent
to further experiments. Her answer was always the same : she
was terrified that any additional experiments "would drive her
daughter away". Price added a brief footnote on the page : *May
1939. There is now a possibility of my attending another seance.*
But this possibility never came to anything.

When war broke out, Madame Z. apparently returned to
France and was "lost to sight". *Fifty Years of Psychical Research*
was duly published and the Rosalie case attracted special notice
in the reviews. Price received a good many letters about it. Professor C. E. M. Joad with whom he had done some entertaining
if not very conclusive ghost-hunting, wrote to him, puzzled and
disturbed, that this was one account he could not accept, one
incident he could not stomach . . . his mind simply boggled at
nude little girls, with pulse and heartbeat, who materialized out
of nowhere "under perfect seance conditions". A Mrs. Beatrice
Cooper sent an account of her own experience—a materialization
of her daughter who had died, like Rosalie, of diphtheria.

There were many other things that occupied Price during and
immediately after the war; and however much the Rosalie case
had shaken and excited him it was after all only one of the
hundreds he had investigated. He ran a small factory during this
time and was very active in civil defence; all this aggravated a
heart condition and in March 1948, sitting in his armchair,
smoking his after-lunch pipe, Price died.

Early in 1949 I was approached by Price's executors, the Mid-
land Bank Trustee and Executor Ltd of Brighton who asked me

whether I would undertake the handling of his literary estate. I was somewhat dubious at first for I was no psychical researcher myself and certainly could not undertake to continue his work. But I was assured that this would not be required; what they wanted was someone who could look after the fifteen books and innumerable articles Price had published in his life-time, arrange for their possible reissue and translation. I was also invited to become a trustee of the Harry Price Library which he had left to London University; more than seventeen thousand volumes, dealing with every possible aspect of the supernatural and the occult and including all his papers, photographs, correspondence etc. It was also suggested that in the fullness of time I might like to write his biography—though Price himself had published several autobiographical works and the personal element was never absent from his writings.

I had met Price on several occasions and written a long feature article about him for a Canadian paper; I had attended several meetings of the venerable Ghost Club which he had revived (and of which I am proud to be a Vice-Chairman); and I knew a certain amount about psychical matters as my father, Cornelius Tabori, a Hungarian writer and journalist, had been involved in several famous or notorious European cases and had preserved for many years a lively interest in the connection of crime and the occult. (I translated and edited some of his material under the title *My Occult Diary*, a book that was published both in Britain and the USA though at an interval of fifteen years.)

In the end I accepted the offer and in 1950 my Price biography was published by Athenaeum Press, London. In it I reprinted almost in full his account of the Rosalie case which I, too, considered one of the most extraordinary in his long career. At the end of this chapter I wrote:

". . . But he had one experience that shook and moved him deeply—an experience that remains an enigma to this day. It is known as the 'Rosalie' case. When I began to sift Harry Price's papers, it was one of the first manuscripts of his I came across, and once I had read it, I continued to search for details or unpublished evidence with growing excitement. I must confess that I have found *practically nothing*. 'Rosalie' had disappeared into thin air, and no trace of her meeting with Harry Price remains except his own account and a few chance references to her in his letters . . . I believe that Harry Price was telling the truth, and that he was both frightened and shaken by his experiences. If Mr. X., whom H. P. has described in his letter to his publisher as a well-known businessman, realizes that he owes a duty to psychical research and to Harry Price's memory, perhaps he will come forward after reading these lines; but unless he or some other sitter at that remarkable seance twelve years ago comes to our aid, the riddle of 'Rosalie' must remain for ever unsolved..."

Some time before the publication of my book a Mr. A. Baird had made a similar appeal in the January 1949 issue of *Light*, a moderate spiritualist magazine published in London.

Both appeals remained without any response. It looked, indeed, as if the people connected with the Rosalie case could not or would not agree to any further publicity or provide any additional proof (apart from Price's report) about the little girl who materialized in December 1937 . . . or of whom Price and the participants of the seance believed that she had become, temporarily, flesh and blood.

In a footnote of my biography I mentioned that there was some evidence in Price's papers that pointed to the seance having taken place in Brockley. But this was a rather vague clue and another pointed to Bromley, Kent.

In any case, though there were repeated references to the Rosalie case in reviews of my Harry Price biography and *Fate* (New York) reprinted the relevant chapter, no further details came to light and it seemed that it must remain one of the many unsolved mysteries and inconclusive cases of psychical research.

Some eight years went by, until in 1958 Dr. Eric J. Dingwall and Trevor H. Hall published their book, *Four Modern Ghosts*.

Dr. Dingwall is one of the oldest and most distinguished psychical researchers of today—a man of many parts who has held, among other posts, that of the Keeper of Erotica at the British Museum, London and has written a pungent book about American women. Pugnacious, assertive, with very firm opinions, he was Research Officer of the Society for Psychical Research in London when Price began his career in the same field. They worked together, quarrelled, argued, sometimes did not meet for years—but seemed to have a sort of hate-love relationship that is not uncommon in this field.

Trevor Hall, Dingwall's co-author, had been a student in Psychical Research at Trinity College, Cambridge and he had written a number of books and many articles, all of which were more or less "debunking" in their general approach.

One of the *Four Modern Ghosts* Dingwall and Hall analysed in their book was Rosalie.

They started by quoting Robert Fordyce Aikman's *Postscript to Harry Price* (published in *Mystery, An Anthology of the Mysterious in Fact and Fiction,* London, 1952). Aikman was highly critical of Price and posed the question : "Could anyone enabled to participate in the almost incredible experience of 'Rosalie' be so lacking in imagination as to abstain from pressing investigation further despite all the restrictions and obstacles?"

They quoted my own comments from the Price biography and then presented four possible hypotheses.

The first assumed that "Rosalie" was a genuine materialization with a voice, a beating heart and respiratory action. If this was true, it held tremendous implications—which Dr. Dingwall and Mr. Hall were quite unwilling to accept.

The second hypothesis was that a seance did take place, more or less as described by Price—but with far less elaborate and careful precautions than he described. This could very well have been one of the series arranged by Mr. and Mrs. X. for the benefit of Madame Z.—or maybe to their own advantage.

The third alternative Dr. Dingwall and Mr. Hall offered was that Price might have been at first deceived by a clever performance but later realized that he had been duped; on the other hand, as was more probable, he may have detected fraud but decided that "Rosalie" provided an excellent basis for a sensational story.

The final hypothesis—and one which the two authors seemed to favour—was that Price invented most of the story in order to make one chapter of his intended book *Fifty Years of Psychical Research* a truly breathtaking one. His reluctance therefore to include it into the book was only pretence.

These were, of course, very serious charges—though not the first ones brought against Harry Price after he died. Nobody accused him of the slightest dishonesty during his lifetime— probably because they were afraid of his immediate, fierce and immediate response—but under British law you cannot really libel the dead and his critics and enemies, of which he had many, now felt that they were free to mount the attack.

Dr. Dingwall and Trevor Hall went to considerable trouble to support their hypothesis—which certainly needed such support for there were a good many facts that did not fit the framework of their theory. And above all there was the psychological difficulty.

In my Harry Price biography I commented on the Rosalie case and wrote:

". . . There seemed to be no normal explanation—provided Harry Price was telling the truth.

"Was he lying? I do not think so. He was not good at inventing tales. The few pieces of fiction (all unpublished) which I have read from his pen show that he was utterly incapable of spinning a convincing plot. And why should he lie? What possible motive could he have had for risking the reputation of a lifetime? Psycologically and morally, this theory will not hold water. Was he, then, mistaken, a victim of hallucination? He had never been deceived by his senses before and was inclined to be over-sceptical rather than credulous. Was there some superbly cunning trickery involved? But why?"

The authors of *Four Modern Ghosts*—though one of them had known Price far longer than myself—brushed this objection aside; according to them Price was quite capable of telling fibs, evolving an elaborate and detailed tissue of lies. They were, of course, entitled to their opinions and as Price's literary executor I thought it only fair to grant them access to the Harry Price Library and all its material.

But there was a far more tangible difficulty. I had, of course, talked to Mrs. Goldney about her meeting with Price on the morning after the Rosalie seance and though I did not mention her name in the biography in this connection, I recorded that according to her Price had "appeared to be deeply disturbed, almost distraught, that he was shaken to the core by his experience".

If Price had invented the whole story, what had caused this disturbance? If the seance had never taken place, why was he distraught by it? If the experience was non-existent, how could it have shaken him?

Messrs. Dingwall and Hall claim, in essence, that Price *did* put on an act for Mrs. Goldney's benefit, that he gave an amazing performance of being upset and perturbed about the seance he claimed he had attended the night before. He was supposed to have done this because, through a series of events that were connected with the work of his National Laboratory of Psychical Research and especially with the series of sittings conducted with the Austrian medium, Rudi Schneider, his prestige had suffered an eclipse. (Price believed that, after a sequence of highly successful seances, he had caught Rudi cheating; this disclosure split the council of his Laboratory, most of its important members resigning in protest. Mrs. Goldney, however, did not resign nor did her friendly relations with Price suffer any change.)

Dr. Dingwall and Mr. Hall built up a very elaborate case to explain away the meeting of Price and Mrs. Goldney on December 16, 1937—but it was hardly a convincing one and the most important person, Mrs. Goldney herself, did not accept it. Nor could they explain why Price had told R. S. Lambert about the forthcoming seance and then reported to him when it had taken place. As a matter of fact, they did not consider Lambert's role at all. Lambert himself wrote in his foreword to David Cohen's book, *Price and His Spirit Child Rosalie* (of which we shall speak in detail later):

"During the last fifteen years of his life, I was on terms of close friendship with Harry Price. He often contributed to *The Listener*, which at that time I edited. We lunched together frequently, visited at each other's homes, and went on trips together, in England and abroad. We regularly discussed his 'cases' and I took part in a number of his investigations, in the role of independent witness. These included the Fire-walking experiment, and the Talking Mongoose case, which subsequently involved me in painful litigation. After my departure for Canada, Price and I continued to correspond frequently until his death. From my personal acquaintance with the man, I can say that Harry Price was generous, straighforward, loyal and honest. His attitude to the phenomena he investigated was extremely sceptical; and he also possessed a highly developed sense of publicity and a skilful pen. These characteristics seemed often to clash. At any rate, they earned him enemies, particularly among his fellow-researchers.

". . . I read with astonishment the statement made by Mr.

Trevor Hall and Dr. Eric Dingwall in their book *Four Modern Ghosts* that in the 'Rosalie' case 'either Price had spun a wilful fantasy or had consolidated the events of several previous seances into one dramatic event'. I at once wrote to the *International Journal of Parapsychology* (Spring, 1960) to point out my personal knowledge of the circumstances attending the 'Rosalie investigation'. I recalled the conversations I had had with Price in 1937, immediately before and after the seance with 'Rosalie'. These were quite inconsistent with the possibility of any deceit or pretence on Price's part. I originally urged him to undertake the investigation. After the first tantalizing seance, I repeatedly urged him to press for a second seance; it being understood that I would accompany him on this occasion, as an independent witness . . .

"To quote from my letter to the *International Journal* : 'Price's attitude (after the seance) was that of a man flabbergasted by his experience. He would neither accept the phenomenon as genuine, nor admit that he had been a victim of deception.' He did however more than once remark to me that he regretted not having taken certain extra precautions at the 'Rosalie' house, to eliminate completely the possibility of deception.

"Price's subsequent reticence about his 'Rosalie' experience, after he had failed to secure a second seance, was perfectly understandable. He had either to confess that he, the arch-sceptic, had been taken in by an obvious fraud; or he must eat the words he had spoken so often and so emphatically in his career against 'spiritism'. Price was unwilling to do either, and therefore he turned his back as soon as possible on the whole unpalatable episode, and tried to forget it . . ."

This is, of course, just as much a theory as any other; but Lambert knew Harry Price well. Perhaps he was echoing what Professor Joad had written in a letter, part of which we have already quoted, after Price showed him the Rosalie chapter in manuscript :

"It seems to me to be the most exciting thing that has happened in the course of your career and, therefore—for you have described it vividly and well—the most exciting thing that appears in any of your books. Personally, I am still incredulous. Of course, I know (*a*) that it was exceedingly unlikely that you were hoaxed and (*b*) still more unlikely that you are lying . . . Unless I were myself to see and to feel, I do not think anything would persuade me that this had in fact really occurred. This, I daresay, is a statement about me, a statement to the effect that I am grown incredulous and prejudiced; yet that is how I feel about it . . ."

And this is how Messrs. Dingwall and Hall felt about it—except that they did not by any means exclude the possibility of Price having lied. Dingwall wrote to him after the Rosalie story had received a good deal of newspaper publicity :

". . . I see your after-dinner story of the materialization has had a wide publicity. It seems odd to me that you never told me a word about this miracle, if it occurred. It is also very odd that in all these remarkable tales there are no names, addresses, or means of checking. I have another one now. One of the most eminent lawyers in the provinces tells me that at a seance at which he was present (no details, of course), a white horse materialized, and walked round the circle. I will suggest to him that your circle should meet his and that we should be treated to the first materialized Lady Godiva . . . What is the real object of telling these tales ?"

The sarcasm was somewhat heavy-handed; Price did not answer the letter. Now, ten years after his death, Dr. Dingwall and Mr. Hall were returning to the attack. In my Price biography I had mentioned that the seance probably took place in Brockley. Dr. Dingwall and Mr. Hall claimed that they had found a letter in the Price Library which contained a reference to Brockley and the Rosalie case. Then they proceeded to try and locate the house of Mr. X. They used twelve ordnance survey sheets covering the Brockley area and the surrounding parts. Using Price's detailed description of the exterior, they chose one in Wickham Road—out of four possibilities. This had twelve front steps mentioned by Price—but unfortunately did not comply with the rest of the details given. Because they could not find a house to fit Price's report (though, of course, twenty years had passed since the seance and the Blitz had altered the landscape in South London drastically), they concluded that Price had just chosen an imaginary house in order to make his story sound more realistic.

Why had he chosen Brockley? Because, Dr. Dingwall and Mr. Hall replied, he and his wife had lived in Brockley at one time; because in his *Search for Truth* Price had described the spiritualist meetings he had attended in his youth in Manor Road, every Wednesday evening; and because he also gave the account of a private circle held in a house in Wickham Road which ended in a fight between a drunken medium and a local plumber.

So Brockley was really a clue to Price's mendacity! He had used a real place for a ficticious story—as, indeed, liars often use realistic details to make their fibs more acceptable. At least this was the argument of the authors of *Four Modern Ghosts.*

The final details Price gave about the Rosalie case included the information that at the end of August 1939, Mr. X. took his famly and Madame Z. on a Continental holiday. During the trip they left Madame Z. in Paris where she was visiting relatives. Then came the outbreak of the war. Mr. X. was at Zurich and he made a dash for one of the Channel ports. He was unable to pick up Madame Z. and had to abandon his own car at Ostend. Madame Z. more or less disappeared in the confusion of the war; nor was "Rosalie" ever heard of again.

Dingwall and Hall found this a most unlikely story; they couldn't believe that anybody would go on holiday in those tense and fateful days of August, 1939. They thought this was another fabrication by Price—who, by this convenient device, provided a complete explanation of why he was unable to obtain another seance with the X.'s and why he couldn't produce Madame Z. or anybody else as a witness that the seance had really taken place. (The thing about the unlikeliness of the holiday hardly held water; I took my family to the Continent during that last summer of peace and got back to England only a few days before the signing of the Russo-German Pact which was the final signal for the holocaust.)

The charges brought by the authors of *Four Modern Ghosts* received a good deal of publicity; as usual, opinions were fairly evenly divided for and against the "genuiness" of the Rosalie case. But except for one man who took up the investigation, the matter would have been allowed to be forgotten, the controversy would have died down.

Some time in 1961 I began to receive letters from a Mr. David Cohen who was a member of the Society for Psychical Research and Investigation Officer of the Manchester Psychical Society. He wanted access to the Harry Price Library and information about various points connected with Price's work. I provided all this, as a matter of course; we had several telephone conversations and finally met. I found him a slim, nervous, freckled, red-haired man who was obviously a devoted fan of Price and his work in every sense of the word and wanted to rehabilitate the somewhat tarnished reputation of his hero.

He set out to disprove the allegations of Dr. Dingwall and Mr. Hall and in 1965, after spending much time and effort on this task, published a book (largely, I suspect, at his own expense) under the imprint of the Regency Press, London and New York, called *Price and His Spirit Child Rosalie*. In several chapters and several supplements he set out to demolish the case against Price; and I must say, in my opinion, he largely succeeded. He obtained from Mrs. Goldney a full corroboration of her meeting with Price on the day following the fateful seance; he established that the letter in the Harry Price Library allegedly fixing the place of the seance at Brockley (written by Mrs. Clarice Richards, a charming old lady and friend of Price) referred to something quite different from the interpretation of Dingwall and Hall; he interviewed everybody who had even a remote connection with the case and argued that an early split between Dr. Dingwall and Price might have provided a motive for the attack on the late psychical investigator by the authors of *Four Modern Ghosts*.

On October 7, 1965, Cohen delivered a lecture at the London Ghost Club—a neutral meeting ground for spiritualists and sceptics—at which I took the chair. He made out a very convincing case for his main contention : that the seance did take place, more or less, as Price described it and that the Rosalie case was still an unsolved mystery, a legitimate subject for further research. Though Cohen showed a certain excessive credulity in connection with his other investigations and a fair amount of naïvety in his approach, he was obviously a burningly sincere and honest man. In his book he offered a modest reward of £25. to anybody "passing on information that will lead to the identity of any of the participants who may have witnessed the 'Rosalie' materialization".

I spent the greater part of 1966 away from England. When I returned, I heard that David Cohen was gravely ill with cancer in a Manchester nursing home. I wrote to him and in reply he sent me an extraordinary document that had reached him in

April 1966. It was handwritten, on lined paper, and postmarked London.

It is such a striking and revealing piece that it cannot be summarized but must be reproduced in its entirety (the first time in print), with its original punctuation and spelling.

London

April, 1966

Dear Mr. Cohen,

I have read your book about Harry Price and his spirit child with interest and; forgive me; with some amusement for I am always amused at the various guesses which are constantly being hazarded about the Rosalie ghost. But then I am in a rather privileged position being now the only living person who knows the whole truth about the seances held in our house thirty years ago. As this long-kept secret concerns the honour of my father, it is a matter of some doubt whether I am justified in divulging it now, particularly as I promised my parents never to do so, but as my parents are dead, and as I have no intention of disclosing their identity, perhaps I may be forgiven for this breach of trust.

I suppose that anyone who did not know my father would think his actions shameful but he was the kindest and most lovable man and the trouble he got himself into was more the result of weakness than of any real defect in his character. Of course, I was only a small girl at the time of my father's trouble and knew nothing of the cause of his distress, but many years later, after his death, my mother told me that it was a case of one deceit leading inevitably to another—one deceit being used to cover a preceding deceit. However, if it had not been for my father's trouble, there would never have been a Rosalie.

My father had a good position; a position of trust, in a City firm and we were living, in the nineteen-thirties, in a fashionable suburb of S.E. London. My mother did not know when or why my father started to speculate on the stock market. She told me that he lost money in what I think she called "stagging" and "borrowed" money from his firm in order to cover his losses. Naturally the time arrived when this money had to be returned and, about this time, my father became acquainted with a wealthy French widow who lived in our neighbourhood. When, some time later, I met Madame I took an instant dislike to her. She was a grasping, suspicious woman and something of a miser. The only soft spot in her hard nature appeared to be a love of her dead child; if such a morbid fixation can be called love. According to my mother, my father suggested to Madame that he could invest some money for her at a high rate of interest and this appeal to her cupidity proved too great a temptation for Madame to resist. But poor father, although he was now able to return the money he had "borrowed" from his firm, was completely in Madame's power. He was able to pay the interest on the money he had pretended to invest, but Madame had to be prevented from asking for the return of her capital, or from making any enquiries about some worthless "securities" my father had given her. My mother told me that she was convinced that had Madame discovered she had been tricked, there was absolutely no doubt that she would immediately have started legal proceedings. However, my mother assured me, that this deceit was merely a matter of time, because my father had cause to believe that he would, within a year or two, be in a position to pay Madame the money she had given him. In fact this is actually what did happen and sometime before the last war, my father persuaded Madame to sell her shares in the pretext that they were likely to depreciate in value. My mother thought this was when Hitler invaded Czechoslovakia, or Austria, because she remembered that my father used the international situation as a reason for the likelihood of depreciation. Of course, some twenty years had passed when my mother told me about my father's financial difficulties, and she was then a little vague about details, but I remember my father returning from the City one evening and saying to my mother with some excitement, "XXXX (word crossed out), we can now exorcise the ghost." This, I now believe, must have been a reference to the ending of a period of great anxiety suffered by my parents.

But I must return to a time about two years before this happy ending, when it was deperately necessary to retain Madame's faith in my father and to prevent her from asking embarrassing questions about her "investments". Unfortunately, for my father, Madame started to show some suspicious interest in her capital and her inquisitiveness had, in some way, to be diverted. As Madame was contantly talking to my father about her dead child, Rosalie, he came to the conclusion that this was the only weak link in her armour; the only interest stronger than her interest in money, and therefore the only interest that could be used to save him, and his family, from disgrace. So my father turned towards spiritualism, purchased some books on the subject and informed Madame that my mother was an amateur medium and that seances were sometimes held at our home.

It was at this time that I was first brought into the deception. My parents asked me to take part in, what they called, "a ghost game" to be played as a harmless joke on a French lady. At first my part in this business was childishly simple. I was to slip noiselessly into the darkened room soon after the others had settled down, take up a position in the corner of the room and answer some questions in a hushed, childish lisp. I was then, at a pre-arranged signal from my mother, to slip silently out of the room before the lights were switched on. But when we started to rehearse the procedure we came up against our first snag. Although my father oiled the hinges and handle mechanism of the door, the latter could not be persuaded to act noiselessly. My father overcame the difficulty by making a small wedge which he stealthily inserted into the door catch when finally closing the door before the seance commenced. A wedge which he removed when opening the door after the seance had ended. Thus I did not have to touch the rather loose handle when entering and leaving the room.

When my parents were satisfied with these rehearsals, my father told Madame that a child voice had asked for her at a seance held at our house. Madame showed great interest and asked to be allowed to visit our home, meet my mother and attend a seance.

I have to admit to experiencing a feeling of excitement and pleasure of the anticipation of this game of ghosts. Perhaps this was reprehensible of me but, it must be remembered, that I was a mere child of ten years at this time and the idea of playing a trick on a grown-up seemed to be an intriguing adventure. This feeling, I have no doubt, came from the child-desire to be important and to be clever enough to put one over an adult world which, the child feels, is constantly exerting its grown-up superiority.

The second snag which my father had to contend with was Jack, our Airedale dog, who was greatly attached to us, as we were to him. Whenever any of the family were in the house, Jack was completely miserable if he could not be with us, whining and scratching at doors until he found us. My father said he could not trust the servants to keep him in the kitchen during the seances, because Jack was an adept at slipping out of any door which had to be opened, even for a second. The danger had to be overcome of his flinging open the unlatched seance door and so father decided to have him in the room during the seances where, as long as mother and father were there, he could be relied upon to remain quiet. Much later my father realized that the presence of Jack at the seances could have been a clue to an intelligent investigator, but here we were lucky for the clue was never discovered, not even, I believe, by any of the many authors who have written about Rosalie.

My mother was, at first, rather apprehensive about these seances and my father had to give up the idea of asking her to simulate a trance condition. She was to play as passive a part as possible and merely to ask certain questions of the spirit, commencing with, "I feel the child is in the room—are you there—are you there Rosalie?" After she had repeated this three or four times, I was to whisper, in as childish a voice as I could answer, "Yes—Rosalie is here."

If I remember correctly, Madame first visited our home for a sitting about two days after the Crystal Palace fire, an event which caused a great stir in our part of London. The seance went without a hitch. I waited in the hall after Madame and my parents had entered the room and I listened for the wireless to be switched-off, which was my signal to slip into the room. I was very nervous and excited at this first seance and nearly forgot to switch-off the hall light before opening the seance door, an omission which could have been fatal to our purpose. The door opened noiselessly at a slight pressure and I crept into the room and waited. I answered about five or six questions, giving the answers which had been suggested

F

by my father : "I am very, very happy"—"I walk in meadows filled with beautiful flowers"—"I play with the other children —they are very kind to me"—"A beautiful lady in shining white looks after us" etc. After Madame had departed, my parents told me that they were very pleased with my perfor- mance—I gathered that Madame was suitably impressed.

Many such seances followed, although I do not think they were as frequent as one a week, as Mr. Price suggested. My impression is that we held one or two a month, usually, if not always, on a Wednesday evening. As the sittings progressed my father became more adventurous, and when Madame asked whether she would ever see her child at a seance, father told her that this might be possible. Thus we began to practise with an electric-torch whose bulb had been covered by one or two layers of blue tissue paper. This I held at chest level, pointing it away from the sitters and towards my face. The very dim, slightly blue light gave a suitable ghostly appearance to my face. Indeed I remember almost frightening the life out of myself when I tried this out in front of my bedroom mirror. I wore a black dress, black stockings and black gloves for this trick and my mother told me that the apeparance of a disembodied face, dimly underlighted in blue, was most eerie. Madame seemed to accept this face as that of her dead child, so I presume that I must have looked rather like Rosalie or, what is perhaps more probable, I looked like nothing on earth and therefore was accepted as not of this world.

After some months my father decided to ask his young brother, Uncle Jim, to help him in this ghost game. I think the reason for this was that Madame had asked whether Rosalie was the only spirit which appeared at our seances, and what had happened before the child had made an appearance. Father, who was always anxious to allay Madame's slightest suspicion, said that several other spirits had spoken, but that her presence attracted Rosalie more than the other spirits, who would, no doubt, return when Rosalie became less insistent. Uncle Jim was a very dear person and the family was terribly distressed when he was killed, in 1942, fighting in North Africa. He was divoted [*sic!*] to my father, as we all were, and eager to help in what he thought was "rather a lark". So Uncle Jim, on occasions, waited in his stockinged feet in the hall with me, and we took it in turns to enter the dark room. He spoke in the voice of Big Chief Eagle of the Mohawk Tribe, or an ancient Chinese philosopher, or any other person who appealed to his imagination. I remember on one occasion he became General Gordon, I think he was reading a biography at the time, and on another, when I had a bad cold, he took the whole seance using one or two different voices. My uncle's sense of humour caused my parents some anxiety. Listening to him from the hall, I had great difficulty in suppressing a giggle.

Some time before my father had thought of producing the spirit of Rosalie, he had told Madame that he had a daughter, but had not mentioned my age. Soon after the seances had commenced, Madame asked my father how old was his daughter and father, always on his guard and thinking that there might be some suspicious connection in her mind between the spirit child and myself, said I was sixteen years old.

Unfortunately, a month or two later, Madame asked why she had never met this teenage daughter and father countered that by saying that I usually attended physical training classes on Wednesday evenings but, no doubt, she would meet me before very long. I believe there were gym classes for adults much publicised at this time and the claim that I attended these classes made it seem impossible that I could have been young enough to have impersonated Rosalie.

However it was now rather imperative to produce a teenage daughter so—what to do?

My parents considered the possibility of bringing a young person into the house to play the part of their daughter, but they soon abandoned the idea as impracticable,—whom could they ask to play this part?—would it not be dangerous to allow the Rosalie secret to go outside the family? It was finally decided that I must impersonate myself, or more correctly, my elder self. I had played the part of a child some years my junior and now I must play the part of a girl, some years my senior.

My mother went to work on me and with the aid of cosmetics, a teenage dress, a padded bust-bodice, a new hair-do and high heeled shoes, brought about a fairly convincing transformation. It is true I was a little short for a sixteen year old, but the high heeled shoes and the hair-do had added some inches to my height. For several evenings I was rehearsed in my new part until I became, more or less, accustomed to moving and behaving without awkwardness. Strangely enough I felt quite at home as a teenager and seemed to put on a new personality with my new clothes. My mother was rather frightened that Madame, having seen my face during some of the seances, would recognize me, the teenage daughter, as Rosalie, but my father said that even he could not have recognized me in the peculiar light of the seance room and did not think it possible that Madame would so so. As the Rosalie seances continued my parents were forced to take greater and greater risks, but they had passed the point of no return and therefore could not retract.

Some two or three weeks later I was introduced to Madame who seemed to accept me without question. This was the first time I had seen her, although we had been in the same room many times. I cannot say I was exactly attracted to this severe, taciturn Frenchwoman. She seemed permanently disgruntled and I cannot remember ever seeing her smile. I remember that at this first meeting we spoke about a coronation which had taken place about a week previously—I suppose this must have been the coronation of George VI because I remember the now Duke of Windsor had abdicated at the end of the previous year.

After this introduction I was in the room for about a quarter of an hour before excusing myself by saying that I was going to my gym class. My mother had bought for me a white blouse and pair of black shorts, their being, I believe, the fashionable uniform for physical training classes at that time, and these had been placed on the sofa in the seance room in order to impress Madame. These I picked-up on leaving the room and, after waiting for a moment or two in the hall, opened and closed the front door before slipping upstairs to remove my teenage disguise. I passed Uncle Jim on the stairs who was coming down to impersonate the first spirit.

For some months after this all went well until one disasterous [*sic!*] evening in, I think, late November. This mishap was entirely my fault. I had become, after so many successful seances, rather over-confident and ignored my father's instructions. He had told me that if Madame asked the spirit anything about Rosalie's life on earth, I was either to remain silent or to say I could not remember. I cannot recall the question that Madame asked me on that evening but I foolishly attempted to answer and, of course, it was the wrong answer. After the seance something like a quarrel broke out between my parents and Madame. She said she was far from satisfied that she had not been tricked and my father said that even spirits could forget instances in their earth life and that it was many years since Rosalie had been on earth. Naturally, I was not present during this altercation, but I learnt about it later, and the upshot of the dispute was, I was told, that father offered to have a seance investigated by a trained investigator and Madame suggested Harry Price.

For the first time since the seances had commenced my father was worried. During the past year he had been reading books on spiritualism and realized that a seance with controls would be the most difficult one we had yet given. So my parents, Uncle Jim and I went into a huddle and worked out a method of procedure. My mother was to telephone Mr. Price, invite him to a seance and extract from him an assurance of secrecy. Considering the danger of one investigation, my father did not want to risk further investigation and should Mr. Price publish our names and addresses it would be difficult, if not impossible, to avoid further investigation and enquiry. Apart from my parents, Madame and Mr. Price, I, as the teenage daughter, and Uncle Jim, as my boy-friend, were to be sitters at the seance. The importance of my being in the room if Mr. Price sealed the door, and father assured us that he would wish to do this, was obvious. There were two reasons for Uncle Jim being a sitter. One, my father thought it advisable to have an extra helper in the room to cover, if possible any minor, or unexpected mishap. Two, he would, as my boy-friend, add testimony to my assumed teenage. Although Madame had heard Uncle Jim speak in several different voices, she had never seen him and therefore he could be safely introduced to her as "young Jim". Uncle Jim was, I believe, in his late twenties at that time but looked very much younger.

My parents and Uncle Jim then discussed the question of what form the spirit should take. My father, after my faux pas, was against my speaking and the materialization of a spirit face seemed impossible because of the difficulty in concealing the torch. My father said that Mr. Price would possibly search the room and the male sitters, and he might ask Madame to search the ladies. Looking back on this seance, it is perhaps surprising that my father thought it possible that Mr. Price would ask Madame to do this but this was because we thought of our seance as being investigated by both Mr. Price and Madame, and did not see it from Mr. Price's point of view. To Mr. Price, Madame was someone to be investigated equally with everyone else in the seance room, and it would obviously be futile to ask one suspect to search another suspect—a point which evaded us at this time.

My father suggested that the spirit should be lighted by hand mirrors coated with luminous paint because these would not require to be concealed. Uncle Jim pointed out that, if Mr. Price wished to handle a mirror, it would be impossible to assure that he would direct its light only to the face and he might see, and recognize the dress of the girl he believed to be sitting opposite to him in the dark. My mother said that I could change into "spirit clothes" but my father very logically said that, should there be a search of the room, "spirit clothes" would be as impossible to conceal as a torch. It was finally suggested that the spirit should appear in the nude—a suggestion I didn't much like but to which I eventually agreed.

It was agreed that Mr. Price should be invited to arrive at our house some considerable time before Madame arrived in order that my father might have time to tell his own version of the Rosalie story before Price met Madame.

We had some days in which to practise our new routine; the most difficult part of which I found was to dress in complete darkness. My mother showed me how I could overcome this difficulty by the careful and methodical placing of my clothes as I undressed.

On the evening of the appointed day Mr. Price arrived. He was, I thought, a charming man although rather ugly and seemed pleased at being asked to attend our seance. I believe my father told him that seances had been held in our house for a longer period than they had, and this exaggeration was, I think, in order to put the beginning back to a time before he had any financial connections with Madame—in case Mr.

Price subsequently discovered these financial dealings. He also told Mr. Price that Rosalie had first appeared to Madame when she was alone and at home, thus suggesting to Mr. Price that the spirit first appeared when there was no possibility of trickery on the part of our family.

The seance held on that December evening nearly 29 years ago has been described by Mr. Price in his book and, although I have not read this for many years, I think he described it fairly accurately. There are, however, one or two points which need to be explained and these I will attempt to remember.

It struck me as very amusing that Mr. Price should take so much trouble to seal the doors and windows when he was actually sealing Rosalie inside the room, and I could not suppress a smile which caused my father to give me a very severe look.

After he has searched my father and Uncle Jim, I had a moment of panic because I thought he might wish to search the ladies and would discover my padded form. In my agitation I lifted my skirt in the attempt to convince him I had nothing to hide and displayed my black shorts; these I was wearing because they were very easy to remove in the dark. My father very quickly commented on these shorts and told Mr. Price I had been attending an adult physical training class, and thus turned my impulsive gesture to some account. As it was necessary that I should not sit too near Mr. Price, my father suggested that, as Mr. Price could not search my mother or Madame, they should sit on either side of him and this was agreed to.

In the complete darkness, I was able to leave my place in the circle and undress in a corner of the room. As my mother had remarkably small hands, we had agreed on the following procedure. After Mr. Price had felt the spirit form, my father suggested that, while holding the spirit's hands, Mr. Price might like those not sitting next to him to speak, and thus assure himself that they were in their proper places. My mother, who had rolled up the sleeves and removed her rings in the dark, then placed her hands in front of Mr. Price, which he held while I returned to my seat in the circle and spoke a few words.

When it came to using the luminous mirrors, my father

asked Mr. Price to commence from the feet and work upwards. This was because when he came to light the face, the mirror would be beneath the chin and therefore the face would be underlighted. We had discovered, when experimenting with the torch, that a face which is underlighted is completely unrecognizable as the same face when normally lighted, and it was obviously necessary that Mr. Price should not recognize my face. But although we were reasonably sure that Mr. Price would not recognize me, we were rather afraid that Mr. Price would think that my face was not that of a six year old. I was then eleven and therefore looked older than six, but he did not comment on this so I suppose my looking slightly older than Rosalie did not occur to him.

I was somewhat nonplussed when Mr. Price spoke to Rosalie because my father, after my unfortunate reply to Madame, had told me that I must not speak at this seance. But as Mr. Price persisted in asking questions, I eventually ventured a "yes", and this reply fortunately put a stop to his questions.

After the seance Mr. Price examined his seals and found them intact. He seemed very perplexed but absolutely satisfied that trickery had been impossible. Madame's suspicions had vanished and once more she appeared to be friendly towards the family, or, at least, as friendly as she was capable.

That night, after Mr. Price and Madame had left us, my father suddenly exclaimed: "Good heavens! The dog!" Jack had been sleeping in his accustomed place before the fireplace during the seance. When my mother asked him what he meant by this exclamation, he replied by quoting a scrap of conversation between Sherlock Holmes and Dr. Watson: "I would draw your attention, Watson, to the extraordinary behaviour of the dog in the night" "But the dog did nothing in the night, Holmes." "Exactly, my dear Watson, that was the extraordinary behaviour of the dog." As my mother was still perplexed, my father explained that, because it is generally believed that dogs show intense fear when confronted with the supernatural, Mr. Price might reasonably conclude that as Jack remained peacefully sleeping throughout the seance, no spirit form could possibly have been in the room; but Mr. Price was no Sherlock Holmes and apparently this point did not occur to him.

We continued to hold seances for the benefit of Madame, for some months after this test seance, but, in the following year, my father was able to repay the money to Madame and my mother lost her power as a medium. My father explained to Madame that my mother was tired and far from well—which was actually the case after so many months of worry—and must have a rest from seances. Madame was not pleased but as we were no longer an obligation to her, this did not concern us. I never saw Madame again but, about a year later, my parents spent some days with her.

My father, in the summer of 1939, had arranged to take my mother for a holiday on the Continent and meeting Madame by accident one evening at xxxxxxx (erased word) the Station, he happened to mention the holiday to her. She asked him whether she could accompany them as far as, I think, Paris, and he could see no way of refusing this request. I was spending my summer holidays with my paternal grandmother and Uncle Jim and only heard of this when they hurriedly returned to England. No member of the family saw Madame again and, to tell the truth, we were not sorry to have done with this reminder of a very worrying time.

Indeed I sincerely wish people would cease to write about the Rosalie affair. I have no intention of giving any clues which might connect me, or my family, with this sorry, and rather reprehensible, business and this I think you will understand. There is now, I believe, no other living person who knows the whole story. The servants were never in our confidence although it is rather impossible to know how much servants guess or find out. However, the cook is dead and our housemaid, I have been told, married just after the war and left England to live abroad.

I think I should in fairness to the memory of Mr. Price, write to Dr. Dingwall and tell him he is mistaken in thinking that Mr. Price invented Rosalie, but I must, of course, remain forever anonymous.   Yours sincerely,

Rosalie

I actually saw this extraordinary letter (or rather, a typewritten copy of it) at Le Piol, the charming retreat near St. Paul de Vence where Eileen Garrett organized her summer meetings for the

International Parapsychology Foundation. David Cohen had apparently prepared several copies of it and sent them to some of the interested parties; but (as I said before) I had been abroad and lost touch with him so I was not one of the original recipients.

There was a select company of psychical investigators present and we discussed Rosalie's "confession". There were considerable doubts about its genuineness—caused, of course, largely by the fact that she did not provide any names or localities. The story was still somehow hanging in the air—we will see before long how much—even though it was a most careful and complete explanation of many (if not all) puzzling details. Some of us felt that it was too much so—as if the writer, whoever she or he was, had taken Price's original report and going through it paragraph by paragraph, had painstakingly provided a natural explanation for everything that had happened.

I wanted to study it at more leisure and when I returned to England, I wrote to David Cohen who was waging a valiant fight against his terrible malady, and mentioned some of my scruples. He replied that he, for once, was convinced of its complete and utter sincerity and genuineness; that though heartbroken because he had so much hoped this would turn out a mile-stone in spirit materializations, he was willing to accept it. He said that he would dearly like to make another appeal to Rosalie to come forward and reveal her identity—but because of his illness was handicapped and unable to do so.

It was then that I asked him whether he could let me have a photostat of the original letter rather than a typed copy I had received in the meantime. He did even better—for he sent me the original letter—and suggested that I should try to obtain the widest possible publicity for it. Perhaps, he said, this would provoke the mysterious lady—who must be in her early forties by now—to give up her anonymity and agree to be questioned by experts, naturally under the promise of total discretion.

I was dubious about it but I promised to do my best. I left England again for a few weeks and when I returned I found that David Cohen, after a most courageous battle, had succumbed to cancer and had died. He was a bachelor and though there was a sister she was obviously not much interested in her late brother's dominant passion for psychic matters.

I felt that I had to fulfil, if possible, his last wish. So I took the Rosalie letter, together with a copy of Price's original report, to a graphologist, one of the most eminent of the profession who works closely and regularly with Scotland Yard. He insisted on remaining anonymous for the very same reason; but he had no reservation about declaring the writer of the Rosalie document "absolutely sincere and genuine". This was an opinion to be respected—but, for the scientific mind at least, hardly conclusive. If it had been a question of identifying a handwriting, comparing two existing specimens, tracing a forgery, we would have dealt with tangible facts. But our graphologist had ventured into psychology and conjecture—and here his opinion, though perhaps more important than that of any layman, did not have the force of final argument, of complete resolution.

Even if this had not been so, I felt that there were some nagging inconsistencies between Price's account and the alleged Rosalie's explanation.

Many of these were concentrated on the problem of age.

Was it possible for a girl to play two parts within the space of half-an-hour which entailed an age difference of eleven years? Rosalie was supposed to be six; Miss X.—seventeen. In reality, by the time the Price seance was held, she must have been twelve. At one end or the other there was a gap very hard if not impossible to bridge. She might have been accepted for seventeen with suitable padding and make-up. But when she undressed, how could her eleven-year-old body become that of a six year old? Biologically, anatomically, these five years represent a considearble difference. There was no indication in Rosalie's account that she was underdeveloped, retarded physically. She might have been a small girl—but she was on the threshold of puberty and "Rosalie" would still carry her puppy-fat. Perhaps Price did not have the opportunity of examining many naked six-year-olds at such close quarters—but he must have been a singularly obtuse man not to notice such differences. And what about the long months during which "Rosalie" changed from eleven to six and then seventeen for the benefit of Madame Z.?

Nor could one accept the switch-over which Price's decision to test the position of the sitters entailed. First of all, Mr. X. couldn't really know that this would happen—if previous arrangements were made, they must have been preparing for a very remote contingency. Secondly, the fake Rosalie would have to move from Price's immediate vicinity back to her place and then back again to him after he called upon her to speak. The transition between her mother's hands and her own must have been extremely quick and smooth—but even so Price, a most experienced investigator and a superb amateur magician himself, was bound to notice *some* movement, some interval of time. And then the young girl had to get back again to take over once more from her mother.

These are only main points—others, after a minute comparison of Price's report (written, remember, immediately after the events) and Rosalie's "confession", would no doubt emerge. But of course Rosalie composed her account some thirty years after the events; she may have forgotten details or remembered them wrongly. However, her letter is such a closely-woven, carefully worked-out structure in which each step, each fact, each circumstance seem perfectly enmeshed, that this defence is hardly acceptable.

If it is a forgery—if it was written by someone trying to discredit Price's opponents or just to climb on a psychical bandwagon—what could the motive? "Rosalie", though she promised to do so, never wrote to Dr. Dingwall. Such an anonymous letter, without any proper clue as to its writer, could bring neither material nor psychological profit. Was it the work of a practical joker? a hoaxer—not uncommon in matters psychic? The handwriting had been compared to that of a few well-known practitioners of this genre and the results were totally negative.

The only solution would be to track down "Rosalie" and confront her with these questions.

This, some highly qualified researchers have been trying to do in the last three years and I have given them some modest help.

More or less parallel with David Cohen's crusade to save or rehabilitate Harry Price's reputation after the attacks upon him, Mr. R. G. Medhurst and Miss M. R. Barrington, both of the Society for Psychical Research, decided to examine Dr. Dingwall's and Mr. Hall's theories about the Rosalie case. Mrs. K. M. Goldney was also involved in this long and often tiresome investigation. The results were summed up in an admirably lucid and concise report by Mr. Medhurst in the *Journal* of the Society (December 1965) after the Cohen book was published. The first thing the investigators did was to look through Harry Price's correspondence around the period of the Rosalie seance. And here they came upon the carbon copy of a letter by Price addressed to Mrs. X. Like many of Price's outgoing letters, the copy did *not* bear the name and address of the recipient. But this particular copy carried at the top a name that was typed directly on to the sheet. And this name was "Mrs. Mortimer". (The letter, dated 13th December, was the one to which we referred earlier, in which Price confirmed the arrangements made for the seance over the telephone and asked whether he could bring R. S. Lambert along.)

The searchers thought that this new clue (which Dr. Dingwall and Mr. Hall had missed or ignored) would lead them to the location of the Rosalie seance—even though they would have to search the entire Greater London area. This is what they did.

"As a first step," Mr. Medhurst wrote, "Mrs. K. M. Goldney undertook the tedious task of copying out the names and addresses of all the Mortimers in the Greater London area who were listed as being on the telephone in 1937 (it will be recalled that one detail in Price's story required that there should be a telephone in the house). In the directory issued at the beginning of that year we found 108 Mortimer entries, and in a second directory issued in November there were eight more. The Post Office Guide was also scrutinized for Mortimers living in the London and suburban areas who had resided in the same houses for nine years, the period during which the 'Rosalie' sittings were said by Price to have taken place."

The result of the long, exacting search—after ruling out public houses, shops, offices, almost all the remaining houses were inspected from the outside, with Miss Barrington covering the southern part of London and Mr. Medhurst the northern one— was rather disappointing. None of the houses fitted Price's description at all closely—hardly any of them turned out to be "substantial detached Victorian houses" and those that were could almost all be eliminated for various reasons.

And here the long arm of coincidence reached forward. For the only house that was even half possible was one in Wickham Road, where the search made by Dr. Dingwall and Mr. Hall ended—though for quite different reasons. This house, No. 21., was a detached, double-fronted Victorian house but many details were wrong—such as the number of windows and steps, it was not a corner house etc.

"We found a similar, tantalizing situation," Mr. Medhurst continued, "as regards the family living in the house in 1937. Mr. Mortimer, who now lives in a seaside town, could indeed have been described as a 'City businessman'. There was a Miss Mortimer—but in December 1937 she was only just fifteen, whereas the daughter of the family was said by Price to have been nearly 17. This Miss Mortimer, moreover, also has a sister two years younger. She says that if anything in the nature of a seance had taken place she and her sister would have been sent to bed and would not have known anything about it. Furthermore, while Mrs. Mortimer has a long-standing interest in psychical matters, Mr. Mortimer does not share this interest at all."

It is worthwhile to pause here and compare the facts in this paragraph—written, of course, well before the Rosalie "confession" reached David Cohen—with the anonymous letter. We know, of course—if we accept the "confession"—that the Miss Mortimer was not 17 but 11 in 1937. Here, again, there is a discrepancy between her alleged age and that of the real Miss Mortimer living at No. 21 Wickham Road whom Mr. Medhurst and Miss Barrington managed to trace and interview. The sister does not figure in Price's account nor in the alleged Rosalie's, who also claimed—in 1966—that neither of her parents are alive.

"A curious circumstance is that in the early nineteen-twenties," Mr. Medhurst added, "Mr. and Mrs. Mortimer lived in Manor Road which, like Wickham Road, was the location of the early sittings attended by Price which have already been mentioned."

At this point another relevant piece of evidence was discovered by Dr. Alan Gauld: a letter from Mr. S. J. de Lotbiniere (Director of Outside Broadcasts, B.B.C.) to Harry Price in which he said: *"I look forward to hearing how the Brockley seance goes."* So Brockley appears to be definitely the place of the "Rosalie" seance—and while the new investigation appeared on one hand to confirm some of Dr. Dingwall's and Mr. Hall's conclusions it pretty well demolished their claim that Harry Price invented the whole business. George Medhurst summed it up:

"It may well be that Price, in fulfilment of his promise to

conceal the identity of the sitters, omitted some vital step in his narrative. It is not inconceiveable, for example, that he was met, and taken to a house other than the one he had anticipated. An obvious alternative possibility is that the telephone number of the house was ex-directory.

"If one postulates the essential truth of Price's story it is not, of course, also postulating the authenticity of the phenomena . . .

". . . Evidently Price envisaged the possibility that the manifestation reported by him was a clever fraud, and this conclusion may be considered to receive strong support from the continued silence of the sitters, which seems otherwise inexplicable . . ."

Mr. Medhurst, of course, could not have known when writing this that only a few months later there would arrive a "confession" that would make things, at least at first glance, less inexplicable. After the arrival of Rosalie's letter all we could do was to try and obtain some specimens of handwriting from those who were candidates for the role of "Rosalie". We used a few perfectly legitimate ruses to do so—and failed completely.

We do not know, therefore, who Rosalie is nor whether the "confession" is genuine—though I, personally, am inclined to think that it is true in the main outlines. But it may well be that the publication of the full text will bring further evidence to light. Close investigation, for instance, has already revealed that Mrs. X.'s Christian name must have been "Edith" for the word "Rosalie" inked over so carefully was not obliterated, only covered. The name of the station at which Mr. X. met Madame Z. just before the war is in the process of being deciphered. Perhaps these two new clues will help a little. But at this time, in the late summer of 1970, the Secret of Rosalie is still to a large extent unsolved—while Price's good faith is vindicated.

POSTSCRIPT

After finishing this chapter, we asked Dr. George Medhurst to comment on its contents. He expressed a very strong scepticism as to the genuineness of the "confession" and made the following points :

(a) Price, after carefully feeling Rosalie's nude body, gives her height as about three feet seven inches. Later he was able to see her in the faint light from the plaques. If the height were substantially greater Price's statement would be clearly wrong. If, however, it is about right it would be quite absurd for a girl of such a height to pretend to be nearly seventeen. Even with "some inches" (due to high heels and hair arrangement) extra she would look like a dwarf.

(*b*) Price was told by Mr. and Mrs. X. over supper a story of the previous seances. It was explained in particular that Madame Z. had first seen Rosalie in her own bedroom in 1925, some twelve years before the Price sitting, and that the sittings had been taking place in the X.'s house for nine years. If the "confession" story, i.e. that the sittings had been going on for just a year, were correct, Mr. and Mrs. X. would not have dared to tell Price what he reports since, immediately after, Price was free to have a conversation with Madame Z. who would clearly be in a position to contradict this information.

(*c*) The "confessor" claims that she, as a teenager, and Uncle Jim (she doesn't say Uncle "Jim") attended their first seance, i.e. the Price seance, so far as Madame Z. knew. However, Madame Z., according to Price "apologized for not being able to admit my friend (Mr. Lambert) to the seance, as they had never risked two strangers at a sitting "in case it frightened Rosalie". Now, if there were *three* strangers as, according to the confessor it would seem to Madame Z., she would surely not merely make a mild apology to Price. The confessor, after all, says that she was a "grasping, suspicious woman", with a "hard nature".

Since then Mr. Medhurst had an opportunity to study Price's original manuscript of the Rosalie case as included in *Fifty Years of Psychical Research*. He discovered that Price had referred in it to Mr. X. as a "hop merchant"—a description which he deleted and then replaced with a "City businessman". Perhaps this opens up a new line of enquiry? There is certainly still a considerable scope for investigation.

Sex and the Occult

During a panel discussion held in 1968 under the auspices of Forum Magazine, the participants reached more or less general agreement that there was a definite link between sexuality and psychic phenomena, that genital eroticism played at least a discernible part in this field—as, indeed, if we accept Freud and his school for our authorities, in all human life. Mr. Peter Underwood, the President of the Ghost Club, pointed out that many mediums had complaints and illnesses associated with the genital organs—though this was little known and discussed. According to him it was an indisputable fact that a good deal of psychic phenomena *was* associated with the sex organs. He had gathered considerable material on this subject and had delivered lectures at Sussex University and elsewhere on *The Sexual Element in Spontaneous Psychic Phenomena*.

Not all experts were definitely committed to the idea. Anita Black, a Cambridge-educated psychologist pointed out that Spiritualists, like many other religious groups, did not have a special attitude to Freud. She explained:

"Looking at the problem in a wider context, Freud's views and his contribution can be divided into two very wide areas. One has to do with the supposed content of the psyche, which in his view was so largely infantilely sexual, and the other has to do with 'transference' in the very widest sense, the 'defence mechanism', the view that a very large proportion of our conscious life is governed by unconscious factors, whatever they may be, and this has a very important bearing on mediumistic communication from any point of view. A medium speaks from sources which are supposed to be from outside his or her consciousness. Now he or she is very apt to think and wish to believe (and very often does sincerely believe) that this communication comes from a communicator, a higher spirit, a spirit guide or something of that order. At the same time, it may be all too apparent to the onlooker that at least some of this comes from the medium's own mind. The medium's interests and pre-occupations may certainly colour the subjects he discussed with his sitter. The only work in psychic research in this area that I know of has been done by Tenhaeff, with Croiset and other *Paragnosts* as he called his mediums. Tanhaeff found that what a Paragnost 'sees' is very often something that preoccupied him in his childhood. For example, a man who, as a child had been abandoned and left with an unscrupulous guardian would be very sensitive in tracing frauds perpetrated by guardians on orphans. Again, another medium who was himself a transvestite, was good at gaining paranormal information regarding transvestites. I do think that there is a link-up between Freudian theories or psychoanalytic theories in a very general way and the para-psychical . . ."

It was a short step form general conclusions to the more specific. It had been established that pent-up sexual energy, especially within girls who were at the age of puberty, often manifested itself psychically. This usually happened during the so-called poltergeist disturbances where objects moved, noises were heard, small fires were started—and the "agency" remained invisible and unknown. In the instances when young girls or boys moved, so did objects around them—though safely outside their reach. Poltergeist phenomena were really an example of a person who was haunted—as opposed to a house.

And, of course, in many poltergeist cases the bed or bedroom played a major part. Here the correlation between the erotic element and the poltergeist phenomena was only too plain. Beds bedrooms and stairs were almost invariably associated with poltergeists—which established a clearcut link. A good deal of research has gone into this question and the definite relationships between some of the so-called "hauntings" and sexuality are now unchallenged by most experts.

Peter Underwood related a case where a couple in love discovered that little blue lights appeared and sparks and articles moved in their bedroom when they reached the climax in their love-making. Some years ago a general practitioner who had spent many years in India told a Ghost Club audience how he had been called to a house which had a quadrangle in the centre, open to the sky—a familiar enough arrangement in the East, and especially in the Madras area. Here frequent showers of stones occurred, a veritable hail rattling down upon this open area. Nothing could be seen from the outside but the showers of stones had been observed inside from many positions. The open space was used for drying purposes and occasionally when the clothes were put out they would ignite all along the line. After he had made careful enquiries throughout the household, the doctor found one girl about the age of puberty who was suffering from unnatural suspension of the menstrual functions. The girl was removed from the house and the phenomena ceased—but where-ever she went the same poltergeist happenings followed her. She was then medically treated and while in a healthy condition, nothing unusual happened. Eventually she was cured. The doctor believed that psychic forces could be stored up in girls around the age of puberty and he related another case in Devon where similar phenomena took place in similar conditions. There is, indeed, voluminous evidence available by now pointing to such an unmistakable correlation between sex and psychic phenomena.

We raised the question of the connection between masturbation and poltergeist phenomena. (By the way, poltergeists appear to be immortal—while many *types* of phenomena seemed to have faded out, have become extremely scarce in recent years, these baffling outbreaks continue to be reported from the four corners of the world.) Underwood recalled a case where a number of adolescent girls, unhappy in their isolated surroundings, became absorbed with masturbation and poltergeist-like phenomena took place : footsteps, door-openings, objects flying about without human agency. When the circumstances changed and the girls became happy and ceased excessive masturbation, the unexplained psychic happenings stopped. Pent-up energy thus seems to be used in a psychic way. As to the explanation of such extraordinary events, one possible theory put forward was that masturbation could be described as a release of pent-up energy and it was possible that some poltergeist phenomena were a direct result of such a release.

By and large, deprivation of love (physical and mental) could also lead to so-called psychic phenomena. If we accepted the psychological truth that love was the basic necessity for a happy man or woman or child, privation of love naturally caused unhappiness. This, in turn, resulted in anxiety and conflicting tensions in the nervous system which, in turn, could lead to both masturbation and subsequently, psychic phenomena. Unhappiness could also cause frustration and there was overwhelming evidence that frustration could lead to so-called spontaneous psychic phenomena. A good example of this was the number of ghostly nuns and monks—whose way of life often led to sexual frustration. No one could deny that there was more than just sexuality in psychic phenomena but a distinct relationship did exist on occasions; certainly not always but perhaps more often than the layman suspected.

The problem of sex was, of course, by no means solved with death. Much had been written and arguments still raged about the somewhat academic question whether male and female ghosts *did* have sexual relations—in spite of the adage about there being no giving or taking in marriage in Heaven. Swedenborg, the Swedish mystic whose voluminous writings about heaven and hell form the basis of a still flourishing Protestant sect, is accepted as the "great authority" on this subject. His major argument with his own established church was that he claimed—in all earnestness and with a peculiar intensity—that sex was one of the preoccupations of the spirits. Actually, Spiritualists range all the way from the Swedenborgian view to the opposite extreme. Some spiritualists might say : "Of course, it depends at which level you arrive after death." In this respect, as in so many others connected with occultism, we're dealing with a tremendous range of opinion—nor does it appear to be narrowing as the years go by. But on the whole a fair proportion of spiritualists believe that there is love and sexual intercourse on the "astral plane". Speaking of such a "plane" or "level" indicates a belief in all human beings possessing more than one body. According to this theory when we vacate our ordinary body, our other bodies survive, still substantial but more tenuous—and at the early stages of spiritual life, are still quasi-physical. Obviously in this intermediary stage there is more likely to be sexual desire and activity than later when the "flesh becomes all spirit".

Peter Underwood and other specialists have claimed that sexual activity can release not only sexual tensions but also the non-sexual psychic tensions which prevent the occurrence of spontaneous psychic phenomena. One case which Underwood investigated in the sixties was one in which a frustrated and unhappy young woman lived alone for some years simply existing from day to day without hope, and without any psychic occurrences. Then she met someone and they fell in love and in the midst of the great outpouring of their love and happiness, psychic happenings did take place. Thus normal healthy sex appears to be able to promote psychic phenomena, though this is, of course, only one theory to account for hauntings or poltergeist happenings. In other cases the circumstances do not fit into the framework of a preconceived theory. "So we revise the theory," Underwood explained, "and then we come across another case which does not fit the revised theory! What we can say is, without any shadow of doubt, sexuality is very much concerned with psychic phenomena, both induced and spontaneous."

"Spiritual love" and "normal love" are conceived to be different things—though such a differentiation depends in what dimension one is supposed to be in. When the spiritualists speak of an astral body, they consider that it has passed from one plane to another—and therefore one's love life has undergone certain changes. Presumably there are a very large number of possible expressions of love—and these include, perforce, the physical and non-physical in the occult sense.

Another interesting fact linked by occultism and sex is that many women become clairvoyants at the time of their menopause. Researchers have found time and again that sexual change or sexual shock are associated with the beginning or the cessation of spontaneous or mediumistic phenomena. It is known that women are more sexually inclined at certain times of the month, often during the pre- and post-menstrual weeks and in some cases of haunting it has been found that the reported psychic phenomena reached their height at those times. In the case of the menopause it is quite likely that the physical and psychological change has a direct bearing on the woman's potential powers of clairvoyance. Medical science, incidentally, has discovered that there are rhythmic contractions which occur every eight or ten minutes inside a woman's body throughout the whole of her child-bearing period. In women past the menopause these contractions are absent. It may be that the onset of this function, at adolescence, is the reason for many poltergeist phenomena associated with girls as they become women. It is quite likely that at the menopause the physical change has a link with the psychical phenomena—or the absence of them. But there is a great deal of work to be done about this whole problem—medical and psychic—before definite conclusions can be drawn.

Mrs. Black added: "If I were forced to theorise, I think I would be more general. Supposing it were true, that there is a tendency for the increase of clairvoyance during and after the menopause. I would try to put it into the same category as clairvoyance as a result of people being knocked on the head, and of the 'phantom limbs' as the result of losing an arm or a leg; in other words, I would be inclined to look on it as a compensatory phenomenon in a very wide context. Supposing one regards different functions, different parts of the body, as in some sense fulfilling the needs of an organism as a whole. If you frustrate, if you stop, if you injure the body at any point, there may always be a psychic compensation, or perhaps occasionally there could be a real break-through compensaton."

Sex also may have a definite connection with the fact that there were far fewer physical mediums than about thirty or forty years ago—though this is a question which is being discussed at greater detail in our next chapter. Peter Underwood suggested that the greater freedom, the wider permissiveness of the fifties and sixties in the field of sexuality may be the cause of less frustration—and it is quite possible that this may have some connection with the lack of physical mediumship. At least there are two undeniable facts here—a more tolerant view of all types of sexuality and a definite scarcity of good physical mediums. Certainly if one assumed that some aspects of psychic phenomena are the results of sexual frustration, then obviously if there is less frustration, there must be fewer psychical phenomena. It's a matter of the source of supply, of cause and effect. It is not something which can be expressed in statistical terms because there are no reliable statistics at any given moment—one cannot say that there were X number of physical mediums in the world in 1930 and today there are so many less.

Once one accepts the distinct correlation between conscious and unconscious sexual motives and so-called "spontaneous" psychic phenomena, there are certain conclusions to be drawn though most of them must be qualified. The only unqualified one, after some twenty years' of special research, is the certainty of connection. Of course it would be quite wrong to say that sexuality explained all psychic phenomena but it does explain some hauntings and it is certainly associated with many polter-geist phenomena. And the force used in mediumship appears to have a very close relationship with the sexual force. Some male mediums have a sexual climax at the height of their psychic performances—without any physical stimulation. Many female mediums have genital disturbances. Some mediums are incapable of producing any form of psychic phenomena *after* having sexual intercourse, much as athletes or football players will perform much less satisfactorily if they have sex before a race or a game. The forces of mediumship and sex are definitely related to one another though the nature and the intensity of this relationship still have to be fully explored. Perhaps we would need a psychical Kinsey Report.

There are certain sexual elements in telepathy where two people who are in general rapport—such as husband and wife—are more likely to be able to communicate; though there is no suggestion that the telepathic one is necessarily a heterosexual relationship. Identical twins, for instance, probably have a stronger claim to communication than a married couple though there is still insufficient material to come to definite conclusions about this.

Hypnotism, while no longer considered an occult phenomenon, still remains one of the techniques of psychical research—indeed, it was the principal technique used by the French psychiatrists such as Richet and Janet who were also interested in psychic phenomena. And a good many of them observed in the course of these experiments that there was between themselves as hypno-tists and their hysterical patients a rapport so powerful that they could apparently exercise some influence on the patients even when they weren't present. In the first instance, this was observed almost by accident. Some of the curious phenomena of hypnotism brought quite a number of nineteenth-century natural scientists and doctors into the field of psychical research—among them a number of Russians. Hypnosis in the first instance was very much part of the research techniques of psychical researchers. Origin-ally it was one of the phenomena that were not generally accepted—just as telepathy and clairvoyance are still struggling for full scientific recognition. When a famous surgeon did an amputation using hypnosis, while the patient sat there smiling happily, the sceptical doctors said : "He's shamming !" And while hypnosis has been proven as not belonging to the field of psychical phenomena, as a technique it has a special relation to psychical research. Unfortunately there are comparatively few competent hypnotists so psychical researchers have not been very successful in their attempts to design more sophisticated experiments.

And here the old chestnut of hypnotic seduction must be mentioned as another link between sex and psychical phenomena— or, in this case, psychic technique. Could a girl be seduced against her will while under hypnosis? The answer seems to be that it could not happen—she would wake up. However, there are experts who think that in twenty cases out of a hundred she may *not* wake up. This view is based largely on experimental evidence and there is still a great deal of argument going on about such experimental situations. Perhaps in such experimental hypnotic situation the subject really knows that the hypnotist is only "playing at it" and therefore refuses to comply with a command she knows the hypnotist does not really wish her to carry out. Experimental situations cannot be taken as necessarily duplicating situations in real life. So at least some experts claim that seduction under hypnosis—though "generally accepted that it cannot be done"—has, in fact, been achieved. However, there are obvious limits—and the idea that a person can be made to do "almost anything" under hypnosis is certainly erroneous, however many thrillers have been based on this premise. For instance, it is highly doubtful, whether someone can be made to commit murder— unless, of course, the intention or inclination is already within him. A classic case was that of the Krafft-Ebing experiment in which a young woman under hypnosis actually fired a gun at the famous psychiatrist—but before she did so, unconsciously removed the bullets. In other words, she obeyed the hypnotic command but she safeguarded herself against committing murder. There has to be some initial basis on which the hypnotist builds. That is why it is necessary to spend some time with a patient or subject. It cannot be done in a single session. What hypnosis can do is to remove certain inhibitions, release certain forces that pre-exist in a person's mind. But these forces cannot be *created* by hypnosis. Sexuality, of course, is part of everybody's make-up and it should be possible to release it, to remove the inhibitions. Unless the woman to be wooed is impossibly frigid, these forces within her may be released, the sexual elements in her psychological make-up can be brought to the surface. Hypnosis certainly can be used by psychologists and psychiatrists in treating patients so that they might be able to uncover sexual facts buried deep in the subconscious—and do this more effectively and quickly. Here sex and psychical technique are closely linked.

So much for the theory. What about practice?

We have referred before to the apparent scarcity of physical mediums—the men and women who, in the twenties and thirties, provided psychical researchers with some of the most spectacular phenomena of materialization, telekinetic and other "exploits".

Many experts incline today to the view that these unusual people possessed an extraordinary amount of what could be described (for want of a more precise expression) psychic energy. Mr. Underwood referred to this during our panel discussion and likened it to sexual energy or potency—though, of course, the two cannot be called identical. What appears to be fairly well-established, however, is the limited total of this psychic energy— as if it were a capital with which Nature endows a person. A capital sum which does not increase, yields no compound interest but is spent—slowly and quickly, according to its employment— until it is all gone. If this theory is accepted and applied, it will explain a good deal about the mystery of the so-called "mixed mediumships" which has plagued psychical researchers for many years and has caused innumerable feuds, quarrels and arguments among them. For as a medium feels his or her powers waning, the chances are that he or she will start to "help out", to fake and cheat. This may explain Eusepia Palladino's famous injunction to those who sat with her during her later years: "Watch out or I'll cheat!" It may even explain the still-debated case of Rudi Schneider who was accused by Harry Price of freeing one arm from the electric control at the very end of an extremely successful series of seances. Defended passionately by other researchers, Rudi's cause is still being championed or assailed some thirty-five years after the events. But whether Price was right or wrong in his accusations, certainly Rudi became less and less interested in mediumship—as he became more and more interested in his fiancée, a pretty girl whom he later married. If his sexual energies had found an outlet in his mediumship, they

were now directed towards a more universal and "natural" goal
—and who could blame him for it?

There have been similar cases where the waxing and waning
of mediumistic power could be clearly linked to sexuality. And
of course, there have been mediums in the sixties and long before
it who used sex to win adherents. At least one American medium
was notorious for making it a rule to sleep with the male
investigators, especially with those whose vigilant antagonism
she had good reason to fear. The result was an obvious lenience,
a relaxation of scientific detachment which inevitably benefited
the lady. She was a kind of Empress Catherine of the psychic
world and it took a very determined man to resist her seductive
charms—though these, too, faded as her reputation declined and
finally she was unmasked as a common fraud by some people
who obviously found truth more attractive than this remarkable
woman.

During our investigations of so-called physical mediums of the
sixties—who should be nameless just because they were all utterly
and completely disappointing—we came upon three obviously
hyper-sexed individuals who were using the obvious advantages
of the seance-room to indulge their propensities.

One was a lady of what the French call "a certain age" who
sported a handsome little moustache barely bleached by
hydrogen-hyperoxide. There were three sitters, all male, in a tight
little circle; the room was very dimly lit by a red-coated bulb
and she urged us to get "real matey" and sit as close to her as
possible because then "the influences would be strengthened".
She had not one "control" but three and their choice certainly
showed that she had studied erotic history—for the first one was
Messalina, the second Catherine the Great and the third someone she addressed rather familiarly as Cleo. (It became evident
that it wasn't Anthony's love but a latter-day sinner, Cleo de
Merode, one of the "great horizontals" of the Belle Epoque
whom she meant.) The medium—whom we might as well call
Madame Zara though that was neither her real nor professional
name—invited the three amorous ladies in turn to manifest
themselves. Not one of them did—perhaps they were otherwise
occupied—but the small, pasty-faced man who sat on her right,
suddenly started to emit the most peculiar noises, half-agonized
and half-pleasurable. We listened partly in alarm and partly in

envy, for a full three minutes as these noises became louder and louder, reached a crescendo and then died away. The medium remarked: "Ah, that must've been lovely, he must've met Cleo or maybe it was Messy, on the astral plane!" The little man said nothing about his experiences; he left before the lights went up so we couldn't tell what effect, if any, the extraordinary encounter had on him. Then the other man, a tall, beefy fellow began to giggle and grunt alternately. "Stop it!" he cried out suddenly. "Stop teasing me!"

"Who's teasing you?" asked the medium, her voice a little unsteady.

"I dunno," the man replied. "But it's too much, I tell you, lady, it's too much!"

He heaved himself to his feet and almost upset the table. The medium pulled at his coat tails and made him sit down again. "It's all right," she said. "I told her to go away. That was Catherine, of course. She's used to having her way. With men, I mean."

It was only a few minutes later that we felt a far from astral hand on our knee whose fingers started a kind of exploratory wriggle. We endured this for a while, in the interests of psychical research—but suddenly we pounced and grabbed the hand around the wrist. It was small and slippery and it managed to wiggle out of our reach. The medium spoke up indignantly at this point: "You were told not to grab, dearie! They don't like that—they don't like it at all!" We said that we were sorry but the spirits were getting too familiar and asked for the lights to be put on. The medium's face was flushed but that may have been due to her exertions to summon the three famous ladies from the Beyond. She collected the agreed fee and we left. The beefy gentleman stayed behind. No doubt he wanted another bout with Cleo, or maybe Messy?

The second medium, holding his seances in a spacious though somewhat shabby living room in South London, was a silver-haired and very dignified gentleman. Before the circle was formed—which, on this occasion, consisted entirely of women—he explained at length and with a great many rather eccentric technical terms (instead of "materialization" he talked of "flesh-becoming") that in order to manifest themselves, return to the cumbersome and clumsy world of the living, spirits had to draw

energy from those who summoned them—both the medium and
the sitters. This they achieved apparently in a number of ways—
through the astral equivalent of fingertips, the toes and the lips,
depending on whatever they found the most expeditious. He
therefore warned his sitters that they might experience such
touches and contacts. If any of them had an objection to such
things happening to her, he advised the person in question to
leave—the entrance fee would be promptly refunded. Though
one or two of the eight women present looked dubious, not one
of them budged, it was obvious that they were willing to make
sacrifices and, if need be, "nourish the spirits" so that the psychic
manifestations could take place.

The medium wore a kind of white robe or cloak which enve-
loped him completely. A broad silver belt spanned his still trim
waist. He waved his long, tapering fingers over the table and the
lights went out suddenly. Only two small phosphorescent plaques
glowed in the middle of the table.

"If you are being chosen as a source of spirit-food," he said,
"please try not to cry out. Just hum a note or tap your heel
against the chair. Sudden, loud noises will frighten our friends
away—and they are coming a long long way to visit us.'

Indeed it wasn't a cry or a scream that interrupted the seance.
It was a loud and unmistakable slap which sounded, loud and
clear, after about fifteen minutes had passed. The record-player,
discreetly muted, had supplied a spirited version of the *Liebes-
tod* and thus the slap was even more startling.

"Wha . . . what's happened?" we heard next the medium's
voice, startled out of its former sauvity.

"You know damn' well what happened, you beast!" an angry
female voice replied. "You and your spirit feeding! I don't mind
nourishing the entities—but *not from there*!"

This cryptic remark broke up the seance—though the medium,
now almost reduced to tears, protested that the young lady had
absolutely no cause for alarm, that whatever happened was a
"purely ethereal contact". As for himself, he was at least six
feet from her, hemmed in by the other sitters—she didn't really
think . . .?

She did and told him in no uncertain terms that he should
call himself lucky she did not go to the police and charge him
with indecent assault.

The third medium with whom we had a seance with such sexual undertones was also a woman but she was young and really pretty. We made the appointment by telephone and she explained that she only gave private sittings—either to single men or women or to a mixed couple but never more. Her fee was by far the highest ever quoted and her address a Mayfair one which probably explained the scale of her charges.

She received us in a highnecked, severely cut dress, her blonde hair brushed back from her forehead, her make-up discreet almost to the point of non-existence, her perfume "out of this world". She first collected the fee—in cash, please—and then offered us a drink. After which she came straight to the point.

"I'm a clairvoyant," she said, "and a very good one. You'll find out pretty soon. But I can only function *after* sex. It's up to you how you want it—singly or as a threesome. I don't mind. Afterwards I will demonstrate my powers. Any objections?"

We explained that we had neither moral nor professional objections but that we were gathering material for a book and therefore should not be classified as her ordinary "clients". Instead of testing her powers, would she mind answering a few questions? No, she said, if they were not too personal.

"Do you consider yourself a proper medium?"

"What else?"

"Not a prostitute?"

"Certainly not. I don't charge for sex—I charge for being a mental medium. But as sex is an integral part of my mediumship, I cannot draw a firm and rigid line between the two, can I?"

"And don't any of your clients abuse this—well, proximity?"

She looked quite shocked.

"Oh no. They are all interested in my clairvoyant powers. At least I hope so," she added with the hint of a smile.

She went on to explain that intercourse "recharged her psychic batteries". No, "auto-erotism", that is, masturbation would not do. It had to be, as she put it, "participatory sex" for the "recharging" to work properly.

We decided to take her word for it. She asked us to recommend her at least to "those genuinely interested in precognition" —and we left it at that.

When the panel discussed sex on the "astral plane", the love-relationships of the disembodied spirits that have "shuffled off the mortal coil", one member quoted the case which Harry Price had recorded (probably with tongue-in-cheek) about the young man who kept on receiving gifts from the other world. These were highly embarrassing and very personal—like a set of rather fancy male underwear, deposited in his lap while he was travelling in a crowded tube-train—and were apparently tokens of affection from a young lady who had died some years earlier and who, apparently, had conceived a mortal (or lethal) passion for the gentleman. This was the more inconvenient because the young man was engaged to be married. Price did not tell the end of the story so we do not know how long this peculiar haunting continued and in which manner it ended. In any case, it was something that the late Thorne Smith, the Rabelaisian creature of Topper and his ghostly friends might have thought up for a plot, or that would have fitted perfectly into one of the books of P. G. Wodehouse. But we came across a similar and, by all accounts, far from imaginary story in—of all places—Chicago where a young musician became involved in a series of far from pleasant incidents. At least they started innocently enough—flowers and small gifts would drop on him in the privacy of his apartment or when he was walking alone on the beach of Lake Michigan. He would find them in the pockets of his overcoat, tucked into his violin case (he was a junior member of the string section of the Chicago Symphony Orchestra), under his pillow. He was puzzled but neither alarmed nor displeased. Until one day a whole series of near-deadly accidents began. Someone was trying to kill him—though he had no idea who and why; and in most cases, after very narrow shaves, he could not trace any human presence, tangible agency behind these attempts. Truly alarmed now, and urged by his fiancée to whom he was forced to tell about his predicament, he went to a medium. During a long and exhausting seance he was told that a "girl-spirit" had fallen in love with him and was showing her affection both by the presents and by the determined tries at killing him—because she wanted to be "united with him in the spirit". Apparently the girl—who had died of an overdose of drugs—had fallen in love with him while she was still alive and lived in the same apartment house—though the young man never even noticed her. All this the medium, a lady of great earnestness and dignity, explained in detail—but she had no advice to offer as to what the young man should do. He considered resigning from his job and moving—but his fiancée pointed out that for a ghost changing her place of haunting should offer no difficulties. He tried to talk to the invisible presence, to argue and plead with her—all to no avail. And then—at least so the story was told—it all stopped suddenly. The young lady-ghost had apparently transferred her affections to a folksinger whom she found more to her liking. Three weeks after the violinist's troubles stopped, the singer was killed in a car accident which no one could explain—for he was a particularly careful driver, road conditions were excellent and there was no conceivable reason why his car should plunge from the expressway into the ravine below.

Si non è vero . . . But who could say that Swedenborg was wrong when he insisted that love and sex survived the death of the body and that the passions were stronger than the flesh? And if he was right, what could be more exquisite and delightful than the love-making of the spirits, unhampered by such things as gravity, metabolism and all the cumbersome ties and processes of our existence? And if there is a mutual, reciprocal influence of the material and spiritual world, the present permissiveness of our society, the break-down of sexual taboos and restrictions, must find its echo in the Great Beyond. If spirits have inhibitions, they should be loosening, too, with the new gospel of total sexual freedom being preached in most countries—if not yet totally transposed into practice.

The field where sex and the occult are almost inextricably interwoven, is that of black magic and witchcraft. Discussing these occult practices in the nineteen-sixties with a British journalist who made a long, special study of them, we were told that during his exhaustive investigation he found nothing supernatural—but he found plenty of sex!

The personification of occult sex, of satanism and the magic of evil, is at this date on trial for life, together with several members of what he called his "family" but what could be best described as his harem. Charles Manson's trial has become a six-ring circus as most trials involving colourful and strong personalities are apt to do in the news-hungry, neophiliac United States—and Manson's case became even more front-page-

featured when President Nixon himself indulged in his favourite
gymnastic exercise of putting his foot into his mouth. Manson,
the frustrated musician; Manson, the footloose wanderer; Manson, the hypnotic male whose women would do anything he
asked them, with the kind of utter submissiveness that was wholly
alien to the mainstream of America; Manson, the visionary;
and finally, Manson the maniac whose supreme test for his followers was butchery and mass-murder. What he promised them
was a kind of black paradise on earth, totally within the experience of the senses; and most of these promises were redeemed
through sex. He wrapped up his undisguised sadism into a good
deal of mystic talk, half-baked parable and lunatic precept.
Drugs were added to sex as another means of achieving the
"mystic union with Evil that is the Supreme Good". It is a
characteristic and odd fact that at the same time Manson dreamt
of financial success, of acclaim and material reward through his
music—which was utterly amateurish—and that the Sharon
Tate murders may very well have been due to the frustration
of these ambitions. But it is obvious that sex and drugs would
not have been sufficient if he had not invented and elaborated
an occult framework for them; a Manichean conception of Good
and Evil, complimentary and each unable to exist without the
other; a rehash of the ancient heresy that no one can be saved
unless he has first sinned which inspired so many sects throughout
history. As Craig Karpel put it in a discerning *Esquire* piece:

> The acid vision blends the illusory vector from good to evil into
> a circle.
>   M'Naghten's Rule, a courtroom test of sanity, does not
> enter into it. Acid heads know very well the difference between
> right and wrong: it is the same as the difference between up
> and down, in and out, clockwise and counter, a direction
> rather than a directive. That is why the leader of the Family
> that is up for offing Tate, Sebring, Folker, Frykowski and
> Parent could be called, interchangeably, God, Satan and Jesus
> by his zombies. There are few acid moralists. What is, is good;
> and what isn't, why that's groovy too.

Thus the occult has been linked to sex and drugs and both
have become fashionable—a trend and a fad within which evil
is being celebrated "with a flair for accoutrement and ceremony

that will be merchandized to all of us in time . . ." As Karpel points out: "Already the beautiful New York ladies of *Women's Wear Daily* are wearing diamond-crusted crucifixes to ward off the fiend." This is, of course, a far cry from the fumblings of the white-haired medium in South London or even the breezy sales-talk of the lady-clairvoyant in Park Lane.

The dominating element in this half-mystic, half-hippy com-bination, is of course LSD or acid—the hallucinogenic drug that can be made at home from readily available chemicals after the briefest study of its preparation and has a fantastic potency in minute quantities. It inevitably links the psychic experiences of a "trip" with sex—even though in most cases it is *sex-fantasy* rather than actual fornication for acid, like most other drugs, is only a very temporary aphrodisiac and actually reduces the *libido*; or rather, turns it *inward*. As a Los Angeles Bible sales-man told Tom Burke:

"If you sense an evil here, you are right, and I'll tell you what it is: too many people turned on to acid. If you make a habit of tripping—well, acid is so spiritual, so uh, metaphysical, that you are going to be forced into making a choice, between opting for good, staying on a goodness or Christian trip, and tripping with the Lord Satan. That's the whole heavy thing about too many people turned on to acid: to most of them, the devil just looks groovier. Acid is incredible—I've been on one hundred and seventy-two trips now—but it shouldn't be available to every-body and anybody . . . Acid does expand the mind. I believe in powers that you can't explain . . ."

Confused, uneducated, conceited (for he, of course, is one of the elect to whom LSD should be available, who can control his reactions), these few sentences are highly revealing. They are the verbal and simplified equivalent of the young man's action who, under the influence of LSD, stepped on a Hollywood freeway and tried to stop the traffic—because he firmly believed that he had the power to do so. Of course, he was reduced to a mangled heap of flesh within a minute or so. Or the young girl who, standing in the middle of a room in New York, on the twenty-seventh floor, suddenly exclaimed: "I can fly! I can fly!" and before anybody could stop her, vaulted over the win-dowsill and plunged to death on the pavement below. Acidheads, LSD addicts, are increasingly getting involved in occult practices

G

and cults—and many of them wear large gold crosses to ward off the very evil which they worship and court.

In America many of these addicts are sons and daughters of wealthy or even extremely rich parents who can indulge their various strange passions. You see them in California and in Florida, in Cape Cod and in Chicago, in New York and in Nevada; they are highly mobile. Their wealth has a high visibility even if its source is obscure.

One of the most striking and most outlandish characters in this constantly ebbing and flowing pageant is a woman who calls herself Princess Leda Amuh Ra, neatly combining Greek and Egyptian mythology, the daughter of Tyndaerus, King of Sparta and the mistress of Zeus who impregnated her in the shape of a swan and of the Sun God of the Nile. One of her hangouts is a huge and private nightclub on La Cienega Boulevard, within a short drive of the famous Sunset Strip. It is called, fittingly enough, the Climax. There the privileged members sprawl on velveteen divans while ancient horror films featuring vampires are projected on the ceiling; or jerking and quivering in front of a twenty-foot high Satan's head, its eyes daubed with luminous paint. All this is more than a little reminiscent of the two adjoining, now defunct nightclubs of Montmartre (near the Place Pigalle) called *Ciel* and *Enfer* which combined witty obscenity with broad blasphemy. Here, sometimes, Princess Leda appears —and she is certainly a good deal more authentic than the phoney erotic setting. Her body is covered with black feathers that appear to sprout from her dead-white skin; her bare breasts (magnificently firm) are little restrained with gold fishnet. She has ebony hair and huge, crazed eyes. As she dances, she seems to invoke the combined ghosts of Salome and Lilith, Cleo de Merode and all the sex-symbols of the past centuries, including our own.

The Acid Goddess, as Burke called her, has a male companion, a dashing young man who might be Mister Universe, dressed in red tights and top boots, his frilly shirt open to the waist, a sword in a scabbard on his lean hip. He is supposed to be an astrologist who charges a thousand dollars for a brief and perfunctory reading. He likes to be called the King just as she is merely known as the Princess. In a city where everybody is playing a part (in the hope that one day she or he might be called to do so in front of a camera) these two walk wrapped in mystery, an aura of decadent and yet powerful sexuality which is nourished by drugs and the occult. And Leda plays her part to the hilt, as Tom Burke's graphic description makes it only too clear, presenting the scene which he has been allowed to witness in the Princess's "castle" high above Hollywood:

". . . The boudoir, painted predominantly black, is large, but the bed is almost too large for it—wide as two Y.W.C.A. rooms side by side, canopied in black bombazine. In the bed, the Princess Leda Amun Ra, doe naked, her skin dusted with pumice, or volcanic ash. She lies on her back, her legs splayed. Her thighs are firm as a girl's. Between her thighs is a full-grown black swan, its neck arched like a cobra's, its yellow eyes fixed, amazed. It makes one harsh, comic noise, like an echo from a rain forest.

"'*I will conceive,*' the Princess shouts, heaving joyously. Half a dozen people have come into the room by now. No one else makes a sound. No one laughs; no one even smiles."

Occultism and sex also merge in the various varities of Satan worship and witchcraft; and these have not only endured into the sixties but seem to be developing and spreading. Much of it is just slightly ridiculous and childish pretense, self-conscious and deliberate "naughtiness". Others are much more intense and much more dangerous. Like the Hollywood party where guests were received at the door with a welcoming drink—a bit of acid and a pinch of strychnine mixed in tomato juice which at least had the colour of blood. They had to empty the cup before they were admitted—for everybody had to be "tripping". Inside three altars were set up; two of them had young, nude boys tied to them with wide leather belts, being whipped by two bearded men dressed in *nun's* habits, looking more than a little incongruous but very determined. For whips they were using heavy black rosaries—and there was no make-believe about the flogging for both boys were screaming and weeping. The middle altar held a girl, barely in her teens, with her arms and legs spreadeagled. A tall man wearing a goat's head was crushing a live frog on her sex and then started to carve a small cross on her naked stomach—just a shallow, superficial cut. Later the party became both wilder and more ritualistic: the young girl was deflowered in a long and elaborately blasphemous procedure and then proceeded to retaliate on the goat-headed chief satanist with the help of a plastic dildo; this was followed by a kind of rock concert with songs whose lyrics were childishly yet persistently sacrilegious and it all ended with the declamation of a visionary creed by the "Anti-Christ" which could only shock those who hadn't read the late nineteenth-century decadents and Satanists.

The Anti-Christ is also a leading character in "the Art of Evil" which neatly links sex and the occult. Its practitioners—some of them not without talent—believe that the Second Coming has already taken place but instead of Jesus it is the False Messiah that has returned. (And here they go back to the legend of Zwi Sabatai, the Jewish False Messiah who was both a historical and legendary figure and played a decisive role in the diaspora's philosophical and religious development.) It is both amusing and characteristic that this reincarnated Satan was supposed to have chosen Hollywood Hills for his headquarters whence he was supposed to have spread his tentacles throughout the world. He is served, so some of his believers claim, by an international organization called the Devilmen who have admitted Satan into their bodies and souls and work for him. (This time a leaf is taken from the book propagating the totally fictional existence of the Elders of Zion, the anti-Bible of the Nazis and anti-Semites; a fabrication that has survived a dozen total proofs of its complete phoniness.) This organization or league is supposed to have become a secret World Power whose members hold key positions in all major governments. But there is still hope for the forces of Virtue and Goodness; the Cross will triumph over vampires and devils.

It would not be America if all this, the close relationship of the drug-achieved psychic experience and sex did not have its elaborate and profitable commercial side. Indeed, the three elements: hallucinogens, witchcraft (whether based on black or white magic) and sex in its most permissive, least inhibited forms, fuse into big business. Whether your special interest is reincarnation, numerology, the Cabala, astrology or karmic law, it is all catered for by scores of shops and hundreds of merchandize items. Crucifixes are sold to the "straight believers" and upside-down crosses to the Satanists. Zodiacal signs are brought by all and sundry; so are voodoo candles and love charms, amulets and incense. Today there are, according to a specialist, well over a thousand bookshops in Western Europe and the United States that specialize in occult literature and in America alone their sales have tripled over the recent years. The owner of the Magical Mystery Museum in Los Angeles who calls himself Arch-Druid Morloch, Bishop F.A.M. (Family of the Ancient Mind) is proud of his large collection of "witchcraft items" and never lacks students at his "college" which offers no less than thirty courses in the occult. He believes that "the public wants to know more about the occult but will only be attracted by the spectacular". Certainly the goods on sale in some of the shops fulfil this requirement—from the carved devil's rosary, versions of the Egyptian ankh (symbol of life and fertility), to the all-seeing eyes, focusing spiritual aspirations; from satanic crosses, usually worn next to the skin; to Lucifer charms used in "summoning the lower sexual spirits". The Minotaur is a particularly popular "love-sex-and-lust" charm and is often combined with a white disc, the replica of the seal of Solomon, representing the highest magical powers of the Cabala. And so it goes, with prices ranging from a few shillings to several hundred dollars. Add to it the various long playing records devoted to the same subject of which the Rolling Stones' recent *Witchcraft* is proclaimed on the sleeve as guaranteed to "destroy minds and reap souls . . ." The same shop that will sell you an ouija board or an "incantatory instrument" will also provide a mojo-bag love charm consisting of "love powder", pure mercury, "Lucky John, the Conqueror, a root" and "love oil". Truly, whether in New York or in London, in Paris or in Franfurt; you are never too far from your "friendly neighbourhood purveyor" of occultism and sex.

The Future of Psychical Research

In such a vast field as occultism trends develop slowly; contradictory or parallel directions are difficult if not impossible to establish. In our previous chapters we have seen how faith healers proliferate—perhaps because even orthodox medicine is beginning to recognize the importance of the psychological element in most if not all illnesses—and psychic surgeons, though mostly working underground, are gaining credence and followers. We have also seen that while there are still die-hards denying the existence of telepathy and clairvoyance, more and more scientists are inclined to accept them as facts while, of course, denying that they have anything to do with survival after death or physical phenomena. Reincarnation appears to exercise a powerful fascination over millions of people who have lost their faith in science— or, to put it in another way, in the beneficial effects of scientific progress. The ancient wishdream of rebirth in another body, but retaining at least some of the memories and knowledge of previous existences, shows no signs of fading. And we have shown how the age-old link between occultism and sex has become enormously expanded through the cult of drugs and the commercialization of psychedelic experiences and gadgets.

There are, of course, other aspects of this huge subject which deserve close attention but we hope to deal with these in other books. While we have presented some non-physical mediums, a systematic survey of "psychics" throughout the world still remains to be undertaken. Not long ago a British magazine offered a prize of £25,000—for anybody willing to undergo tests under rigorous conditions in various psychic disciplines. Almost four hundred applications arrived and, while the sifting and testing of the claims is bound to take a long time, it is obvious that there is no dearth of men and women who believe themselves to be possessors of supranormal powers and talents. Dowsing appears to have been largely removed from the area of the occult by the development of a dowsing machine which is also in the process of being investigated but of which there are highly promising preliminary reports. Poltergeist cases are still being reported in the daily and specialist press from all over the world. And, as we have seen in various connotations, the occult is still "big business" —growing by leaps and bounds and not likely to diminish as long as people seek certainty about the future and refuse to accept the finality of death.

In order to gather some "educated guesses", we have talked to some veteran psychical researchers and asked their opinions about present and future trends, about discernible and hermetic changes in techniques, attitudes and approaches.

Our first subject was Mrs. K. M. Goldney, a Vice-President of the Society for Psychical Research who has spent some forty years active in the various branches of psychical research and has been, for almost thirty, a Council Member of the Society. She has known many important mediums and has worked with other well-known psychical researchers. A lady of very firm opinions, great erudition and the saving grace of a well-developed sense of humour, she is not the one to mince words or gloss over unpleasant facts. At the same time one has the feeling that she still has the fresh eagerness of youth, anxious to be convinced of the genuineness of phenomena if the criteria are up to her high standards—still hoping to find new experiences, new openings. A veteran, too, of many battles that seem to be an intergral part of psychical research, she has managed to keep her objectivity and detachment in difficult situations and often violently controversial arguments.

"Have there been any significant changes in the general trends of psychical research during your long experience?" we asked.

"Yes. There has been a considerable change. When my husband and I retired from India in 1930, Harry Price was running his independent laboratory, and he investigated a whole succession of mediums of all types. There seemed to be no difficulty in obtaining interesting mediums for investigation; whereas now, and for a long time, it has been impossible to get, or even hear of a worth-while physical medium. I have enquired at Spiritualist societies and have spoken to a good many individual Spiritualists about this, and even in the case of mental mediums they have all told me 'No, Mrs Goldney, there is nobody whom the SPR would consider a really first-class mental medium for research purposes. We have nobody who could compare with Mrs Piper or Mrs Osborne Leonard. We have a staff of good second-class mediums but not a single "Mrs Piper" or "Mrs Leonard".' And if one asks about a physical medium—well, they have apparently disappeared."

"Do you think this has something to do with recent or new legislation in connection with mediumship—or with people who profess to be mediums? In former times it was, on the whole, difficult to prosecute a fake medium—while more recently . . ."

"I don't think it has to do with legislation. Both the best-known Spiritualist societies in London—the *Spiritualist Alliance of Great Britain* and the *College of Psychic Science* (formerly the *London Spiritualist Alliance* and now changing its name once again to the *College of Psychic Studies*) maintain a staff of mediums. These mediums are giving clairvoyance demonstrations to groups of sitters several times a week—indeed, the SAGB holds several meetings each day. There is no shortage of mediums from that point of view (excepting physical mediums). But there is certainly difficulty when you approach them to discover whether there is even a single medium for research purposes. Mr Douglas Johnson has been a welcome exception. But in the past the only worth-while research in this country (incidentally producing the best evidence for Spiritualist claims), was by the *Society for Psychical Research*, working with well-known mediums for years on end."

"What other changes, if any, have taken place?"

"There is another very noticeable change. 'Healing' has come to the fore enormously. Very many striking cures are claimed and there is a need for serious research here by doctors who are also familiar with psychical research. But the rules of medical etiquette make it difficult to obtain the co-operation of doctors. On the other hand, healers do not always seem to realize the force of alternate valid hypotheses which are offered by spontaneous regression of symptoms and by the almost 'miraculous' cures effected by suggestion. Healers are bound to obtain 'cures'! After all, exactly the same kind of wonder cures are claimed by Roman Catholics (Lourdes and elsewhere), by the use of Suggestion (Coué and his disciples of the Nancy School), by Christian Scientists, and by Spirit Healers. From the research point of view that has to be taken very seriously into account. Still, there is definitely material crying out for research here."

"Do you think that it's a question of physical mediumship in particular, and the highest order of mental mediums, dying out and disappearing? or is it perhaps a more critical approach on the part of researchers that prevents them from coming forward?"

"There has always been a critical approach so far as the SPR is concerned and yet, as I said, the best mediums have collaborated with us for years on end in the past. Whether the *Zeitgeist* is not conducive to psychical phenomena, or whether some sort of fear of having their diminished powers put to the test is responsible, it is difficult to say. One can only note that mediums for research purposes were readily available in the past, and now are not; and that is so in spite of the fact that many researchers want nothing more than to see the phenomena established."

"Is this restricted to England or is this a global situation?"

"So far as physical and really first-class mental mediums are concerned, my enquiries when I have been in America and in Europe have shown the same pattern. There is a great deal of activity in America, but of a different type altogether : poltergeist cases are investigated as occasion offers, but mostly research is on laboratory lines with subjects not claiming pronounced psychical gifts."

"Has the type of psychical researcher changed? Are other sorts of people attracted to this field? Or is it the same type of person that was engaged in this field, say thirty years ago?"

"Speaking for the SPR again, there are careful investigators of the same kind as in the past. But I think they are not prepared to waste their time investigating what is palpably rubbish or with mediums unwilling to co-operate adequately. If there was a possibility of serious research with a worth-while medium, I am sure there would be eager researchers! But such investigations as have taken place in recent years have been disheartening. But there is more to be said here. Simpler investigations of the pioneer type of the past, are of little use today. One needs statistical evaluation and those competent to carry it out; computers and the facilities only readily available in university circles. No doubt a certain amount of preliminary work could be carried out in private premises, but if we are to get any worth-while results in the future, it will demand highly trained university

194 *Beyond the Senses*

personnel. And this means adequate funds, which are hard to come by for this subject! America is much luckier than Britain in this respect. But even so, with all their activity, there are no startling results over there—no Mrs Pipers, no Basil Shackletons!"

(Basil Shackleton was the subject whom Dr Soal and Mrs Goldney investigated in 1941–1943, and who proved to possess remarkable telepathic powers. See p 50 proceedings, Vol 47, *Experiments in Precognitive Telepathy*. By S. G. Soal and K. M. Goldney).

"But do you think there is really a valid explanation why a physical medium like Rudi Schneider does not exist today?"

"I don't think there is a 'valid explanation' for this fact. You can put forward the theory, as I said, that we have today more sophisticated methods of investigation such as the infra-red viewer for seeing in darkness, and dubious physical mediums obviously would not wish to expose themselves to that! Or it may be an unexplained factor in the 'Zeitgeist', since the decline is in both mental and physical mediumship. I don't think the infra-red viewer would have been a hindrance to Rudi Schneider. I never knew him object to any form of control—he never seemed to ask, or want to understand, what control was to be used. I attended a fair number of sittings with him, both in Harry Price's laboratory and in his own home in Braunau, and I think most people who sat with him a large number of times considered his physical mediumship was genuine. Lord Rayleigh's Presidential Address (SPR Proceedings, vol. 45) on *The Problem of Physical Phenomena in connection with Psychical Research*, discussed the experiments Drs Eugene and Marcel Osty had carried out with Rudi in France and described their work as 'one of the most valuable contributions ever made to our subject', and he was obviously impressed with Rudi Schneider's possession of apparently paranormal powers."

"What about Stella C.? She, too, was most co-operative when she worked with Price, wasn't she?"

"Yes, but that was in the 1920's. If we could produce another Rudi, or another Stella C. now, we would all be delighted. But I did not know Stella C. Her work with Harry Price took place while I was in India."

"So it isn't impossible that within the next 10 years, say, somebody of the stature of Rudi Schneider or Stella C. might be discovered?"

"Not impossible, of course. But I should think the odds were definitely against it."

We told Mrs. Goldney that we have followed Dr. Gaither Pratt's work with Pavel Stepanek in connection with clairvoyance, precognition and other allied fields; wasn't there a falling-off of his psychic powers after a certain period?

"Pavel Stepanek has certainly been a bright spot in the experimental stage in recent years. He works in Prague and his experiments were originally carried out under Dr. Milan Ryzl, who now lives in the USA. Dr. Gaither Pratt (University of Virginia, USA) has made several visits to Prague to continue experiments with Stepanek there, and not long ago Stepanek went over to America and worked with Dr. Pratt and others at the University of Virginia. He has never produced such spectacular high scores as Shackleton did, but what is outstanding in Stepanek's case is that his telepathic ability has continued over a longer period of time than did Shackleton's—indeed, he holds the record in this respect in laboratory tests. Further, he has been able to score positively not only with the investigator to whom he is accustomed, but with a succession of visiting investigators—a very great advantage from the research point of view. Visiting investigators have been welcomed by him in Prague from several countries, including Britain: Dr. Beloff from Edinburgh University and an SPR Council member, has been one of them. As you say, there have been ups and downs in his successful scoring and periods of negative results. But experiments with him in America in 1968 have shown very curious and interesting patterns in his 'focusing effect' on targets and we must all hope that he will maintain his ability through further years of research."

"Do you feel that during the last twenty or thirty years psychical research has achieved a certain measure of academic recognition—which seemed almost impossible in the twenties or thirties?"

"I don't know that I would put the question quite in that way. If you examine the list of SPR Presidents since the Society was founded in 1882, you will see a large number of scientists of the highest rank. Both our present President, Professor Rushton, and the last President, Sir Alister Hardy, are Fellows of the Royal

Society, and there have been several earlier Presidents with this highest of scientific achievement and honour. The subject is a complex one and cannot be judged in a cursory examination; for that reason many scientists have been unable to devote the time to examine our material adequately. Some have done so and formed an adverse opinion. I can't say I blame them! The whole situation is so puzzling that, had I not taken part myself in experiments with Shackleton on the one hand, and Rudi Schneider, the physical medium, I think it likely I would incline to an adverse opinion myself! And here I would like to add something about which I feel strongly. Psychical Researchers use the same material as do Spiritualist societies. But it is natural that the latter attract the best mediums there are to their staffs. Yet one can search their Journals over years in vain for any reports worth the reading. The outstanding opportunities they have had for furthering our knowledge in this subject have been wasted; and their pages are filled with merely anecdotal material or essays and poems! What a waste of opportunity! I suppose psychical researchers have many sins to answer for too; but that would seem to be a big one for them to answer for! Yet the situation here is worse than that. Some years ago two anonymous S.P.R. donors offered £1,000 for a genuine psychic phenomenon in physical mediumship. Not only was it not claimed, but prominent Spiritualists warned mediums not to apply for it. (Maybe they were wise: the Spiritualist scene showed only probable frauds in that domain). But at the present time a £25,000 prize has been offered by a popular magazine for anyone producing genuine psychic phenomena of one kind or another to the satisfaction of an investigating body, which includes several SPR Council members. This is a very large sum of money, and if mediums feel they don't like to compete for money prizes, there is no obligation on them to claim the award even if they satisfy the judges. On the other hand there is more than one Spiritualist project in dire financial straits to whom such a sum, if handed over, would about save their lives. Yet recently it was advertised that a 'Direct Voice' medium (I won't mention his name) had given demonstrations of Direct Voice phenomena which had been taken down on a tape recorder *every week for seventeen years.* Yet when this medium was approached by an SPR Council member, and specifically urged to apply for the prize, and demonstrate the validity of his claims, he refused. I myself telephoned the editor of *Psychic News* (the most widely read Spiritualist journal) and begged him to use his influence with this medium to make good his claims. The editor also refused to do this. Can one be surprised that many people form an adverse opinion of the whole subject when such claims are openly made and yet the opportunity to demonstrate the *bona fides* of those claiming these powers is wilfully refused.

"It is a sickening situation for those of us who long for the subject to be furthered and accepted in the scientific world. Both psychical researchers and Spiritualists have surely a *duty* in the matter. You may remember, Dr. Tabori, what Myers wrote when he was discussing D. D. Home's phenomena : "Such phenomena as those under discussion belonged properly neither to Home himself nor to his sitters, but to science as trustee for mankind." (SPR Journal, vol. 4, p. 252). Binding words—"as trustee for mankind". But turning to America, a notable event has been achieved there in the past year : the Parapsychological Association, of which I and several other SPR people are members, was accepted as an affiliate of the *American Association for the Advancement of Science*."

"You travel a great deal and have visited Russia, we believe. Do you know anything about recent work in this field in the Soviet Union?"

"Yes, I have been to Russia twice in the last year or two. But each time I went with an organization unconnected with psychical research and with a very full programme. So I had no time to make any contacts. Naturally I keep abreast in my reading of reports of what is occurring in the USSR. But three delegates from the SPR attended a psychical research conference in Moscow a couple of years ago. Unfortunately the arrangements went badly astray, and those interested in this subject in Russia cannot have an easy time. There have been excellent surveys of the situation in the USSR : see for instance Dr. Milan Ryzl's long paper in the inaugural issue of the American magazine *Psychic* (June/July 1969) entitled *ESP in Eastern Europe and Russia*; and Nikolai Khokhlov's paper entitled *The Relationship of Parapsychology to Communism*, in *Parapsychology Today*, Vol. 1, 1968 (edited by J. B. Rhine and Robert Brier, New York)."

"Were they not experimenting with hyperaesthesia—seeing

through the skin, and various similar physiological and psychological approaches? But when one of us made an attempt to visit the appropriate institute in Moscow in 1965, he met with a very frosty reception. Do you think that if any work is going on, it's more or less conducted 'under wraps'?"

"That's quite probable I would conjecture. But even when it is openly conducted, the authorities swerve from approval to disapproval it would seem. I remember when Russian scientists were quoted as deriding parapsychology as 'the interest of a decadent bourgeoisie'! Then some article in an American magazine led them to believe, apparently, that the Americans might be on to something useful through telepathic communication in the military or space-travel fields! Great activity then ensued in various Russian universities. You remember Professor Vasiliev's book *Experiments in Mental Suggestion* was translated into English and published by Mr. and Mrs. Gregory's *Institute for the Study of Mental Images* (1963). It is extremely difficult to get a coherent account of what is happening in Russia, and there would appear, as I say, to be alternating swings of official approval and disapproval."

"What about Europe? France and Germany in particular."

"Well, the Parapsychological Association held its 1968 Annual Convention at Freiburg University. Dr. Bender of that University was host to the P.A. for the occasion and the arrangements were first-class. There was a very large attendance of delegates from various countries. I attended, together with other members of the SPR. Summaries of the many papers read were published and it provided a splendid opportunity for American and European researchers to meet and discuss their work together. The investigation of some extremely interesting poltergeist cases was reported——"

"Which happened in Germany and were fairly recent?"

"Yes. One was in Rosenheim (Germany) in 1967, another in Bremen. Both cases seemed very remarkable and full of interest. But as usual the investigators were not able to continue the investigation as long as they would have liked to do."

"What about France?"

"I myself am out of touch with the French work. But one of our SPR Council members, Renée Tickell, has recently visited France and had discussions with workers at the Institut Metapsychique. And although not exactly 'France' in the sense you mean, Mrs. Garrett has come from New York to her European centre on the French Riviera and has held annual conferences there with delegates attending from all parts, and this has been of immense benefit to workers in different fields who met each other there. Alas, immediately after the Conference held in September we got the sad news of Mrs. Garrett's death."

"What do you think of Rosemary Brown?—the lady who composes music inspired, she says, by dead geniuses such as Beethoven, Liszt, etc., who use her as their physical agent."

"That is a matter for musical experts to pronounce upon, and I see there is much difference of opinion among them on this point. So I don't think it a matter primarily for psychical adjudication. But she is not the first in the field! Recently an SPR Council member, Brigadier Spedding, turned up a description in the *Annals of Psychical Science of* 1906 describing similar claims in France by a M. Aubert, who produced musical compositions in the 'style' of dead composers, claiming he was inspired by them. When the Oscar Wilde scripts were produced by automatists, I think most psychical researchers felt that imitation of a well-known author with a distinctive style did not demand a psychical explanation. If this were so in the literary field, I do not see why it should not apply in the musical field. All depends on how ignorant Rosemary Brown is, and has always been, of musical knowledge. People who can 'play by ear' without being able to read music—seem 'miraculous' to me!—but it is not 'miraculous' in fact."*

"You have probably heard that in the United States the mass interest has become especially pronounced among young people who have turned against rationalism, materialism—all that they consider part of the Establishment. It is almost a political attitude, this preoccupation with the occult and psychical. Have you followed this development?"

"I have read about it, certainly. But what is the use of such groups to this subject? I suppose people who have worked as long as I have in this field don't set much store by people who haven't troubled to read up the subject properly. They say 'I think' and 'I believe' with great emphasis, until you have to ask

* See Rosemary Brown's *Unfinished Symphonies: Voices from the Beyond* (Souvenir Press, London)

them what work they have done, what they have read of others'
work, to justify their 'beliefs'. The answer is usually a lemon—
in slang parlance. They think so just because they think so. I
can't imagine that the groups you speak of in America could
contribute anything to parapsychology. As you say, it is some
sort of political or psychological attitude on their part and they
don't appear to be groups from which one can expect much help
of a practical sort! On the other hand, occasionally I have come
across really keen youngsters who are reading and questioning as
much as they can, and one wishes there were more of that sort."

"We didn't mean to suggest that young people today are
particularly interested in serious psychical research. What seems
to happen is that they are turning in increasing numbers to the
occult, the supernatural, the irrational—as a form of revolt.
Because of course the irrational is the extreme opposite of the
Establishment, it does not demand any discpline, it does not
claim any authority. Thus we get the preoccupation with Satanism, with black magic, with drug-induced trances—which can
lead in extreme cases to such horrors as the Hollywood murders,
mass suicides and various destructive cults. Do you feel that this
is a significant trend?"

"I think it is a most unfortunate trend, though undeniably
it exists in a section of youth. Surely no sane person could do
other than deplore this trend? By their very appearance they
can hardly claim to be taken seriously. They look dirty, unkempt,
and as if they had taken the antimacassar from the sofa, cut a
hole in it and put their heads through for a garment. That hardly
seems to me the type of person who can be taken seriously. But
they don't, thank goodness, represent the average, though they
are the ones that make themselves conspicuous. I think, too, that
their many appearances on television foster this eccentricity and
pander to it. It is a great pity. Possibly, they have had freedom,
education, money—too quickly, in too short a time, without
gradually acquiring the self-control and discipline which should
go with these things!"

"Do you see a connection between psychic phenomena and
drugs?"

"Well, Aldous Huxley in his *Doors of Perception* seemed to
advocate taking LSD and even substituting it for cigarette smoking. He had himself luckily experienced pleasurable and

interesting results with his experimental LSD 'trip'. Presumably he had not realized that such drugs can have very different effects on different types of people; and medical reports would seem to establish the trend now is one that must be stopped, because of the dire effects it has on many youngsters. After all, when they do reach a parlous state and need medical and hospital treatment, the cost of this comes from the tax-paying public so it is very much our affair!"

"Then, as you see the immediate or even the more distant future of psychical research, do you think that it is going to settle down to a more sedate, statistical, large-scale academic approach rather than dealing with individual mediums?"

"Well, what I have already said indicates my views on that. There is a tremendous increase of interest in the subject and a lack of material to experiment with fruitfully. I think that the Spiritualist societies, and the Churches Fellowship for Psychical and Spiritual Studies—both such organizations will, I think, continue to flourish, particularly the CFPSS which has had a quite phenomenal growth and support from Bishops since it was founded in 1954. But as regards serious research in experimental parapsychology, it will be a question of whether there are the necessary funds forthcoming to finance a worker at a University. The Hon. Secretary of the SPR, John Cutten, has recently started a fund for this purpose. It is a small beginning but it *is* a beginning; and if only a good subject would present himself for experimentation, one might well look for a hopeful future. But I confess that the situation in Britain since the war has not led me to optimism."

Mrs. Goldney ended on a rather pessimistic note; Peter Underwood, President of the Ghost Club (founded in 1862) for over ten years, was somewhat more sanguine. Underwood has conducted world-wide tests in telepathy and extra-sensory perception, investigated scores of haunted houses, representing the "middle-ground" attitude between extreme scepticism and uncritical belief.

We asked him partly the same questions, beginning with his views on the main trends of psychical research in the fifties and sixties.

"These trends," Mr. Underwood replied, "have been, in my view, away from the search for proof of life after death and towards an understanding of the workings of the human mind. The thousands of reputable experiments conducted in America, and to a lesser extent in Britain, seek to discover whether or not there is some force or perception that can cause or 'see' things other than through the five senses; to the almost complete exclusion of the investigations for concrete proof of survival after death that absorbed so many researchers for so many years. Another trend in these two decades is the upsurge of faith-healing in Britain and 'spirit surgery' in South America. With the scarcity of other forms of psychical phenomena, the startling and spectacular 'spirit surgery' captured the imagination of the public and there are numerous alleged operations of a very puzzling nature that took place in varying conditions and in the presence of witnesses of varying responsibility and judgment. Unfortunately, as with physical mediums, there have been charges of fraudulence and deception which are all the more puzzling as most of the practitioners of this type of healing refuse direct payment. The increased interest in faith-healing in Britain is largely due to the efforts of one man, Harry Edwards, whose commendable work warrants praise and admiration—but it is extremely difficult to establish beyond reasonable doubt and to complete satisfaction that cures have taken place due to his or his assistants' ministrations."

Underwood also thought that the rarity or virtual disappearance of physical mediums might be partly due to the introduction of infra-red apparatus. But he added :

"Physical mediums work today almost exclusively in private home circles where controlled conditions are neither welcome nor practicable. But apart from the infra-red developments, other factors should be taken into consideration. It has been suggested that mediumship runs in cycles and that we are at present in the middle of a mental mediumship-cycle but that physical mediumship will return in due course; it has also been suggested that physical mediumship in itself is of a low order, an inferior level and that we have now progressed to a higher form of mediumship, the mental form. And if there is anything in the correlation between sex and mediumship, it may well be that the sensible and open present-day attitude towards sexual matters prevents frustration and the 'bottling-up' that could have been conducive to physical mediumship some years ago and especially during the Victorian era when physical mediumship was at its height."

"Do you think that this is also the reason for the general emphasis on faith-healing?"

"Not entirely. I think this emphasis on faith-healing and 'spirit surgery' is partly because of its spectacular presentation and apparent successful results. Whether it is the case of a South American swilling whisky before an 'operation' or chain-smoking while he is performing it or whether it is in the seemingly clinical surroundings of some of the healing 'sanctuaries', there is an indisputable appeal to the emotional and the unknown which attracts great masses of people. The old seance-room phenomena were limited to those who obtained entry to the circle; a visit to a professional clairvoyant is often fraught with anxiety as to whether the 'mystic' will really perceive the innermost depths of one's being and discover what is often not very praiseworthy or noble; but in faith-healing and 'spirit surgery' considerable attention is focused upon the individual as a patient and most frequently it is within the individual's authority to declare whether he has been relieved or cured. With the increasing and continuing rejection of organized religion throughout the world, faith-healing tends to fill a void in many people's lives, where reliance on someone other than themselves, a practical demonstration of some outside power, beyond their fellow-men and the requisite devout concentration—and perhaps, gratitude—are all fulfilled."

"What about the passionate interest of to-day's youth in the irrational and therefore the occult?"

"I would hesitate—unlike some of my contemporaries—to try and give reasons for the actions of to-day's youth who, incidentally, are better informed, more self-reliant and independent and certainly more open-minded and enquiring than the youth of any previous generation. Their tremendous interest in the occult is probably one more indication of their refusal to accept anything without trying to find out the why and the wherefore; surely a worthy and commendable approach. In their search for a meaning to life when religion is more and more rejected, they experiment with drugs, with mysticism, with way-out dress, with sex and with the world of the occult and psychical research which is the study of the mind; and the mystery of mind is at the root of all these matters."

We asked Peter Underwood whether he agreed that the centre of psychical research had shifted from Europe today?

"There is certainly more intensive and very important work on psychical research being done in America to-day," he replied, "than anywhere else in the world but in the solid examination and qualitative study of *all* aspects of the subject Britain still probably leads. These islands have far more reported ghosts and haunted houses than any other country and whether this is the result of our Celtic blood, our island isolation (in mind as well as in body) or simply that we are more credulous—or more psychic—is a fascinating subject for study in itself! The serious study of psychical phenomena began in England with the foundation of the Ghost Club in 1862 and the Society for Psychical Research twenty years later and if we are not the centre of psychical research to-day (and it may well be that we are) we certainly have the people for this tremendously important subject—though perhaps we do not have the money nor the facilities that our American cousins seem to find always for their activities. I have noticed that psychical researchers in other countries have sometimes pronounced judgments and declared final results of their experiments which, on reflection, have proved erroneous—whereas the British Society for Psychical Research has a very good record in this respect and only once, having published a report on a particular study undertaken by its members, has the Society had to publish a contradictory one. This exception was the notoriously biased report on the Borley Rectory haunting (published in 1956) which attacked Harry Price and was full of errors and inaccuracies. In a subsequent report (published in 1969) Harry Price was completely vindicated and the haunting remains one of the great enigmas of spontaneous psychic phenomena."

"Could you indicate the leading psychical researchers of to-day?"

"I am not sure that there are really leading psychical researchers—certainly there is no one with the interest and the opportunities to investigate psychic phenomena with integrity and originality of some of the past investigators. One of them, alone, succeeded in making the study of psychical research respectable and put poltergeists, the investigation of mediums and the investigation of haunted houses on the map for all time. I have long been impressed with the work of Professor H. H. Price, former Wykeham Professor of Logic at New College, Oxford and our discussions and a visit to a haunted house together, have convinced me that he must rank as one of the foremost psychical researchers alive to-day; a fact that the Society for Psychical Research recognized when they elected him President from 1939 to 1941. In recent years I have been particularly impressed with the work and approach of Professor A. R. G. Owen, Ph,D., of Cambridge; he seems to possess just the right amonut of academic learning and practical commonsense that is so necessary and so rare in psychical researchers. In the literary field Dennis Bardens' excellent studies merit serious attention and represent extensive research and meticulous attention to detail. Dr. Eric John Dingwall must be mentioned as a leading psychical researcher, although his real subject is abnormal sexology, and he was telling me recently, he has given up psychical research and that if he had his time over again, he would not study psychic phenomena. On the statistical side the work of George Medhurst, B.Sc., stands almost by itself as thorough, painstaking and always objective. Mrs. Eileen Garrett has been the fountainhead of psychical research in America for so long that one tends to forget she was English and probably one of the most experienced and knowledgeable genuine psychics of our century. And then there is Mrs. Muriel Hankey whose knowledge of mediums and mediumship is probably unrivalled."

"Has there been any rapprochement between psychical research and spiritualism?"

"There is a committee drawn from spiritualists and psychical researchers which meets periodically and deliberates current problems but, personally, I do not think there has been any real rapprochement between the two in recent years. There will always be the dyed-in-the-wool spiritualist who refuses to submit to any kind of investigation and there will always be the sceptical psychical researcher who will admit to nothing that he has not witnessed under controlled conditions. I must confess that I was surprised when a spiritualist followed my address on *Sex and Psychic Phenomena* at a conference on psychical research recently and began by saying that he found he was in agreement with practically everything that I had said; so perhaps there is hope after all for a rapprochement although I do not feel that there will ever be complete unanimity."

"How do you see then the future of psychical research in the seventies and eighties?"

"With the enormous upsweep of interest in the occult and all branches of the paranormal the chances are that there will be a break-through in some sphere—most probably in extra-sensory perception where an American scientist has recently claimed that plants react to human thought; several governments are also exploring the possibility of the use of ESP in espionage and other 'unfriendly' activities. Personally I have never been entirely convinced that the dead have returned to the land of the living in any shape or form—but if there is life after death I think this might be proved within the next ten years. In any case I think it likely that our knowledge of apparitions and of the human mind will certainly have supplied a wealth of interesting information and perhaps some of the answers; although I recall a prominent spiritualist telling me with complete conviction twenty years ago that survival would be scientifically proved beyond any shadow of doubt within the next five years."

"Do you think that space travel and its technology will influence this development?"

"No, not in my view."

"What other elements do you see in the near or distant future?"

"During recent years, in various writings and particularly in lectures to my fellow-members of the Society for Psychical Research and at various English universities, I have drawn attention to the indisputable correlation between sex and psychic phenomena; a field of research that yields rich dividends and very definite results. This is applicable to practically every sphere of paranormal activity."

(We have, of course, discussed this subject and presented some of Mr. Underwood's view, in our previous chapter.)

"It has always been evident in mental and physical mediumship," the President of the Ghost Club continued, "to a greater or lesser degree; one of the most famous of all physical mediums used to reach sexual climax at the zenith of his psychic manifestations and mental mediums, too, have been known to achieve sexual satisfaction—while the instances of mediums with ailments of the genital or reproductive organs are legion. In telepathy and ESP experiments it has been shown that sexual objects (or objects with sexual associations for the participants) have yielded exceptional results. Poltergeist phenomena have long been established as usually being associated with an adolescent girl or boy and when these persons reach maturity, the apparently paranormal phenomena cease. In some cases of alleged haunting it has been noticed that reported incidents coincide with the periods of menstruation in a member of the affected household; in others the height of sexual activity has been paralleled with flashes of light—reminiscent of seance lights—and with the unexplained movement of objects. Investigators of physical phenomena, including Professor Thirring of Vienna, Dr. Schrenck-Notzing, the German parapsychologists and Harry Price, the English investigator, have been aware of this relationship but little real work has been done on the subject before my own investigations which leave me in no doubt that a relationship does indeed exist which extends to all branches of psychic phenomena, a correlation that may well prove to be significant when we eventually resolve the mystery that is psychical research. I have no doubt that the study of psychical research is among the most important work that man can undertake—for if the phenomena are satisfactorily established, then our ideas of life, personality and mind, perhaps even of space, matter and time, are inadequate and will have to be modified to include the new facts. That day has not yet arrived; it may well come within the next twenty years . . ."

Mr. George Medhurst, a prominent member of the Society for Psychical Research, has done a great deal of patient and distinguished work in the various fields of psychical phenomena. He has also participated in a number of international meetings (he was one of the British delegates at that ill-fated conference in Moscow) and has written some penetrating and well-balanced studies on a number of aspects of contemporary and historical phenomena. We talked to him in the presence of Miss M. R. Barrington who has been associated with him, in particular, in the long and arduous detective work connected with the Rosalie mystery. We asked more or less the same questions as we put to Mrs. Goldney and Mr. Underwood but during the discussion explored a number of other, adjoining issues; and while some of the conclusions inevitably overlapped, there was a good deal of fresh and unexpected view-points that emerged during our long talk.

To Mr. Medhurst the main trends of psychical research in the fifties and sixties have been, on the whole, negative.

"A number of cases have arisen in which serious experiments were found to have considerable holes in them. Additionally, attempts to repeat the early types of experiments have failed more and more. For example, paranormal effects under hypnosis have virtually ceased except in cases in which one has to doubt the accuracy of the experiments. A number of people who seemed to be good investigators, went to elaborate pains to repeat their earlier tests and experiments—and got purely negative results. While the popularity of psychical matters is rising, I think the convincing evidence is decreasing and being whittled away. Sorry to sound pessimistic, but that's what I think."

"So you think there is a general decline—a paradoxical situation of more and more interest existing in less and less happening or in less and less actual research?"

"Yes—with exceptions that are worrying because they're becoming almost unique. Thinking of ESP test in particular there appears to be only one person in the world who apparently produces reliable results—and that, of course, is Stepanek, tested among others by Dr. Gaither Pratt."

"Isn't it a question that this particular man is known and reported—while there might be people in some countries doing equally valid work whose results are simply unpublished?"

"That's always possible but then one wonders why an experimental search doesn't produce anything nowadays whereas in the past it used apparently to produce most impressive results. When Pratt and Woodruff in 1939, tested some twenty-five students they found one, who produced enormously significant results and, four more who produced useful results. Well, it doesn't happen nowadays. And some members of the Society for Psychical Research did at one time a mass test and out of twelve hundred people we found no one."

"We have discussed the practical disappearance of physical mediums with some of your colleagues and some of the theories advanced in explanation were, for instance, the development of the infra-red viewer and various other electronic apparatus which may have accounted for this. But then, others said that the really great physical mediums would have been quite prepared to accept such advanced control and would have still produced remarkable phenomena. Which of these two views would you be inclined to accept?"

"I am inclined to the second one. As much as anything this comes from the D. D. Home results. Over many years, Home achieved his results in good light—this seems beyond doubt—before anybody, including people of high academic reputation. I think this was true of some other mediums. One thinks, for example of Anna Rasmussen who was producing her effects in good light and if the description is accurate, there seems to be no way by which the results could have been obtained normally . . ."

(Anna Rasmussen was a Danish lady whose main 'speciality' was to make suspended steel balls move at a considerable distance from herself, within a glass cage which stood on a pedestal cemented to the floor; she could vary the movements according to request, clockwise and anti-clockwise, up and down, forward and back.)

Miss Barrington added here : "Think of the Eusepia Paladino sittings in Naples, supervised by Feilding, Baggally and Carington. For the most part they seem to have taken place in pretty good light which is specifically described. I can't see that the existence of the infra-red viewer could have made any difference to the results in this case."

"Another theory which was put forward," we suggested, "used the parallel of having cycles in the weather—the climate heating up or cooling down—and claiming that there well might be cycles in physical mediumship. We might be, it was said, at the nadir of such a downswing."

"I don't think that's sensible at all," Mr. Medhurst said. "Because impressive mediums producing results under test conditions flourished from, say, the eighteen-fifties until about the second world war, and it is since then that they have apparently disappeared. Madame Kulagina in Russia, may be an exception, and though no really adequate or satisfactory tests on her have been reported, there are films which are, to some extent, interesting. Materialization mediums? Well, in *Psychic News* during the last few months a certain gentleman, Gordon Higginson, was described as having produced full figure materializations at public or semi-public meetings. But he doesn't seem to be prepared to be tested and for that matter he doesn't seem to be willing to apply for the £25,000-prize offered by a British magazine."

"It is rumoured constantly," Miss Barrington told us, "that there are materialization mediums in Brazil who produced enormous phantoms that march backwards and forwards through the bars of cages and there are reports signed by a dozen doctors to this effect . . ."

"Whereabouts in Brazil?"

"I could not tell you but reports appeared in *Psychic News*. Again one mustn't completely sneer at the story put about that physical mediumship is cast aside by mediums in favour of healing. Because physical mediumship in the past has been extremely well-witnessed and I believe there was a document signed by over a hundred reputable citizens testifying to the authenticity of Willi Schneider's mediumship. Now that convinced nobody else of anything, and the feeling may have become ingrained in researchers *and* in mediums that there is little sense in trying to prove physical mediumship by pointless exhibitions so they might as well do something useful—whether people believe them or not. This might be a little naïve but I think it may deserve some sort of consideration."

"As if there had been a sudden pronouncement that, say, from January 1st onwards, there won't be any more materializations but instead healing slipped discs or malfunctioning kidneys?"

"I don't know that it is quite as definite as that," smiled Mr. Medhurst. "It is true that a number of spiritualists are said, in effect, to have changed their minds about the type of activity they are prepared to undertake, but this doesn't sound like evidence to me. Healing is in a sense an awfully easy thing to do, because many, people, who are treated will, at least for a time, actually benefit by it."

"When orthodox medicine has, in fact, failed them?"

"Yes and I suspect that many mediums have turned towards this kind of activity for this reason. Bearing in mind also the quite devastating criticisms mediums had to endure in the past in connection with physical phenomena—even if the particular medium happened to be genuine. I think the vast majority of mediums would nowadays, tend consciously or unconsciously to prefer healing—because there an accusation of fraud can't be made—except of course in the case of psychical surgery, which is another matter."

"Is it perhaps a case of a psychological placebo effect that makes spirit healing so popular? Just as in the testing of any new drug about sixty-five per cent of the results must be discounted because results would be achieved even with sugar or water, as long as the patient felt that the doctor's or experimenter's attention was concentrated on him, on his complaint, whether for five mintes or an hour . . ."

"Well—may I slightly contradict myself? I suggested that psychic healing has 'taken over'. But then perhaps we ought to remember that already in the last century the Christian Scientists were producing effects strikingly similar to present-day psychic healing. So perhaps one shouldn't suggest that this is an entirely new development."

"So psychic healing is the continuation of an old tradition and it does not replace physical mediumship? And physical mediumship has faded out quite independently of this continuing process of spirit healing?"

"Well, of course, Christian Scientist healing did not quite have the same spiritualist background; it was supposed to be a purely 'Christ-effort' as it were, whereas the spirit healing is supposed to be done by deceased doctors—so one can't make too close a comparison . . ."

"Is it always deceased doctors? Aren't there Indian chiefs, exotic sages, who are supposed to do the healing?"

"Yes, in some cases. Red Indian guides, Chinese mandarins, Hindu gurus, will suddenly say that they want to try healing. There was a long series of sittings I attended during the late forties, at which we had assorted physical phenomena, including a heavy table repeatedly going up several feet in the air, though in total darkness, I am afraid. I can't say now that all this was completely convincing evidence. But the ancient Chinese guide— who claimed to have lived about a thousand years ago—quite suddenly one evening decided that he wanted to 'cure'. We had to bring patients for him to heal, we were told. And in fact we did find three or four. One of them was a girl I knew who was a Lesbian and very worried about it. She was terrified when she was left on her own but she couldn't talk to people. She was a civil servant in London—and hated the place, but couldn't leave.

She had her psychopathological treatment but it had produced no results. I brought her along to these sittings with some trepidation. She had eczema on her hands, both hands had to be bandaged and we couldn't hold her directly as she sat in the circle, she had to be held by the arms . . . Her so-called 'treatment' was merely a conversation with the guide, about twenty minutes per session. We didn't really see anything wonderful happening at the sitting but, the eczema disappeared, she seemed in a far happier state and she moved to St. Ives where she started some business of her own; I kept in touch with her for a year or so and she seemed to be doing wonderfully. What this proves, I really have no idea."

We asked Mr. Medhurst whether he, too, had any views about the intense interest of young people today in the irrational—and, by association, in the occult?

"I think that youth today is very badly unbalanced, feels for various reasons that there is no secure future," Mr. Medhurst answered. "I think that the strong possibility of a future nuclear war has really penetrated their minds, and while they know little or nothing about mysticism, occultism, or psychical research, they feel that this is a possible way round . . ."

"Round the insecurity?"

"Yes, and an escape from the totally unsatisfactory situation of the world."

"Do they perhaps also feel that occultism might offer them means to defy authority? After all, the spirit world, if they believe in it, is hardly likely to interfere directly with their daily concerns, their permissive way of life?"

"Oh, I don't think it's a matter of the spirit world, it's their own powers they are concerned with. Many of them, for instance, believe that they have psychical powers they can use for their own ends and influence other people."

"How do drugs enter into this?"

"I think psychedelic drugs might be involved—though this is not a field I have explored myself. It may be of course, that many youngsters who do not take drugs, have seen accounts of the trance-like state produced by them. Maybe they feel that *without* any drug they can achieve this condition and have quasi-paranormal experiences through occultism."

"You mean that psychical experiences might replace drugs if

they can achieve them—rather than such paranormal experiences and powers being attained through drugs?"

"I am only guessing but I think many of them would like to have some unusual experiences, without resorting to drugs."

"This is possible—though, at least in the United States, the truly horrifying regular accounts about the fate of drug-addicts do not seem to deter many young people from trying a new thrill, from experimenting. Their attitude is, of course, rather like the chain-smokers who say, well, *I* am not going to get lung cancer or that of the alcoholic who says, *I* know when to stop. Perhaps the young of today have become disillusioned in science which they blame not only for the menace of nuclear war hanging over them but also for other things which are really the consequence of technology and industrialization—like pollution. Do you think that this may be the reason why they turn away from the world of fact and tangible, though unpleasant, reality to what may be called the world of dreams, of imponderable, instinctive, non-rational experiences? Would this explain the very considerable, still growing interest in all things psychic both in Europe and, to an even greater extent, in the United States?"

"Oh yes, I think this fits very well. This is the kind of thing that I would expect to be the motive."

"Which country do you consider the centre or the main centre of psychical research today?"

"This is undoubtedly America. There is far more psychical research—or what is claimed to be work in this field—going on there than elsewhere. There is a certain perhaps surprising amount going on in Russia—but far less, certainly, than the American activity. Experimental work is going on in this country —always so far producing negative results."

"You have been to the Soviet Union, I believe. Could you tell us what is going on there—as far as it is possible to make out?"

"Well, I went to what was announced as a sort of conference in 1968. There must have been, at a guess, forty or fifty Russians present—I gather, from all over the country. A fair amount of experimental work had been carried out, some of it is even reported in quite authentic-looking publications. For example, there is a technical magazine of good standing concerned with radio engineering and over the last three or four years there have been a number of papers published in it which, the results, if the experimental conditions were satisfactory, would be rather impressive, and apparently these are being taken seriously."

"Were these concerned with telepathy?"

"Yes."

"And they reported positive results?"

"Certainly."

"And how did your conference in Moscow go?"

"I am afraid it went off with some difficulty. There were two delegates from the Society of Psychical Research, I being one of them. Until the very last minute we couldn't get a definite date. At one time we were told that the conference would last a week— so we arranged to be there for what we hoped would be the correct week! When we arrived, we had considerable difficulty in tracing a man called Naumov who was supposed to be the organizer of the meeting. Finally we found him and he came to see us. He spoke no English but he brought an interpreter. It appeared that the conference had finally been reduced to two days; the first day being *our last* day in Moscow. It turned out on that particular day that *Pravda* published an article, containing a heavy attack against psychical phenomena, particularly against physical effects. It appeared that this was printed in *Pravda* because the conference was about to be held; in fact, the second day was officially prohibited. The first day, apparently, could not be banned in time. There was a film of Madame Kulagina's physical mediumship which was to be shown at the conference; then it turned out that some government agency had forbidden its projection. So we had to have a series of talks which concerned various experimental results."

"Were they all by Russians?"

"No, not quite. We, my colleague and I, hadn't expected to speak but we were told at the last moment that we must so each of us produced something in a great hurry. Dr. Gaither Pratt also delivered a lecture. Two American lady writers, who had been totally unable to locate the site of the conference and whom I managed to direct there through an accidental meeting also presented short papers. There was, in addition, a fair number of Russian speakers—though nothing had been properly organized or arranged. And it did appear that there is a strong rivalry between various groups of people who are either interested in psychical research or attempting to carry out experiments."

"But the Soviet Government, because of its strongly materialistic philosophy, is strongly opposed to all this?"

"Oh no, I wouldn't say that. Not at all. Up to a point there *is* government support. And the reason for this is very curious. It relates to the alleged experiments in telepathy carried out under the auspices of the United States government between the nuclear submarine Nautilus and some spot on the American Continent— as to precisely where, the accounts vary. It was claimed, it appears, that strongly significant results had been obtained. This, it seems, interested certain circles of the Russian Government from the military point of view. And it is for this reason that support was given to psychical research and telepathic experiments. As it turned out, the thing was a complete fiction—the story about the Nautilus and American telepathic tests was invented by two French journalists and published initially in France whence it was picked up by other publications. But the Russians don't appear to know that—not to this very day."

"How do you see the general direction of American psychical research, which you consider the most active, in the next few years? What will be the general trends?"

"Of course, I didn't mean to say that the work done by the Americans is the most important. I only wanted to indicate that there is a great deal more work being done in America than in any other country. Whether the results are of value seems to me very much a different matter. The major difficulty, of course, is that no American subject is known who under good test conditions can produce statistically highly significant scores in ESP so other things have had to be tried. Detailed distribution of the score, even if the total score is not statistically significant is the kind of thing that is being looked into . . ."

"What would such a detailed distribution of the score entail?"

"You have to look at the arrangement of the hits and scrutinize runs for a different type of pattern."

"Apart from the very large number of ESP experiments, what other trends do you see in American psychical research? Have they also resigned themselves completely to the apparent lack of physical mediums? Are they more interested in clairvoyance or the practical applications of ESP than any other approach?"

"The interest is almost entirely in ESP rather than physical effects—and I think this is because there is nobody prepared to produce physical phenomena."

"What do you think of Dr. Stevenson's work in the field of reincarnation?"

"The type of reincarnation that he believes he has discovered is something unusual. In the past reincarnation has involved the idea that one is reborn every hundred or every two hundred years. The results that Stevenson is finding suggest the death of a person and his or her virtually immediate reincarnation in a new baby, as it were. This is something really new. I know only a little about these researches. I know that there has been some criticism about the results reported; it has been said—and I don't know whether this is justified or not—that Stevenson would not have the right sort of contact with the people with whom he was dealing. But I wouldn't like to voice a definite opinion about this particular field."

"Whom would you name as the leading psychical researchers of today? Who do you think will carry the torch in the next ten or twenty years? Whose work has impressed you most?"

"Well, I would put Dr. Gaither Pratt very high, because under Professor Rhine he has carried out something approaching thirty years of careful work; most of it producing negative results. Now that he is no longer associated with Rhine, he still has an excellent background, working under Professor Stevenson and he and his students are doing most interesting work. I think he's a most reliable man. Dr. Gertrude Schmeidler's interesting sheep-and-goats work has been very lengthy, very complicated, very carefully done. She is attached to New York City College, still working in this field, trying many variations on her method of experimentation."

"What is her special field?"

"ESP, generally and 'sheep-and-goats' experiments in particular. She divides her subjects into two or more psychological types and then checks whether the ESP scores are divided between these groups to a significant extent. The theory predicts that the 'sheep' will score significantly more hits than the 'goats'. This is, of course, vastly oversimplifying the whole thing—"

"Are there any psychological types that are half-sheep and half- goats?"

"So I believe—and this is part of her complications."

"What about Britain—if this is not too close home?"

"I would have thought that here Dr. Beloff is the outstanding man. He has done, with his students, an astonishing amount of experimental work over a fair number of years. I am sorry to say that to my knowledge *all* his results are purely negative. But he continues to believe that ESP is an authentic phenomenon and goes on with his work. I am impressed by the wide variety of the types of experiments he has carried out. Incidentally, he has visited Stepanek in Prague with whom Dr. Gaither Pratt has done remarkably well in the past and, I am sorry to say, has quite failed to get positive results."

We asked Mr. Medhurst whether he saw any sign of a drawing-together between psychical and spiritualism?

"There has always been a connection, right from the beginning. Sir Wililam Crookes, for example, who was primarily a psychical research man, was also very much involved with spiritualism and also, I am sorry to say, was the subject of violent attacks and vindictiveness. This kind of thing has gone on right the way through. There have been others linking the two sides. Drayton Thomas was certainly a spiritualist but a careful worker in the field . I don't think things have really changed or are likely to. There are people on either side who are flatly against the other camp but then there are also people somewhere in between, on neutral ground."

"Do you think this is likely to change?"

"Well, it *would* change, of course, if for example there should be concrete evidence as regards survival after death and as regards communication with the 'other world'. This hasn't been forthcoming during the long period since psychical research began. A lot has been obtained that is of great interest, possibly very suggestive—but nothing definitely conclusive. If this happened quite suddenly, then of course there would be a sort of coalescence between the two opposing sides, but not otherwise."

"Then your general summary of the future trends is that of more modest aims, there will be more concentration on mental than on physical phenomena and that perhaps, with new techniques, more significant results might be achieved? But is there any particular point you would like to make in connection with this over-all view?"

"There is a highly negative point. It has been believed in the past that there have been a small number of ESP experiments which could be regarded as conclusive—three or four early American experiments—and perhaps two sets of experiments in this country. But with readily testable ESP apparently disappearing—certain people became interested in looking more carefully into what is recorded concerning these experiments, aiming at a reassessment. Now I won't go into details—but in my opinion one of these early experiments will have to be discarded. Something very unfortunate has been discovered in connection with this particular research and there will be a publication about it in the not-too-distant future. Perhaps this will extend itself—maybe these conclusive experiments will begin to look weaker . . . "*

If the future of psychical research does not look too rosy, it does not mean that the world-wide interest in occultism is likely to weaken or fade. And of course, psychical researchers themselves do not entirely agree as to the shape of things to come. The world still echoes Hamlet's words about the things in heaven and on earth that the human mind cannot encompass.

THE END

* It is with deepest regret that we must record the death of Mr. Medhurst in January 1971.